D1565788

Managing
Knowledge Workers

Managing Knowledge Workers

Unleashing Innovation
and Productivity

A.D. AMAR

QUORUM BOOKS
Westport, Connecticut • London

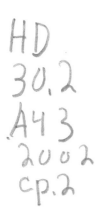

HD
30.2
A43
2002
cp.2

Library of Congress Cataloging-in-Publication Data

Amar, A. D. (Amar D.)
    Managing knowledge workers : unleashing innovation and productivity / A.D. Amar.
    p. cm.
    Includes index.
    ISBN 1-56720-448-1 (alk. paper)
    1. Knowledge management.   2. Intellectual capital.   3. Knowledge workers.
    4. Employee empowerment.   5. Labor productivity.   I. Title.
    HD30.2.A43   2002
    658.3'044—dc21   2001019871

British Library Cataloguing in Publication Data is available.

Library of Congress Catalog Card Number: 2001019871
ISBN: 1-56720-448-1

First published in 2002

Quorum Books, 88 Post Road West, Westport, CT 06881
An imprint of Greenwood Publishing Group, Inc.
www.quorumbooks.com

Printed in the United States of America

The paper used in this book complies with the
Permanent Paper Standard issued by the National
Information Standards Organization (Z39.48-1984).

P

To my parents,
Prem Datt Shakir, Esq., and Kaushlya Devi Shakir,
whose love and sacrifices formed
my character and me,

To my wife, Sneh Lata Amar,
whose encouragement has resulted in
the culmination of this work, and

To our sons,
Harpriye Amar Juneja and Januj Amar Juneja,
who are our future.

Contents

Illustrations

)

Preface

During the last decade of the twentieth century, we saw a big increase in the use of knowledge in managing organizations of all sizes, in all industries. This knowledge has played an important role in designing their product and service lines, conversion systems, and promotion and distribution systems, among others. It has created a number of employees whose primary work function is to have updated knowledge within their area of specialization and then employ it to find applications that will benefit their organization in its performance. Many organizations have created a separate department with the main responsibility being to keep up with the knowledge as and when it develops and to propagate it to other appropriate sections of the company so that they are not left out in their attempts to find new knowledge applications in their business.

We have come to know employees who gather, process, develop, and apply knowledge as knowledge workers. They make up those who work in a company's information technology division, research and development division, corporate planning and strategic management department, product design and promotion division, operations research area, and among a host of other areas of any organization—for-profit and not-for-profit. They are not like the workers that we have come to know since the advent of the job era. They are different in many ways, with regard to what they bring to the organization and what they do. Because of these differences, it is important for firms to manage them differently from workers that corporations have previously known.

The focus of this book is to understand the differences that highlight knowledge workers from other workers and learn how best to manage them and the organizations—small or large—in which they work so that such organizations can get the most out of them. The book also focuses on the usual management functions and adapts them to these organizations—called knowledge organizations. Since this area of study is still in its infancy, there is not much research that is directly applicable to the management of these organizations. Many of the principles recommended herein for knowledge organizations are either taken directly from some business practices or have been deduced from what happens in the knowledge environment.

Since knowledge organizations are still evolving, and the understanding of and the research on them is ongoing, few managers, academicians, or researchers know how best to manage them or their employees. Only a very few have dedicated any effort to understand the differences in managing knowledge organizations and traditional organizations. Those who are aware of these changes are experimenting with different styles through the monitoring and switching of management practices on a regular basis. Whereas a very small number of them have achieved some success, most others have simply faced frustration. The struggle on how best to fit their organization and employees with market demands and available opportunities is still ongoing. Those organizations in knowledge work that have achieved any business success have done so due to the dynamism of their products and markets, not to the prudent and efficient management of their organizations. As "knowledge business" markets become more competitive, their survival could become a management struggle. Only those who set up their operations for the effective transaction as knowledge organizations, in particular, for the effective employment of their human element (the most important resource of any knowledge organization), will grow and become industry leaders. Currently, the pressure on most knowledge organizations from the constantly changing business environment is so great that it does not allow them to put their organizational issues in proper perspective. Effective leaders have to make meaningful adaptations to their management style in order to put their organizations on the road to prosperity. Once turbulence ebbs in the knowledge environment, the main reason for the success and failure of any organization in this business will be its management style.

The main theme of the management of knowledge organizations is how to make employees think, research, and apply—how to make them innovate and create. Whereas in most traditional organizations all these elements are helpful, though not essential for survival, in knowledge organizations they are their thread of life. Knowledge organization managers have to know how to make their employees more innovative, creative, and functional in a turbulent environment and how to change them from those who read a blueprint and follow a methods sheet in executing their jobs, without much responsibility of the consequence beyond their concurrence with the blueprint.

The broad function of this book is to help managers set up their organizations so as to utilize their employees' knowledge and get the most innovation and highest productivity for the organization. Specifically, the book is written to serve three purposes. The first is to serve the needs of managers in organizations or departments whose one main input or output is knowledge. They may be working for organizations in industries such as biotechnology and pharmaceutical research, information technology, or for any department of any organization that has to depend on human innovation and creativity for its success. These may include one of the departments we listed previously. Secondly, this book is written to serve all managers of all generations who have to work with the employees of younger generations, in particular those belonging to Generations X and Y. This book focuses heavily on them as employees because they will comprise the future labor force—the future that belongs to organizations that use human knowledge. Thirdly, this book is written to help managers rewrite management principles to understand how to manage in the changed realities since their business school lectures on management fundamentals. They may rediscover some of the facts in a more organized manner in this book, since it rewrites some of what they have learned without reference to these newer generations of workers.

This work is organized into 12 chapters. The first one builds a foundation in knowledge organizations. It compares them with traditional organizations and emphasizes what is needed for their success. The next two chapters comprise the second section of the book. They focus on knowledge workers, primarily the characteristics of the members of Generations X and Y—the majority of the knowledge employees who have either joined the workforce during the era when knowledge organizations arose or those who are going to be entering the workforce during the current decade. The next section focuses on knowledge work and its organization. In three chapters, it covers the design aspects of knowledge work, how to group and assign knowledge work to workers, and how to organize large-scale knowledge assignments. This section also includes instruments that can be used to assess and prioritize work for the redesign. (Additional copies of these instruments may be ordered by writing to the author at The Stillman School of Business, Seton Hall University.) The fourth section consists of the management of these organizations. In five chapters, this section covers such important management functions as planning and decision making, leading, motivating, controlling, and morale management. This section has been made specific to knowledge organizations so that all of the principles suggested for these organizations have been contrasted with traditional management. This section also covers elements of designing a control system for these organizations. Since morale problems are more serious in knowledge organizations because of their environment, a full chapter in this section has been devoted to assessing and managing the morale of knowledge workers. The last section, one short chapter, covers the future of the field of knowledge organization management.

This book is written for both professional managers of knowledge workers and academicians and researchers working in the field. With that in mind, I have tried to stay away from turning it into an esoteric reading—a dissertation or thesis where the emphasis is on proving to the reader that the presented ideas connect with the literature. Further, to avoid any hindrances in getting the message across, I have taken out statistics, survey results, and excessive, unnecessary citations. Any readings that have been borrowed from and may add further to the subject have been separated and given as References at the end of each chapter for those who may like to explore the subject on their own.

Keep an open mind while reading this book. I have freely integrated human behavioral principles, relationship practices, and management.

ACKNOWLEDGMENTS

There are a number of people without whose assistance this work would have never been completed. Since this work has stretched over a number of years, it is very likely that I might have forgotten to mention all those who have helped in this pursuit. To cover that possibility, I ask for their pardon before I start compiling this list. These individuals are Christopher L. Bruschi, Laurel B. Moller, and Mathew F. Slaski, all of the Stillman School of Business, Seton Hall University; my colleague and friend, Richard J. Hunter, Jr.; my son, Harpriye Amar Juneja of S.G. Barr Devlin, for making comments to improve the content; my publisher Eric Valentine of Quorum for coming up with insightful suggestions on an earlier version of this book; my copy editor, Nadia Blahut; and my wife, Sneh, and son, Januj, who tolerated a huge pile of trashy papers all over the house during this period. Of course, the responsibility for any errors and omissions is all mine.

Section I _____

KNOWLEDGE
ORGANIZATIONS

Chapter 1 _____

Knowledge Organizations and Environment

It is almost impossible for any present-day organization to compete in global markets without making an efficient use of knowledge in its operations. Most organizations are making the use of knowledge in its most obvious forms, such as scientific developments, computing and information technology, and the Internet. However, there are others that have to regularly deploy new and creative knowledge to function and survive in their field. They utilize knowledge, discover applications, and develop technologies to make their or other organizational operations and functions more effective and efficient. Human creativity and innovation are very important inputs to their processes. These are the organizations—complete firms, one department, or just one section of a department—that we call "knowledge organizations." These firms use the most recent scientific and specialized knowledge, electronic computers, and information technology as primary inputs into their operations. Also included in this category are organizations that engage in producing knowledge and applications to be utilized by others (i.e., their outputs contribute to knowledge that becomes inputs in other organizations). Therefore, any organization that either uses knowledge or produces it is classified in this book as a knowledge organization.

Knowledge organizations require skills derived from freethinking and unbounded actions of those working for them. They grow on skills that bring about uniqueness, newness, and creativity. Typically, these organizations are heavily dependent on scientific research, electronics technology, system design and management, information processing and transmission using the Internet, and other knowledge media. In their simplest form, they may be the developers of the Internet applications for electronic commerce for research and development (R&D) departments of traditional organizations for market research or product development and promotion departments of any organizations. At a higher level, these organizations are the ones in knowledge application development, design, medical research, electronic and computer hardware design, software applications, biotechnology, and pharmaceuticals, among others depending on human knowledge and the latest scientific and technological developments.

Management of knowledge organizations is different from the management of traditional firms. There is an urgent need to revisit and assess principles and practices of management as we have learned during the last few decades and determine their suitability for the management of these organizations. Moreover, there may be a need to decide if these principles and practices can be transferred exactly, or only after they are adapted, or should they be fully discarded as unfit and be replaced with newer more pointed and more appropriate theories and techniques suited to these organizations.

However, before proceeding with any development of the management for organizations that use knowledge as a main input factor in their processes, such as the knowledge firms and research and development organizations, we must build further understanding about them. We have to know more about these organizations to understand how best to manage them. In particular, we should know their work requirements, the job skills that they demand to execute the work with up-to-date contemporary resources, the prevalent environments that surround their work, and the characteristics of employees and other people who possess these skills and could be prospective employees of these organizations. Because the people who possess the skills these firms demand or who are working in the knowledge environment are different from the employees of traditional organizations, it is important for us to know how these firms should work with them.

KNOWLEDGE ORGANIZATIONS VERSUS OPERATING ORGANIZATIONS

The most obvious difference between knowledge organizations and other or traditional organizations—let's call them "operating" organizations—is their need for human creativity and innovation. First, innovation is the central arena in which knowledge organization competition plays out (Mandel, Carney, & Reinhardt, 2000). Whereas these organizations need innovation from every member at every level of the organization, for operating organizations, innovation could only be a "good additional input" to their processes. If they have a specific innovation, it may prove to be very beneficial to their bottom line. Nevertheless, if they do not, it will not cause a great negative impact. For these reasons, at least at the present and for some time to come, the principles and practices of management of these two types of organizations are going to be different. These differences are significant and fundamental. However, we know that in the future all organizations will need the management skills of the knowledge organizations because they will all be significantly driven by knowledge. Until then, these differences in management must be clearly understood and applied to knowledge organizations to get the most out of the talent and ambition of the knowledge employees.

The second important difference is the role of human resources in these organizations. Human intellect is the major strength of knowledge organizations—not money. It is for this reason that young and "inexperienced" men and women from colleges can start knowledge business companies with multibillion dollars in market capitalization. What these people bring to the firm—including their dreams, visions, and ambitions—counts more in making them work and succeed than the dollars these firms can raise from venture capitalists or the general public.

Since innovation is the most important input, and human intellect the most important capital, management of these organizations has to focus on how to put the two together in their operating system.

Paradigms of Knowledge Organization Management

The underpinnings of the management style of traditional or operating organizations are set in the writings and conceptions of researchers and thinkers like Adam Smith (1776), Frederick W. Taylor (1911), Henri Fayol (1949), Max Weber (1947), and Abraham Maslow (1943, July). (They can be collectively classified as the twentieth century management models.) Extending the applicability of twentieth century models to knowledge organizations that operate in fully redefined markets and new environments is too simplistic. The demands from electronic business and the environment that surrounds it require responses and responsibilities from workers that organizations following one or more of the management models of the twentieth century simply cannot provide.

Knowledge organization works on the paradigms that contradict the twentieth century models, which flourished during the birth and growth of the large traditional corporation—the "job era." When the management style that is practiced in contemporary operating organizations was being developed, intellectual preparation of a large majority of the worker population was low. Most people did not possess the intellectual preparation essential to make decisions relating to the formulation and execution of an organization's objectives and the management of its processes. This reality of the time created a need for organizations to have a set of employees who, because of their preparation, did only intellectual work for the organization. Any work that required muscle or skill was usually given to people with little or no formal education. This type of work constituted the bulk of jobs in those organizations. It earned them revenue, paid their bills and, later, generated profits and dividends for their stockholders. The intellectual work in these organizations was classified as "burden" or overheads, because it was paid from the revenue generated by the muscle or manual work.

This practice of dividing labor in traditional organizations is unfit for the knowledge organization. The division of work principles of the previous century will have to be fully reversed for efficiently carrying out knowledge organization work. A large number of employees in these organizations should be engaged in intellectual work and a small number should be engaged in what we knew as "operational" or manual work (Amar, 1998). Under these circumstances, continuing to follow the management techniques and styles of the last century is bound to fail. Neither knowledge organization work nor environment nor workers of the twenty-first century are suited for this type of management.

KNOWLEDGE ORGANIZATION CHALLENGES

In the future, every business will require the same traits and characteristics that are today typically associated with knowledge organizations. In fact, by the second decade of the new century, every business is going to be so reliant on innovation that the term "knowledge organization" itself will become obsolete. The resultant changes in organizational behavior and management will totally scrap whatever we have learned from the management of operating organizations and the theories of the last century. Human behavior is going to drastically change. Organizational behavior models of the last century will not apply. We will have to come up with new techniques and styles to fit the changes coming, or we will struggle and be doomed to ultimately fail.

Employee Characteristics

From Different to Unique. The management of operating organizations has been technique-based. These techniques model management as a science or a system in which humans fit as input, thereby creating a man-machine scientific system or, in other words, a factory. Although behavioral scientists of the second half of the twentieth century suggested modifications to this system by highlighting the differences in humans, unfortunately, they also became enamored with models and patterns and typed human behavior and the standardized management responses in each case. Management, as we traditionally know it, bases everything on commonality. Both for practical reasons necessary for the implementation of controls and for the sake of simplicity, it does not accept the existence of unique differences among humans in either their physical capabilities or behavior. This premise worked until about the middle of the twentieth century. Later, when it became essential to accommodate women and minorities in the workplace, this commonality premise had to be relaxed somewhat. Macro differences in the human element of the work system were accepted and allowed to coexist but only as subordinate to these commonalities. Nevertheless, they discarded the assumption of full uniformity among humans. Organizations took the lead from psychology in understanding these differences and in exploiting them for enhancing their organizational productivity. It worked for most of the second half of the twentieth century.

However, in knowledge organizations, just focusing on human differences based on demographics, or even psychographics, is not going to help them achieve full contribution from their employees. Every assumption of uniformity among employees of a knowledge organization is too simplistic and inconsistent with the realities of the coming generation of employees and should be discarded at the organization's door. Knowledge organizations should look upon every employee as uniquely and extremely complex and accept that there are no common patterns beyond a few very basic physiological ones. Knowledge organization managers should assume that the uniqueness of each human being is going to be so prominent that theorizing or systematizing it will result in a lack of the full utilization of one's potential.

From Organizational Goals to Individual Goals. Knowledge organization managers should know how to fit job and organizational priorities into the needs of the individual employee. For a knowledge organization, the concept of organization takes a fully new meaning. A knowledge organization is not a collection of people working together to achieve goals set by others. It is a number of people with diverse individual goals working together to achieve the fulfillment of their *own* goals using the organization as a vehicle. In this process, they allow others working with them, and the organization they are working for, the ability to achieve their goals. The primary aim of knowledge organization employees should not be the achievement of the organization's goals but the fulfillment of their own goals. A knowledge organization will work only if there is this overlap, otherwise this relationship of employees and knowledge organization will be broken up—by their employees. In this regard, knowledge organizations take a major departure from the operating organizations.

From Group to Self. Until the job era began, both in Eastern and Western cultures, humans placed the highest priorities on family, community, and society. In the job era, job and organization became most important for employees. Their bosses and their satisfaction with their work behavior took the highest priority in the employees' lives. Their families took second place, especially in the West. The communities and society were eliminated from the top priority list altogether. This readjustment of human priorities gave organizations and their bosses the most power over the individuals. Employees practically lived at their and the organization's mercy.

Knowledge organizations are changing all this. Knowledge organization employees are guided by a new priority; the most important thing to a knowledge organization employee is his or her individuality. Everyone or everything else is secondary—be it family, job, organization, boss, community, or society. Knowledge organization employees accept things that suit their fancy or are seen by them as fulfilling their needs. They put all their physical and psychic energy into achieving self-satisfaction. On the other hand, anything that does not help them get this will be discarded, and no amount of motivating factors will be able to achieve the intended purpose. Any group—whether formal or informal—will not succeed in exerting enough force essential to alter their determination in this regard.

A knowledge organization manager must first understand each individual employee's needs and motivators and then attempt to address them independent of all other work-related factors.

Opportunity for All. Knowledge work has very little about it that can be monitored or routinely checked. Thus, in order to keep knowledge workers motivated, it is essential that the same opportunities for personal and professional growth, that have been offered traditionally only to officers or other key personnel in companies, be offered to everyone in a knowledge organization.

A knowledge organization must allow knowledge workers to design their work in a way that they find interesting to them, and it should manifest a work environment that is controlled by the person whose work it is.[1] The aim of a knowledge organization should be that, one by one, all factors that constitute work environment are steadily weakened. Its ultimate goal should be to eliminate the work environment factor by factor, and eventually altogether. Ideally, there should not be any factors, forces, or conditions imposed on a worker that he or she does not directly or indirectly control. Only when an organization succeeds in achieving this, can we say that it has no work environment. That, in simple terms, would be the formula needed to unleash innovation and realize productivity gains from knowledge workers. This will be particularly true of the new supersmart generation of workers that is attracted to knowledge organizations.

THE PHENOMENON OF KNOWLEDGE WORK

The changes in human behavior in general and the behavior at work in particular that are expected during the next few years are not only a concern of knowledge organizations, but will also have some impact on every organization. These changes are a worldwide phenomenon. Such changes in human behavior have been observed in inhabitants of the remote Himalayas, the deep forests of the Amazon, the inner urban areas of London, and the suburbs of New Jersey. Since knowledge organizations are drawing their employees from all over the world, and especially from certain developing countries, it is important that they understand these changes. In fact, the magnitude of behavioral change that is occurring in "backward" civilizations is far greater than in the industrialized world. The work demands of knowledge organizations have evolved into a global generation of workers with a worldwide culture.

Basic Ingredients of Knowledge Work

Every job in a knowledge organization should be designed and guided by the fact that all knowledge work is intellectual work. Thus, a job that is not intellectual enough will not contribute to knowledge work. Such jobs should not be allowed in a knowledge organization. In principle, that is the criterion for the selection of a job for direct inclusion in a knowledge organization. Other support, routine, or operational jobs should be permitted in a knowledge organization only if they require, at least for half of their total time, an effort that is intellectual in nature. Even knowledge organization jobs that are classified as "manual" or "physical" should require analysis, decision-making, creativity, and other intellectual skills that were typically needed for the white-collar jobs of the twentieth century. There should be no manual jobs in knowledge organizations.

Simply for the survival of their organizations, knowledge organization managers should regularly revisit processes, tasks, and work assignments to make sure that each job has a significant innovation component in it. Ideally, each job should be loaded with an intellectual component. All tasks in a knowledge organization job should be intellectual.

A knowledge organization has to encourage and facilitate revolutionary changes unlike the *kaizen*, a Japanese management practice, that achieves success through numerous organization-wide, small-scale improvements in service or product design, transformation, and distribution processes. Kaizen worked for operating organizations because it helped them move their products and services up a small notch through better quality, slightly better functionality, or superior customer service. That is not the case in knowledge organizations. They cannot survive by making small improvements. Their success lies in just-in-time, massive, revolutionary changes, no matter which they affect—their own division or that of their competitors.

A knowledge organization's future lies in designing new and revolutionary services/products; devising innovative, efficient transformation and maintenance processes; and establishing a unique means of getting these products/services to markets and customers. The dictum "innovate or perish" is eminently true for knowledge organizations.

Innovation: Hard and Soft. Innovation will come to the rescue of knowledge organizations in many forms. It can range from the design of products and processes to how to manage them or how to uniquely motivate employees. Here, we refer to the former innovation as hard innovation, whereas the latter is called soft innovation. Innovating new products, machines, tools, and the processes to make them are all examples of hard innovations. Hard innovation is very important, but equally or even more important is soft innovation. Soft innovation entails devising new ways to manage all organizational inputs in general; however, the most important of them all should be human resources. It requires an understanding of the mind, behavior, and sociology of the people through whom the organization will achieve its goals. As stated earlier, since every individual in a knowledge organization is unique, managers will have to be innovative in getting performance that will consistently contribute to the achievement of the organization's goals. The managers of the future will have to be extremely soft innovators to be successful.

Innovation as a Competitive Advantage. A basic theme guiding the design and management of a knowledge organization is that innovation is the winning competitive advantage for its success, and to achieve competitive advantage, management will have to practice a style that will breed mutualism between employees and employers. Such mutualism is created through human symbiosis at work, which develops a management system that emulates relationships that are in congruence with basic human nature.

How much mutualism an organization has to practice for its success depends on how much a knowledge organization it is in comparison to its competitors, its position in its industry, and how far and how soon it wants to be a full-fledged knowledge organization.

Knowledge Skills

The employment skills of the twentieth century are not necessarily critical for organizational innovation in the information and electronic age. In fact, the ones we have known as marketable skills from their success in the management of traditional organizations, especially the ones of the twentieth century, are of little use in knowledge organizations. Even the basic skills such as reading, writing, and arithmetic may become irrelevant for knowledge organizations before we enter the second half of the twenty-first century. Computer skills will be redefined. Skills such as programming, system analysis, and system design will become obsolete.

Skills that will be the most important for knowledge organizations are those that are associated with the intellect of the individual. Presently, these skills are hard to teach and harder to assess. The challenge that institutions of higher learning worldwide will face will be their ability to equip their pupils with these creativity skills. Those universities around the world that will succeed in devising and revising curricula emphasizing these skills will be able to take over the leadership of the education for the twenty-first century and beyond. These skills, in six basic classifications, are described in the following section. Employees possessing these creativity skills will enable knowledge organizations to engage in ingenious actions to bring about innovation and productivity.

1. Skill to Refract. The creative skill to refract is required to understand and work with supracomplexity by identifying differences between many similar looking physical and metaphysical variables and all their interrelationships. Intellectual explorations will result in encounters with such physical and discarnate entities that, due to the lack of our experience with them, will appear to be similar. With refractivity, one will be able to see minute differences and be able to divide a set of all identical-looking elements into several subsets in accordance with their discovered microattributes.

Refractivity is an essential creativity skill needed to give new understanding to physical and nonphysical variables and to find creative encounters to interact with them.

In some form, mostly at the macro level, the skill to refract has been in use for inquiry into physical and life sciences. Its use in all other fields of arts and sciences will tremendously increase. In fact, opportunities in the future will mostly arise by successful applications of refractive skill in all areas of human concern, including business, economics, and human behavior in organizations.

2. Skill to Work with the Abstract. Innovative outcomes will require understanding and the transference of studies, knowledge, and experiences from one known field—manmade, natural, supernatural—to another field, known and unknown, which is under study or application. For the success of comprehension and communication in the complex technological environment of the future and to use unique means to represent existence and interrelationships among the physical and metaphysical, organizations will need their employees to possess the ability to work with the abstract. This creative skill is aimed at simplifying the process necessary to understand, record, and disseminate complexity. Science has used abstraction in modeling scientific phenomena. Knowledge organization management will need to be able to abstract conscious and subconscious physical, economical, social, and psychological human interactions and work with their abstractions.

3. Skill to Connect. Innovation generates opportunities through unveiling the existence of commonalities among apparently different physical and discarnate entities. The creative skill to connect can result in enhancing overlaps and plugging in voids. The ability could be used to see relevance among otherwise apparently diverse entities and help find innovative solutions to psychological, social, and physiological problems that constitute any system. The ability to connect can be very well exploited to give a positive overture to any social or psychological metaphor.

Connectivity reveals unique scenarios. This skill has been in use in organizations for several management functions but there has been no formal training to impart this skill or develop tools to assess its presence. In engineering, it can be used for product development, whereas in marketing, it can be used for product promotion.

The field of organizational management has many examples that illustrate applications of this skill. One very popular example is that of a California-based inventor of magnetic imaging technology who failed to connect it to the marketplace and sold the patent to a Japanese firm at a throwaway price. In turn, this firm connected the technology with the marketplace by developing it into videocassette taping, resulting in a number of successful products, such as the VCR and the camcorder.

At the sociopolitical level, U.S. president Ronald Reagan very effectively utilized creativity through the skill to connect in putting his message across to the masses during his successful election against his predecessor President Jimmy Carter.

4. *Skill to Extend.* The creative mind can take intelligent knowledge from one plane where it is well known and may be mature to other planes where it has not yet been discovered. In fact, this skill will extend the life of any physical or discarnate entity to perhaps infinity.

In organizations, through the ability to extend, a manager can turn every opportunity into an inexhaustible source of newer applications. The business world has many successful applications of this type of creativity. One example is drawn from General Motors. Technology engineers at Cadillac Motor Car Division extended the use of fiber cable from its prevalent application in the telecommunication industry to turn on a signal marker light. Cadillac engineers made use of the fact that, with fiber optics technology, light can be made to travel in bent and crooked lines. They used it to send light signals to several spots inside and outside the passenger areas of Cadillac to keep the driver apprised of the functioning of the marker. This multiple locale transmission of a single light source eliminated the necessity to have many bulbs perform the same job independently and guaranteed a foolproof operation of the turn signal system.

5. *Skill to Manipulate Time and Space.* This creative skill requires the ability to work with two important inputs of the physical world: time and space. Their manipulation occurs through concurrent functioning of several human faculties. It is the ability to comprehend a myriad of physical and discarnate variables with all possible interrelationships at any point in time and to regress or extrapolate them along the time or space dimension to any other point. Primarily, this skill gives one the ability to operate variables in these two dimensions through conceiving, imagining, and envisioning. It enables one to connect past, present, and future, first, in searching for real and fortuitous factors that relate to a given physical and/or abstract element and, then, understanding interactions among them along the time dimension. This skill helps create a host of scenarios in new light that has never been previously understood.

The twentieth century analytical technique of economic forecasting that extends variables from the past into the future to enhance human vision will be of little help in assessing and developing innovation. As we know, by function, it only extends the past and does not look into the future. For almost all other purposes too, this technique, in the form we know it presently, is going to be of very little help in understanding the shape, size, and pace of the changes coming in the future.

6. *Skill to Disseminate.* During the twentieth century, from written messages as the major means for spreading thoughts, man used electronic communication for getting "messages" across. Coding, transmission, and decoding have been utilized in sending messages from the sender to the receiver. This medium of communication became very popular, even though it never ensured accurate transmittal. The real aim of the sender is to send his thoughts, sometimes subconscious to himself, into the thoughts of a targeted receiver—thought-to-thought communication, which is the real aim of the dissemination. Due to the process and medium of transmission currently deployed, there is neither a surety of accuracy nor efficiency in this passing of thoughts.

Creative skill to disseminate can achieve this goal of transmission. A fast, effective, and efficient way to spread thoughts to the precisely targeted audience is achieved through *perception dissemination,* which may or may not need a medium. This requires creativity on the part of the sender. Moreover, on the part of the receiver, it requires the creativity to decipher the sender's perception.

To some extent, managers engage in perception dissemination on a one-on-one basis or even on a group basis through their physical presence. For each separate communication situation, creativity can produce a unique way for mass dissemination of perceptions with or without physical presence. These may use means that are nonsensory and utilize nonphysical mediums. Chapter 10 on organizational controls deals with some of these minute details in the context of knowledge organizations.

There are certain examples from organizations that illustrate some applications of this type of dissemination. During the 1950s and 1960s, when the Japanese were making serious attempts to proliferate their international trade, they used unique ways to disseminate the perception of the availability, low prices, and the quality of their products among prospective buyers. One way they achieved this was by shipping superior quality consumer goods with conspicuously given producer information on each item itself to fictitious addresses overseas, mostly in the developing countries, with instructions to the authorities to appropriately dispose of the merchandise if unclaimed by the addressee. As has been a standard practice in these countries, these unclaimed goods were auctioned at throwaway prices to local merchants who brought them to the marketplace at prices comparable to the throwaway prices they paid. The Japanese got an effortless, relatively inexpensive introduction of their products to their targeted markets. Later, many individuals from these markets sent orders for those goods.

It is now evident that there are organizations that are engaged in the use of the above given knowledge or intellectual skills as their main input to conduct their business, or they produce knowledge as their main output—what we called knowledge organizations. Since these skills are different and their employers' expectations from them are different from the traditional organizations, we have to manage them differently. Moreover, while much has been written about the innovation in organizations, there is not enough written about a clear, succinct management style that should work in these organizations.

The remaining chapters in this book describe and critically assess the suitability of management principles and practices for these organizations. Also covered are the usual functions performed by managers, such as motivating, leading, controlling, modifying behavior, and maintaining employee morale at a high level.

NOTE

1. Work environment is used here in the context it is used in organizations. A definition of work environment is given in the Glossary at the end of this work. A detailed description and discussion of work environment is given in other sections of this work.

REFERENCES

Amar, A.D. (1998, March). New worker and work management. *The Mid-Atlantic Journal of Business*, 34(1), 1–3.
Fayol, H. (1949). *General and industrial management* (translation). London, UK: Pitman Press.
Mandel, M.J., Carney, D., & Reinhardt, R. (2000, May 15). Antitrust for the digital age. *Business Week*, pp. 48–49.
Maslow, A.H. (1943, July). Theory of human motivation. *Psychological Review*, 370–96.
Smith, A. (1776). *An inquiry into the nature and causes of the wealth of nations* (Modern Library Edition, 1937). New York: Random House.
Taylor, F.W. (1911). *Principles of scientific management*. New York: Harper.
Weber, M. (1947). *Theory of social and economic organization* (A. M. Henderson, and T. Parson, Trans.). New York: Oxford University Press.

E-Business: Selection and Adaptation of Products and Services for the Internet Commerce

A.D. Amar

Despite the fact that the current century is still ongoing, it can be declared with almost full certainty that the Internet will be the most important invention of the twentieth century. It has influenced every discipline from the fine arts to delicate surgery. For some fields, it is forcing revision of fundamental guiding principles. However, one area that is being altered more than any other is commerce—the sale and distribution of goods and services. Foundation principles and practices of business are being shaken to their very roots by the Internet. Business discipline is being reinvented to adapt to the realities of the Internet. Further, over the next decade or so, the Internet will force a new thinking on everyone and everything directly or indirectly connected with business. How well a business—of any form or size—repositions itself in the marketplace and adjusts its practices, in light of the evolving principles because of the Internet, will decide for it the difference between success and struggle for survival.

For quite some time to come, the Internet, almost like a catapult, will continue to launch new opportunities for business such as never before. New business frontiers will be opened because of the Internet. Typically, when phenomena of this magnitude arise, there is much to be gained by being first to venture into the new territory. Moreover, even those pioneers who fail to cope with the environmental tumult come out with substantial gains. The Internet is a phenomenon that holds out that promise. The sooner a business incorporates the Internet in its primary operations—in other words, ventures into electronic commerce (e-commerce)—the greater will be the opportunities available to it. Moreover, to be able to continue to avail itself of the opportunities offered by the Internet, the firm should see that all its aspects, from accounting and finance to operations, be formalized and redesigned to exploit the Internet. If a firm cannot adapt to the Internet, or even worse, if it believes that its business is not suited to the Internet, then it could very well be working toward its own demise. This would be the moment for a firm to ask for the right help, or, in the alternative, to shift its leadership to those who accept the Internet with an aggressive perspective. Those who take an indifferent approach will lose their customers and markets to other firms, most surely the ones that would be operating from a dynamic "Internet perspective."

The biggest impact of the Internet on business will be transforming business to what is classified as "true competition" in economic theory. Everything that is applicable for industries operating in true competition will be valid for every business. The Internet will generate all characteristics that make business truly competitive: a large number of competitors, easy entry and exit, fewer intermediaries, less regulation, highly competitive prices, and freely available information. It will tremendously reduce the operational impact of both oligopoly and monopoly. An Internet-based business can operate without the resources and capital needs of a traditional business.

While the Internet is suitable for any business, given its operational characteristics, certain businesses are more appropriate for it. The biggest hurdle in starting an Internet business is selecting and adapting a product or a service that will best exploit these operational characteristics. Whereas some products or services are best suited to the Internet, others may be adapted to fit the Internet operations. In fact, the success of an Internet business will depend on the suitability of the product or service selected for the e-business. On the other hand, it will depend on how successfully the product or service has been adapted to the Internet operational characteristics.

Presently, with e-business in its infancy, it is easy for a firm to find a product or a service for which the Internet demand has still not reached a saturation stage. Of course, at the next stage in e-business, when all suitable products and services will have attained their saturation levels, new opportunities will arise only through innovative adaptation of those products and services to e-business operational characteristics. The task will be truly daunting.

Based on the ease with which firms can enter and capture a share of the existing market through employing e-business, products and services are categorized into four classes: (1) defined characteristics products, (2) defined functionality products, (3) dimensionless products, and (4) free functionality products. These classes are arranged in order of their suitability for the Internet; the first one is the easiest in terms of suitability and the last one is the hardest to transact using the Internet.

(1) DEFINED CHARACTERISTICS PRODUCTS

This category includes those products and services whose characteristics have been fully defined—*whole characteristics set*. In this case, the individual trading firm enjoys no discretion in defining any characteristic of the product or service. This constraint on the firm with regard to the product definition gives the customers full confidence to purchase it. A product in this category is a standard product that is the same no matter what source a customer acquires it from. Most of the branded, mass-manufactured for-stock products will fall into this category. Some specific examples of products in this class will include a prescription drug, a new videotape or audiotape of a certain title or by a particular artist, a certain edition of a book by a particular author, or a one-ounce Golden Eagle gold coin. Some examples of services that belong in this category are a hotel room with certain characteristics for a given night, such as a room with two double beds at the Waldorf Astoria in Manhattan for the night of March 16, 1999. Another example may be a British Airways first-class one-way ticket from London to New York by Flight BA117 on March 16, 1999.

Products and services in this category are the easiest to sell using the Internet, as the market is already established. In this case, the e-tailer (electronic retailer) firm is only displacing the traditional retailer. In marketing, the only competitive advantages that firms develop are low prices and earlier delivery, since all functions and quality are assured by the full definition of the product characteristics. Mostly, firms will be competing on the basis of price. In fact, that is what will make or break a deal. It is extremely hard to make a reasonable profit in such businesses. Unless they develop some product synergy or substantially raise the trading volume or succeed in eliminating competition, firms in e-tailing in this category will rarely succeed in making returns at a rate above the industry average. To gain competitive advantage based on faster delivery, firms may maintain a larger on-hand inventory, but that will increase the cost of doing business and will make it difficult for them to maintain a good rate of return.

The Internet success stories of the book retailer Amazon.com and other auction houses, such as eBay, and uBid, belong in this classification. However, there is no long record of accomplishment to base future production of success.

(2) DEFINED FUNCTIONALITY PRODUCTS

Products and services that are designed to serve a particular function with limited constraints and some flexibility are grouped in this class. These Internet products and services are created through the adaptations of existing products and services by relaxing almost all characteristics that constrain their sale to a typical Internet buyer. In fact, these adaptations accommodate all changes to enhance their suitability to market them on the Internet. Like any other innovative creation, these adaptations will require redesign of the products or services and will need to create unique marketing plans to give Internet buyers confidence to make purchases.

There are a number of examples taken from various industries that fit this classification. From the travel industry, there are an open round-trip ticket between London and New York; a five-star double-bed hotel room in Manhattan, good on any day a room is available; and a one-week mid-sized car rental good until used. An example from the entertainment industry may be a General Cinema movie ticket for the screening of a certain movie, valid until used. Other examples from this category may include jewelry items, such as a women's one-carat diamond platinum ring or a pair of 18-carat gold earrings. Others may be designer apparel, or a one-ounce gold bar. Services in this category might also include one-way taxi service from John F. Kennedy airport to central New Jersey on a given date.

(3) DIMENSIONLESS PRODUCTS

These products are designed to perform a function without any constraints on the product characteristics as were the ones used in previous classifications. They are aimed at mass merchandizing and carry a longer shelf life and maximum appeal to a maximum number of customers. Through redesign and repackaging, standard, traditionally marketed products and services can be adapted to become dimensionless. This adaptation adds value and gives customers the necessary confidence to buy them on the Internet. Due to the nature of dimensionless products, their creation may require collaborations among firms and industries. A very good example of this would be an airline ticket good for travel with any of a group of airlines to anywhere within the United States.

While on the one hand longer shelf life due to adaptation increases the attractiveness of dimensionless service products to the buyers, on the other hand it increases the after-purchase storage period. The increase in the storage period decreases the rate of redemption of these service products by their buyers, which results in reduced cost to the selling firm due to the cash flow benefits. The airline ticket example given earlier provides a very good application of this concept.

To expand it further, let us follow up on some other examples from the previous classifications. A dimensionless product from the travel industry will be a one-night hotel room of a certain class anywhere in the United States. From the banking industry, a credit card with a set finance charge, a home mortgage at a particular rate, and a personal noncollateral loan at a given interest rate are examples of products in this category. From the entertainment industry, an example of a dimensionless product would be a movie ticket good for any showing at any movie theater anywhere in the United States, with no expiration. Through proper design and collaboration among firms, any product or service can be turned into a dimensionless product.

(4) FREE FUNCTIONALITY PRODUCTS

Products and services that are custom produced or require customization, including a large number of personal services, are categorized as free functionality products. These products or services are designed to perform a specialized, unique function. They are defined by units of a generic function, such as an hour of a licensed plumber, rather than a whole comprehensive job, such as replacing a bathtub.

A few products, such as custom-tailored apparel, construction of single-family houses, and renovation projects are good examples from this category. Services such as provided by a doctor, a lawyer, a consultant, a plumber or an outpatient or clinic visit will also belong in this category. Firms can adapt these services as product units, such as the hours of lawyer consultations and the number of visits to a doctor's office, and sell them on the Internet.

There are many opportunities for all firms, both new and established, to grow and prosper using the Internet. The resultant turmoil that will be caused in business will not only redefine business, it will change the landscape of the American corporate world with new brand names, icons, and success stories. Entrepreneurship and risk taking will again flourish and become the watchword of American commerce.

Source: Reproduced in original from *The Mid-Atlantic Journal of Business*, 35, no. 1, March 1999. Published by Division of Research, W. Paul Stillman School of Business, Seton Hall University. Reprinted with permission.

Section II ————————————————

KNOWLEDGE WORKERS

Chapter 2 —————————————————————————

Sociology of
Knowledge Workers

In a study released in May 2000 by Radcliffe Public Policy Center, it was revealed that 84 percent of employees in their 20s and 30s—members of Generations X and Y, those most likely to possess marketable recent knowledge—had a family-friendly work schedule as a priority in selecting their jobs. About half of all employees included in this study said that they valued altruism in choosing jobs—the availability of a chance to help society or their local communities was a very important component in their picking a job (Smith, 2000).

> O' it's so confusing.
> Did the surveyors get it right?
> Did they say altruism?
> Altruism as a factor in the selection of a job?

Of course, yes. This is the new generation of workers. If an old-time manager knew the results from this study, he would be flabbergasted. In fact, he would find all the reasons to flaw the study. Nevertheless, that is how the new generations, X and Y, are behaving.

The essence is that the understanding of the sociology of the new generation of employees is very important in recruiting, retaining, and getting optimal performance from them for all the organizations. Nevertheless, it is especially important for knowledge organizations, because these generations have practically a monopoly on the main input needed by them. Recognizing this fact, this chapter discusses how sociology aspects affect knowledge employees' work behavior and details the challenges that managers are facing or are expected to face in the workplace due to the sociology of these new generations. This chapter also models work behavior and personalities of employees belonging to Generation X (Gen Xers) and Generation Y. It studies socioeconomic dynamics that have caused these changes and relates their behavior to the most prevalent characteristics in their personality. Three broad personality topologies are given to help managers of these organizations to *initiate*—mind managers should never really typify—their understanding of the work behavior of knowledge employees.

The biggest challenge that management of knowledge organizations confronted during the 1990s, and will continue to face in the future, came from changes in work behavior of the new generations of workers. These employees, even though young, have superior knowledge and skills, more so than the managers who are supervising them and who have the responsibility to create the environment in which they work. If management understands their psychology and sociology and knows how to work with them, it can make them the supersmart employees it dreams of, but if it does not understand them, then it can turn them into sloths. Communicating similar feelings in *CEO Sound-Off* (1997, July), the owner of a California manufacturing organization relates his experience with Gen Xers who are coming out of college and working for him by stating that they "aren't getting the right opportunities or aren't being asked to use their abilities. That's more the problem than that they are lazy. We have all Gen Xers here. They work really hard."

NEW GENERATIONS AT WORK

This problem will be further aggravated when children born between 1977 and 1994—Generation Y, or Generation Nexters as some prefer to call them (Zemke, Raines, & Filipczak, 1999)—join the workforce. While a few of them have joined the workforce in 1999, 2000, and 2001, most of them are currently in schools or colleges working on their first degrees. The behavior of Gen Xers and Generation Y is fully different from that of the generations of the early- to mid-twentieth century and much different from that of the Baby Boomers. Generation Y is even different from early members of Generation X. The future of the next few decades, and particularly the current decade of all organizations that are engaged in the searching and applying of knowledge, will depend on them. In fact, they will be laying the foundation on which the worldwide economic growth of the current century is going to depend.

Due to the availability and prevalence of computing and automation technology during their developmental years, and their knowledge and fascination with the Internet, Generations X and Y have superior command over knowledge, especially the technology knowledge. Members of these generations, particularly Generation Y, have command over the Internet, says Don Tapscott (1999), the author of *Growing Up Digital*, because unlike their predecessors who only "passively" worked with technology or enjoyed traditional electronic media, they do not just observe the Internet, they participate as well. They actively engage it. They interact with it. They are the users and the producers. The success and proliferation of the Internet and technology depend on an estimated 88 million people in the United States (Shannon, 1998), most of them belonging to these new generations. The biggest difference between these and past generations is that Generations X and Y are the first international generations. The Internet has made it possible to gauge people in all parts of the world by one set of norms like never before in the recorded history of mankind.

Because of their successful generalization of human behavior in the past, managers will quite likely ignore most perceptible differences that these new generations have from their predecessors. A large number of these managers still continue to rely on outmoded managerial and behavioral theories and practices of the twentieth century. Instead, managers should be ready to know their employees' unique behaviors and adapt work—the knowledge work—and the work environment to suit them. They should not allow their management styles to be guided by old, deductive psychological and organizational behavioral theories. The behavior of these generations is far more dynamic. Managers should revisit their management principles and business practices and modify them or just eliminate them if they are found invalid for these new employees and the processes of knowledge organizations. Based on the limited observations made, the safer move for them would be to assume that none of the well-practiced management techniques and principles of the last century will be suitable for employees from the new generations.

These facts create urgency for knowledge organizations to have a working understanding of the mind and behavior of Generations X and Y and of how to avail themselves of the great potential these generations have to offer to them. To assume that members of these generations are just like other employees would be a fatal flaw committed by any firm employing them. Data have shown that their work expectations and how they derive satisfaction from it are different from Baby Boomers. From a Conference Board survey of employee satisfaction, Koretz (2000) reports that in a period of declining job satisfaction, the happiest workers are from Generations X and Y, and the least satisfied are Baby Boomers, with the former having a satisfaction rate of 55 percent and the latter, 46.5 percent.

Understanding the minds of Generations X and Y employees will assure knowledge organizations that they will be able to fully utilize this bright generation coming to work and, further, that subsequent generations of workers will also be productive, since the behavior of Generations X and Y employees is expected to continue to mold future generations.

Observations on the personality of Generations X and Y have shown that these new workers are too smart to be led into the type of "coexistence arrangement" at work that their predecessors—especially the Baby Boomers, who continued to be productive contributors to the success of their employers—embraced without any concerns. This new generation of workers will operate under fully new rules. Knowledge organization managers will have to learn these rules and operate by them in order to evolve a work relationship that will unleash the minds of Generations X and Y for innovation and productivity gains for the organization.

RESPONSIBILITY AND RELATIONSHIPS

Even though we know that with each succeeding generation the age of responsibility—the age at which humans are ready to assume responsible and leadership positions—has declined, never has there been such a big drop from one generation to the next, as we are seeing in Generations X and Y. Members of these generations are ready to take up leadership and top decision-making positions at a much younger age than their predecessors have—in fact, younger than at any other time. Generations X and Y are expected to cut this age still further.

Whereas Baby Boomers, in spite of their vow to change the world, ended up accepting it practically exactly as it was, members of these new generations appear to possess all that is needed to actually change it—in their own way. They have matured at a much younger age than their predecessors did, due for the most part to the way they were brought up. They have experienced the pressure to grow up faster, along both psychological and physiological dimensions. It has happened mostly unwillingly, mainly because their resistance to this pressure to change has been unsuccessful. The changed family structure, needs, and norms did not leave room for any alternative but change.

There is nothing "traditional" about Generations X and Y. They are the first generations bearing the full effect of having career mothers, who worked full time outside of the home. Sociological surveys have revealed to us that most members of these generations have not had either a mother or father available to them when needed. They were left on their own to explore and establish relationships outside the parental bond. This experience has made them redefine human relationships—devising some and eliminating others.

Traditionally, the most powerful human relationships emerge out of natural bonds, such as those offered by parents and siblings. These relationships are guided by ethics, commitment, and responsibility, that is, *ethical relationships*. This is what past generations had mainly known. Generations X and Y have not experienced these relationships in the way their predecessors did and, hence, do not perceive relationships traditionally. Further, Generations X and Y members give a new interpretation to two other human relationships—*emotional relationships* and *sensual relationships*. Both of these relationships are primarily voluntary and emerge out of emotional dependence and sensual gratification, respectively. These relationships have greater importance to Generations X and Y members than do the ethical relationships. In fact, according to a survey, a large number of the members of Generations X and Y do not want their parents to be present with them. They want to be left alone and be able to move on their own at a young age.

Generations X and Y: Family

Largely, the sociological changes of the twentieth century are the cause of the emerging new behavior of these generations coming to work for knowledge organizations. Ironically, most of these changes actually have been in response to the work demands from jobs in large, complex organizations. These demands have resulted in new work rules that have affected the formulation and maintenance of the family—the most important building block of any society. The changes relating to this formulation have been so significant that the meaning of family itself has been totally changed during the last century. Moreover, this revolution is still on.

The first half of the twentieth century redefined the family unit because of man entering the job market. From the undisputed head of a home-based, family-run independent operation, man became a fully controlled, subservient worker whose life depended on and revolved around the whims of others. This forced the family to rebalance essential roles and responsibilities. While the family unit barely learned to adjust to this new reality, large organizations pulled women away from home to fill their need for additional help. As women came to work, eventually organizations placed them in the same condition in which they had put men a generation ago. The end of the family unit as it had been known and understood for several centuries drew nearer. That commenced a redefinition of other social and biological relationships.

Generation Y is the first full product of these newly emerged human relationships and the roles of those playing these relationships. Further, changes in family relationships, such as the marriage of two "independent" persons, single parents, same-sex parents, same-sex marriages, unwed parents, biological parents, surrogate parents, and artificially inseminated parents, will give new meaning to all relationships and will have an important bearing on the management of organizations employing them.

As the end of the job era extends further into the twenty-first century and labor-intensive operations in organizations further diminish, thereby requiring far fewer workers to produce the same number of goods and services, there will be more leisure time and a reemergence of the importance of "belonging to a sociological unit" among people. The form that it will take is still uncertain. No matter, there will be greater stress on playing the required familial roles and assuming responsibility in personal relationships. This behavior will eventually extend to other human social relationships. There will be additional sociopsychological changes occurring. How and to what extent these changes will affect the new family and whether they will revive the roles and responsibilities of the family of the pre–job era will decide human relationships in the future. This should be a very interesting area of study. There is almost no chance that society will return to the old family model. Most likely, family will evolve into something new that may rest in between the pre–job era family model and the model of the late twentieth century family. Slowly, the new family model will acquire some resemblance to the pre–job era family of the late-nineteenth to early-twentieth centuries.

We still do not know which way the family unit is headed: pushing further in the direction set by the last century, taking an about turn, or evolving in a new direction altogether. If the past were any predictor, we would assume that the family of the twenty-first century is going to be unique. Managers will have to observe these changes and adapt their management styles to be consistent with them.

GENERATIONS X AND Y: PERSONALITY

The Generation X and Y eras have seen the onset of a time during which rules of behavior have been totally revamped, not only the ones relating to work but also those prescribing dyadic relationships, such as parent-child, husband-wife, and sibling-sibling. These changes in general attitude and behavior are also going to impact relationships in other contexts, such as community, broader society, politics, professions, and other human functions in all possible spheres. The impact that these changes will have on work and the preparation for such changes that their employers will have to make should be of great interest to knowledge organizations and are covered in detail in other more relevant sections of this book.

Personality Traits

Members of Generations X and Y present an extremely wide range of behavioral patterns—in fact, a universe of behaviors never before demonstrated by any other generation. Making generalizations about their behavior would simply be naive. Each of them is unique; a generalization of any type would be counterproductive. Before deciding how to respond to situations, managers will have to know the value system of each in order to successfully get the most innovative and productive behavior from him or her. Managing Generations X and Y members without understanding their value system will result in the failure to utilize their ambitions and talents to the fullest extent.

The attribution of family traits of members of Generations X and Y to their organizational behavior and performance may be too risky and misleading. Nevertheless, it is very important for a manager to be aware of all possible variation patterns in their organizational behavior and the traits that mold their personality. At the least, this will make the manager aware of what he is rejecting and what to accept in its place.

Some of these important traits and their development during the growth of Generations X and Y from childhood to work age are discussed below.

Misguided by Some Standards. As a rule, the greatest influence on the development of human beings has always come from home—the people who have known them throughout their formative years. These individuals typically have been family members—parents, grandparents, siblings—and other close relatives whose lives have been interwoven. They have been motivated by their desire to achieve what was good for those whom they were guiding. Generations X and Y are the first full generations that have not experienced this personality developmental process. For many of these members, there was no "home" or "family" of the kind that the generations before them had known. Consequently, many members of this generation grew out of childhood without learning many of the standards of behavior that were passed down from the past generations to the new generations. They engaged in formative interactions with several other individuals and groups, making up for the incomplete and inconclusive formative influence of the home or, in some cases, in total substitution of the home. This lack of satiation of interaction with family members, and the failure to get answers from home, resulted in more inquisitiveness and increased confusion and dissonance about the standards of behavior among members of these generations. Whereas Baby Boomers revolted against what they did not accept as "right," many members of Generations X and Y genuinely do not even know what is right and what is wrong. Those concepts have simply not been passed down to them. The principle that any society should assume responsibility for all acts, good or bad, performed by its members is truly applicable in cases of those belonging to Generations X and Y. These people are sincere, motivated individuals who wanted to learn standards and values, but had no one there to teach them. Their value-free development has actually increased their interest in understanding and learning normative behavior and values. This inquisitiveness has sent them seeking answers from others within their reach—mostly individuals who are misguided or confused themselves and should not be approached for such answers in the first place.

"Confused" Value Systems. Many managers and other observers of Generations X and Y behavior have noticed a lack, or laxity, of values among its members as compared with the value system of past generations, including the Baby Boomers. In actuality, it is a misreading. In spite of the "value-free" and/or confused-value upbringing of Generations X and Y, as was natural to occur, members of Generations X and Y did develop values. In fact, they have a much stronger value system than their predecessors; however, it is a different value system. Since preceding generations failed to convince them of the superiority of their value systems, Generations X and Y members have struggled with their value system in isolation. Their younger members are still struggling. They are developing and discovering values on their own. In search of these values, many of them rediscovered faith and spiritualism,

sought refuge in religions, adopted fundamental religious values, or been re-born as believers in God and prophets. With many members of Generations X and Y, this has resulted in a value system that is quite contrary to that of past generations. This lack of congruence is wrongly interpreted as a value vacuum.

Members of Generations X and Y will continue to experiment with new and different values and evolve them as we proceed into the twenty-first century. This evolving value system will continue to be different from the value system of past generations, which will continue to be "confused" by the value system of Generations X and Y. Generations X and Y will defy all that has been so dearly held by their predecessors. There will be virtually a revolution in the value system that will keep sociologists, psychologists, anthropologists, ethicists, and educators busy studying, rationalizing, modeling, and theorizing the motives behind the development of the Generations X and Y value system for a long time to come.

Generation Y will finally bring about the social revolution that the Baby Boomers have longed to do, however, with an outcome of their own choosing.

Very Technology Smart. As a generation, members of Generations X and Y are smart, ambitious, and intellectual as compared with previous generations. Their intelligence is reflected in many nontraditional ways, from breaking into Pentagon computers to organizing and leading inner city street gangs in Central Los Angeles. In addition to the ways traditionally accepted as intelligent, some members of Generations X and Y are reflecting their intelligence in so many new ways that the available intelligence measurement instruments, such as the IQ test—the Stanford-Binet or the Wechsler Intelligence Scale for Children (WISC)—cannot even assess. Such measurement requires a new understanding of intelligence itself. The unique ways that Generations X and Y members have reflected intelligence have forced a new thinking of intelligence and have initiated new research to measure it.

To take advantage of Generations X and Y intelligence, society will have to involve them in the attainment of productive social goals. Organizations will have to redesign their work and create an appropriate environment for the realization of these goals. A proper understanding of the psychology, communications, and actions of Generations X and Y can help organizations employ their talents to unleash tremendous innovation in bringing out new, unusual products and services at a productivity level that will defy containment. On the other hand, failure to utilize their talents could make their intelligence disappear quickly or, even worse, turn into something counterorganizational and antisocial. Timing will be of the essence in this regard. If not offered the appropriate milieu for success, Generations X and Y will shed motivation that will be almost impossible to revive.

This new generation of workers poses a challenge to society: how to keep so many bright young minds occupied. It is the problem of plenty—plenty of talent. Smart, ambitious minds with a "different" value system could be the biggest danger to any society. Left idle, it could potentially be what we have historically known as the "devil's workshop."

Sense of Omnipotence: "The Power Is with You" Syndrome. Generations X and Y achieved a sense of confidence and *success* at an early age through their *victories* at video games and computer interactions. The tough games they "overpowered" and computer problems they solved gave them a sense of potency to resolve any tough situation. Age was not a barrier to them. This confidence, combined with the independence that was effectively "forced" on them, made them grow up. They feel that they can handle any situation and solve any problem—social or organizational—without any help, either from members of their generation or past generations.

Most members of Generations X and Y still treat the real world as virtual reality. This "out of touch with reality," compounded with confidence and the sense of "the power is with you," is what organizations can groom into constructive imagination and innovative behavior at work. Video games and computers taught five very important skills to Generations X and Y that very few successful organizational managers of the previous generations possessed. Collectively, we call them *"the power is with you"* syndrome. These skills are:

(a) *Problem abstraction:* One very important skill that managers worked hard to acquire, or went to top-notch business schools to learn, was how to model business reality to comprehend problems and arrive at solutions and methods for their implementation. Most members of Generation Y mastered this skill before their tenth birthday! Electronic games and computers have given them a perspective to conceive of problems with imaginary and simulated variables, an essential skill to understanding complex real-world problems, especially those of knowledge organizations.

(b) *Micro focus:* Organizations all over the world invest huge amounts of money to have their managers trained in skills essential for focusing on issues and achieving goals without allowing themselves to be distracted. However, in spite of such training, many managers cannot attain the desired level of the ability to focus. A large number of Gen Xers and members of Generation Y have perfected this skill to a micro level. They can allow themselves to be so engrossed in an activity that they could care less if the rest of the world exists. They have acquired this expertise through the power of electronic games. They have learned how to stay on an issue and then focus only on what is relevant to that issue, and ignore whatever else is irrelevant or on the fringes of the issue at hand.

(c) *Optimal solution:* A large number of managers, especially in government and public sector organizations, attempt to resolve issues only to the extent that they cease to be *issues* anymore (i.e., making sure that they do not make headlines and are successfully removed from the public sight). In such organizations, there is almost never an attempt to look for optimal solutions. Training at engineering and business schools emphasizes the importance of searching for and implementing optimal solutions. By their characteristics, these solutions are hard to both find and implement. Members of Generations X and Y began their lives with an understanding and achievement of optimal solutions. For them, each problem situation could result in either achieving and implementing an optimal solution or in total failure. There was nothing in between. They learned it from electronic games and computers. They learned that there is one right solution that brings success and everything else is wrong and cause for failure. They also learned that these outcomes are not influenced by emotions and that implementation only understands commands that fully comply with one predetermined—maybe unknown to them—set.

Members of Generations X and Y know how to cut the irrelevant and unproductive, skip the unnecessary detail, and get straight to the right solution.

(d) *Quick response:* The fourth element of "the power is with you" syndrome is the ability to make a quick response. Members of Generations X and Y acquired the dexterity to give quick responses through their experience with computer and electronic games. They faced tough competition when playing these games. They knew that just being correct was not enough; they had to be right and they had to be quick or miss the narrow window of opportunity. They knew that whosoever made the first correct response "won." They also knew that if they did not respond quickly, the conditions totally changed and the whole effort became worthless. A correct response that was late was a thud, not a response.

This should be the ability that companies want their top managers to have in order to compete in a world where the one who is first is usually the winner.

(e) *It is the Karma:* Generations X and Y members learned that when it came to electronic games and computers, the only actions that mattered to their success and failure were the ones that *they* took. No one else could make any difference to the outcomes of their actions. They alone controlled their actions and, further, they controlled only their actions. Once a step was taken, the outcome was certain—an outcome that was very specific to the step taken. Nobody could avoid it. Moreover, the consequence—good or bad—was for the person who acted, not for anybody else. They knew that there were no pardons and that there was no kindness. To win, they had to do the right Karma; nothing could be achieved without it. They also learned that no one could be blamed for their loss and that victory came through learning and improved actions. The power came after that.

To them, that is exactly how responsibility is accounted for and productive organizations are run for success.

Given that these five skills are present in a job applicant, there are no other basic abilities that knowledge organizations will need in an employee responsible for uniquely solving its knowledge problems of the twenty-first century. All that knowledge organization managers have to know is how to successfully transplant these abilities present in Generations X and Y members to work problems of their organizations so that these turn into productive work skills. A knowledge organization has to accept that there is only a fine line between the abilities essential to play and win at these games and the abilities to solve technology problems of real life. Organization management has to look for members of Gen Xers and Generation Y who have excelled at these games and make them cross over with these skills to organizational life. Even so, these Gen Xers and Generation Y members will have difficulty managing the Baby Boomers due to the latter's lack of technology experience. Says one Gen Xer who is a human resource manager for a manufacturing company, "The differences in characteristics—such as Xers being more diverse, high-tech, results-oriented and, of course, the definition of 'loyalty'—seem to be a roadblock at times when trying to have a positive influence on an organization" (Adams III, 1999). Knowledge organizations may actually engage in the development of video games and virtual reality models to abstract real-life situations to enable Gen Xers and Generation Y members to solve them uniquely. It will also be a good training tool for managers for the generations following Generations X and Y.

Selective Commitment. When it comes to organizational commitment from Generations X and Y, different managers have different experiences. There are those who are fully confused about their sense of commitment and do not want to express any opinion on this issue. Then, there are those who fall on either of the two extremes: They may describe Generations X and Y members as totally void of any sense of commitment, or they may praise them for taking their commitments so seriously. Surprisingly, both of these observations of Generations X and Y members could be correct. Their behavior on commitment draws from their value system. The existence of these extremes is explained by the fact that these new generations of workers, in contrast to their predecessors, are fully internally controlled. Members of these generations independently set their goals and then work with full commitment for their fulfillment. If externally set goals, such as the ones from their organizations, are in congruence with those that they have set for themselves, then they will work for their attainment with great commitment. If such congruence is lacking, they will act fully indifferent, with or without letting others know their mind or the reasons leading to their indifference. When Jason Lundy, executive director of marketing and strategic planning at *Esquire* in New York, says about Generation Y members, "They often act as if they are doing you a favor by working for you," he simply conveys his experiencing of this lack of congruence on the part of some members of this generation working for him (Mui, 2001). This behavior is consistent with their sense of independence.

The commitment of Generations X and Y members, in most work situations, will have to be won over by their organizations on the terms and conditions laid by them. As a rule, winning their commitment, even on their terms, will be worthwhile for the knowledge organizations.

Stoic and Determined. The new generation members, in particular Generation Y, possess strong willpower that they have acquired from the way that they were nurtured. They have been brought up in an environment that did not allow for any accommodation. In this environment, requests and pleadings did not change the obvious outcomes—pleasant or unpleasant. This is the behavior that they have learned, and this is the behavior that most of them reflect. Just the way that their mother, when they barely recognized her, had shown determination in treating them the way she saw fit—by leaving them to go to work in spite of their cries and begging—electronic games and computers later treated them in the same way. There was no consideration in their treatment either. Members of Generations X and Y are replicating this behavior to deal with the real world around them. To them, life is a chain of fixed linkages of almost predetermined acts and outcomes operating within a controlled, limited, and definite set. Further, their behavior reflects that, in order to cause the occurrence of a certain desired outcome at a certain time, working backward, they must engage in the correct acts provided by the appropriate linkages with them during the right "time window." There is no deviation, no mercy, and no pardon. Moreover, the set is exhaustive and there is no other way to affect these outcomes. This belief can influence their behavior both ways, positively and negatively. The positive aspect gives them a character of strength through a feeling of efficacy and a sense of responsibility. The negative aspect makes them continue to grow with these inconclusive linkages. They extend this model to all others, even those from other generations who do not have these beliefs. It can quickly make them lose motivation and become extremely despondent. Such a feeling can come on even a faint belief that they did not "play" things "right" and, hence, the outcome will not be the one desired. It furthers a sense of despair due to the belief that nothing could change it—the "*it is all over*" syndrome. It is this syndrome that can make Generations X and Y members inflict extreme tragedies both on themselves and on others.

Because Generation Y members have experienced that they could not sway others from their determinations with the emotions that they reflected, they, generally, do not allow themselves to be swayed by the emotions of those with whom they deal. They have learned to make objective decisions and to stick with them. Easy-going, flexible decisions with room for accommodation of the Baby Boomers are not what they have experienced and are not what they will reflect to others around them.

This type of behavior, not only on the part of Generations X and Y, but also, in general, is going to gain strength as we advance into the twenty-first century. Generations X and Y members will treat their children the way they themselves were treated, making the future generations even more stoic, determined, and strong-willed, thus further strengthening this behavior of the mid- to late-nineties into the future.

Disdain for Authority. Management researchers already know that an authoritarian model of management may work only weakly in motivating and getting work from workers in general, but they will soon learn that, in the case of Generations X and Y, this model will become fully ineffective. In fact, a manager should discard it altogether while dealing with Generations X and Y members because it is going to be the most counteractive force in unleashing their talent and in gaining their commitment.

Throughout their development, members of Generation Y have had practically no exposure to authority. The first and most appropriate exposure gaining their respect for authority that could have come from their parents never came. Their parents were not there to direct them. There could be several reasons for this: The parents were (a) too busy for their children, (b) unsure of their own abilities to provide meaningful contribution to solve their children's "complex" problems, (c) too old to assert, or (d) believed in nonassertive treatment of their offspring. The latter may be truer for parents of the Baby Boomer generation. In the future, with the child-bearing period pushed even later into parents' lives, this syndrome will become more pronounced. Aging parents have greatly contributed to the lack of experience with authority and discipline of Generations X and Y. Older parents in general are more passive with their offspring and eschew the use of authority.

The second exposure that can teach children respect for authority comes from grandparents, but the diminution of family to nuclear size during the twentieth century did not allow this to occur for members of Generations X and Y.

The third common source of respect for authority, though to a lesser extent, comes from older siblings. A reduction in the number of offspring per couple during the Baby Boomer generation either did not allow members of Generations X and Y to have siblings or allowed them to have only one. This resulted in an absence of a sibling experience or in a relationship of equals—without any real responsibility and authority on the part of any sibling—replacing the sibling relationship in which there was a hierarchy with authority.

Parents of Generations X and Y members made sure that evasion of authority on their children continued outside their homes also. During the preschool years of members of Generations X and Y, their parents forbade any external challenges to this lack of exercise of authority. No teacher could use force or authority on Generations X and Y members. The same pattern extended into their school years. During their school years, teachers and staff who decided to use authority on Generations X and Y members realized that the use of force actually backfired with the same or even greater force. Eventually, they accepted that the use of authority on Generations X and Y members would not work to anyone's advantage.

There is no reason to believe that the use of authority in organizational settings in making Generations X and Y members learn work behavior will be effective. Some managers will attempt to assert their wishes on Generations X and Y members, until they realize that it is inconsistent with their personality and goes against realizing innovation and productivity from them. Managers should know that modifying behavior of this generation with the use of authority is not an effective alternative. Generations X and Y may become effectively engaged in achieving organizational goals through reason, subtle motivation, appealing emotion, but definitely not through autocratic behavior and overt domination from anyone, especially from those belonging to any generation other than their own.

Generations X and Y members will accept only one uniformly applied model of work behavior. They will force organizations to develop a symbiotic behavior consistent with this norm. That is why this book, in later chapters, recommends the human symbiosis model as an effective way to operate knowledge organizations, since the future of these organizations depends on the effectiveness of Generations X and Y employees.

A New Kind of Discipline. Generations X and Y members do not have the same kind of discipline that past generations had. The difference lies not so much in the degree of obedience that they do or do not have. To them, the presence or absence of the discipline trait depends on the reference point used in persuading them to obey. They themselves will first set a reference point and rules of behavior, then will conform to them and, according to that, will consider themselves disciplined. To them, conformance with rules set by others is not a question of discipline; it is subjugation, which, they believe, is inherently wrong, as it is good neither for themselves nor for those who wished them well. To them, their predecessors' brand of discipline amounts to boundaries, and they do not want boundaries for their spirits or for their minds or actions.

Moreover, this discipline is not what managers should encourage because it is not needed for producing and deploying knowledge and, in fact, its presence may actually impede the primary goal of knowledge organizations. A knowledge organization manager should not attempt to make them "disciplined." It is this "lack" of discipline that makes them so suited for the innovation functions. This behavior is apropos for assignments that have not been previously handled successfully. Members of Generations X and Y, with a strong presence of this trait, will give new definition to problems and find unique, new means to solve them by trying the unusual, the forbidden, and the nontraditional.

Disciplining members of Generations X and Y comes from inside, and it would be good to leave it that way. The best strategy needed to manage them depends on the assignment that they will undertake. If the work is well structured, the closeness of fit between the value system that they avow and the one that the organization proclaims may dictate their suitability for the job. However, if the work is not fully structured, the optimal strategy to manage them is to leave them with their value system and let the organization act as a facilitator rather than as a mentor.

If their value system converges with the requisites for the success of the organization, members of Generations X and Y will provide the kind of commitment and adherence that will be much more advanced than that of their predecessors. If not, then managers may take the second approach to keep them innovative and productive: Label them "rebellious," and give them the freedom to form their own little organization within the organization. This new little "rebellious" organization should be given the toughest work in the organization, and the manager will get most of it completed successfully and in the most efficient manner.

In later parts of this book, we will deal with ways to understand and design work to provide a good fit between work and the individual personality of each member of Generations X and Y working in knowledge organizations.

Lonely, Shallow-Rooted. During the many generations preceding Generations X and Y, social evolution of humans has slowly transformed man from a gregarious, enmeshed herds-keeper to a self-centered, self-dependent individual. The way members of Generations X and Y have been brought up has further hastened this process. The sociology and technology of their generation has promoted physical, psychological, and social isolationism among them. A large number of Generations X and Y members have never really *belonged* to someone with whom a meaningful, long-term relationship could be developed. So many of them have never been even close to enough people to build a family.

Generations X and Y members do not have the same concept of belongingness and closeness that past generations had. These generations give a new meaning to human belonging. In this context, traditional participants in strong, long-lasting stable relationships, such as the ones between parents, grandparents, siblings, spouses, and offspring, have had their roles redefined during the later parts of the twentieth century. Moreover, the evolution is still on. These new definitions do not require that having a meaningful relationship means developing spiritual, psychological, or even physical bonds essential to bring about closeness for which every human being has longed. Both the societal and personal environments in which every one of these important role-players has functioned during the later part of the twentieth century have not allowed the resources necessary for the development of the bonds that eventually lead to close relationships. Most members of these generations had been left alone to struggle and find their own answers—untested, unproved, and probably wrong—to the kind of problems that humans have faced since time immemorial. In this new setup, when members of these generations needed help during their development, at the most, as a gesture of concern, they were given the advice to seek professional counseling or join support groups of similar lonely strangers. The only companion many of them have known is their pet cat or dog.

GENERAL PERSONALITY TOPOLOGY

Variations in human personalities during the current century are going to be greater than they have been in the past, not only due to the fact that the process of human psychological evolution has sped up but also because the sources that help form human personality have increased. Although almost all members of Generations X and Y reflect most of the traits given above to some extent, how these are grouped, prioritized, and applied makes them different.

In spite of the fact that all members of Generations X and Y are different and unique, a topology may give a manager some base to start the process of understanding them. It is a good gross classification that may later be fine-tuned to better understand each one of them individually. A study of these topologies should help managers reduce the immense complexity in understanding human behavior at work. One may then devise strategies in dealing with them. However, by no means should one assume that members of Generations X and Y can be fit in these topologies.

Based on this concept, we can group dominant traits among Generations X and Y members into three personality topologies described below.

The Rationalist

The first personality type describing members of Generations X and Y is derived from the theme directing their motives and is labeled "the rationalist." It is expected to be the most common of the three topologies characterizing them. Objectivity seriously drives all behaviors reflected by this type. Reason, logic, and rationality guide those belonging to this category. They will argue for or against the issues, not consistently ending up on the same side of the same issue. All their decisions are made at the material level. They need proof before they will accept anything. Even if they apparently seem to agree without proof, in dealing with members belonging to this type, a manager should insist on showing them data, inferences, and other evidence in support of his arguments. They believe in what is presented in a systematic, logical way, such as in writing or through a planned presentation. Opinions, others' experiences, and anecdotes do not convince them or influence their thinking.

Their experiences with money surround most of the rationalists' objectivity. All their objectives are in dollars and cents. Further, they measure everything by the yardstick of money and believe money can get them everything. To a large majority of them, money is the most important thing because, according to their experiences, it gets them whatever they need. The rationalist members of Generations X and Y think that riches can gain them recognition, respect, education, brains, oratory, health, good looks, friends, and everything else imaginable in this world.

Strange as it may sound, the rationalist treats money, on the income side, as if it were the most important motivator and, on the spending side, as if it had no worth at all. To the rationalists, value is what they exchanged for money, and its value depends on how much money it took in the exchange. Anything that takes less of their money is not as good and anything that takes no money is not good at all. The rationalists belonging to Generations X and Y will not be thrifty like their parents were.

In organizational settings, the rationalists will allow themselves to be managed and controlled only if they are convinced that the consequence of the act will lead to an outcome of value to them. To convince the rationalists, a manager will have to use either straight economic reasoning or a logical rationale, impressing the importance of their act to many others and explaining why their role is so important in its achievement. In general, all decisions a manager makes that are expected to influence the rationalist must come with a lot of explanation. Logical communication will win them over. The rationalists have a sense of self-potency. They perceive that all reality around them is a sequence of interconnected, logical actions that are simply a consequence of the efforts of their doers that they consciously put in to achieve their objectives.

A manager may find this personality topology well suited to undertake general management and other organizational functional areas, such as those relating to systems analysis and design, market development, customer service, engineering, production, distribution, finance, and accounting. They will be well suited to undertake assignments in autonomous work groups, where they will emerge as instantaneous leaders and will bring the group to success.

The Rebel

The second personality category of Generations X and Y members includes those who will not accept any way other than their way for everything. Nothing will make them change their minds or their decisions or stop them from engaging in acts that they have decided to engage in, irrespective of whether these acts result in success or failure or are right or wrong. The result of these actions, either to them or to others, is of no consequence in their decision making.

They do not adapt to their environments, such as the ones around their formal groups—home, school, and work—or even those surrounding their informal groups—friends and social affiliations. They refuse to accept the existence of any factors or forces that control them. They also refuse to accept the occurrence of any changes in these factors or forces that go contrary to their set beliefs. Instead, they work against these unacceptable changes and attempt to change them to fit their perspectives. It is this rebellious behavior on their part that gives them the label of "the rebel."

Their rebellion starts primarily in the home, against their parents, and then extends to all others who do not exhibit the behavior that they consider right. During their years of rearing, they developed a dislike for those around them who did not fulfill their responsibilities toward them (for example, not being there for them when they needed them), especially their parents. When they were children, it started with a feeling of hatred for what took their parents away from them, such as their parents' jobs, desire to make more money, responsibilities outside their homes, and so on. Later, in many cases, it turned into hate against their parents for not giving higher priority to their needs. Many parents became victims of this rebellious generation.

As a reflection of their rebellion, these members of Generations X and Y formed relationships of their own with whoever was there for them or

whoever tried to develop closeness with them. The rebels give greater importance to these self-formed relationships than to any other relationship or
money or, for that reason, anything else material or nonmaterial.
Selectivity drives them. Their selective perception is reality to them. The
rebels treat selectivity just as the rationalists treat objectivity. Because they always see what they want to see, it is hard to discourage this personality type
in Generations X and Y from undertaking tough and unrealistic assignments.

The rebels rarely lose motivation. This type of behavior can be a big con-
tributor to their success on appropriate assignments in organizations. The
rebel's personality contributes likely success on many tough assignments. The
rebel is likely to be best suited to undertake independent assignments in organizations in areas such as research, design and applications, product development, promotion, and sales. The rebel is uneasy and unable to operate in
an environment where groups operate together because the rebel is used to
succeeding in an unbounded environment. The rebels may function well as
leaders of groups created by them; they will rarely succeed working in a group
others have formed, either as one of its members or as its leader.

The Sensualist

The third topology of Generations X and Y personality includes those who
are fascinated by what looks and feels good. They go after sensual pleasures and
believe it to be their biggest motivator. They engage early in their lives in one
or many kinds of pleasures derived through the senses—sight, sound, touch,
taste, and sex. It is this behavior on the part of Generations X and Y members
that is used in classifying their personality as the sensualist. Mostly they use sensual pleasure as an escape from the incompatibilities in their early lives. Not only
did they engage in smoking cigarettes at a very young age, but they probably
smoked marijuana and used other drugs also. Most of them crave close, meaningful relationships that they did not get from their families. They end up engaging in escapism either as a way to please individuals whose relationships are
important to them or simply to forget the unpleasantness of their surroundings.

The sensualist puts pleasure-seeking at the top of all priorities, and anything that impedes this pursuit is set aside—in many cases, it could be personal morals. An owner of a New Jersey marketing agency had the sensualist
personality in mind when he described his experience with Generations X and
Y in a *CEO Sound-Off* column published in *Inc.* magazine this way, "I have a
hard time with Generations X and Yers. Some are great, but most do not
think they have to work hard. Building a career is not their priority. They
spend most of their time on the phone making social plans" (*CEO Sound-Off,*
1997, July). This observation truly describes one side of the sensualist character among the members of Generations X and Y.

Sociology is most important to the sensualists. They want to develop ideal
relationships and do their part to create perfection in their establishment. The

way that others relate to them makes them derive a special meaning from social relationships. Through their roles in these relationships, the sensualists want to set examples for those who do not relate to them, as they believe those relationships should have been. This is how they relive the relational past in their lives. During their past, they did not get cooperation from others in letting them establish meaningful relationship with them, in particular their parents and siblings. This deficit moves them to set an example through their idealistic role in the relationships that *they* formed. Many of them, in that attempt, get into serious sexual relationships in the early parts of their lives and get into trouble through teenage pregnancy, divorce, and other consequential economical, social, and professional problems. In some cases, these add further frustration to their efforts to idealize relationships, and they become impregnated with a sense of failure. This continued effort on developing satisfying relationships turns some of the sensualists into idealists in all their relationships and behaviors, socially as well as at work, whereas others develop into total failures for both of them. In the latter case, they eventually lose the importance of all relationships.

The sensualists do not develop much attraction for money. Use of money as a motivator is unlikely to work for them. In an organizational setting, the best motivator would be a reactivation of their insatiable desire to prove their ability to establish and maintain relationships.

By having the opportunity to work with people whom they like, the sensualists could give high productivity and innovative outcomes, especially in areas such as public relations, advertising, and aesthetic designs. The sensualists can be very effective in teams, if the teams consist of those whom they like; otherwise, they will be total failures.

The sensualists make all their decisions (personal, professional, and social) based on their likes and dislikes. The criteria of evaluation of their decisions are based on the amounts of satisfaction that they derive from the outcomes of these decisions.

SOCIOLOGICAL ANALYSIS

From this chapter, we have learned that the sociology of workers, in addition to their psychology, plays an important part in deciding the right work assignments for them in a knowledge organization. This consideration can help a manager draw right work-worker matches that should achieve superior work performance and satisfied employees. Even though the understanding of worker sociology is very important for all organizations, it is especially so in organizations that are using and/or producing knowledge as a main factor in their processes. Their workforce does not fit the patterns of typical employees that managers have developed from their past experience. This difference primarily arises because their employees belong to the newest human generations, Gen Xers, and Generation Y.

To assist managers of knowledge organizations, we have analyzed and narrated the sociology of members of these generations and have found it to be different from past generations, such as Baby Boomers. We have also derived nine character traits and three personality types that are prevalent among them. A manager, only as a starting point in the understanding of the sociology of employees belonging to Generations X and Y, should consider these character traits and personality types in understanding his employees. He should analyze employee sociology with a tenuous belief in this topology. It is likely that no employee may actually perfectly fit any of these types. However, most of them will possess a sociological profile that would be some sort of mix of these nine traits. No matter what the exact final sociology of an employee is, this analysis should add to the manager's understanding of employees' needs and behavior. He should remember to treat it as a starting point.

The traits and personality topologies given here are based on the observation that all Generations X and Y members are intelligent and can become the most productive people that business has known in many generations. This fact would be of especial significance to knowledge organizations. To them, Generations X and Y members will provide an abundant source of skills and intellect that they need for the successful functioning of their organizations. The responsibility to productively deploy their skills lies with knowledge organizations and their managers. Managers should know these members, understand them, and redirect their focus and energies to where they will become the best innovators, creators, and contributors to their organizations. If managers fail to connect with them, then society could lose a whole generation and it may take many generations to recuperate from this setback in human history.

REFERENCES

Adams, J.T., III. (1999, December). However, what about Gen Xers who manage boomers. *HRMagazine, 44*(13), 8.

CEO Sound-Off. (1997, July). What entrepreneurs are telling *Inc.* about employee motivation. *Inc.*, p. 105.

Koretz, G. (2000, November 13). Economic trends: Yes workers are grumpier. *Business Week*, p. 42.

Mui, N. (2001, February 4). Here come the kids: Generation Y invades the workplace. *New York Times*, p.1, Section 9.

Shannon, J. (1998, August 27). Prepare for the Net generation. *Marketing Week, 21*(26), 22.

Smith, A.K. (2000, November 6). Charting your own course. *U.S. News & World Report*, pp. 56–65.

Tapscott, D. (1999). *Growing up digital: The rise of the Net generation.* New York: McGraw-Hill.

Zemke, R., Raines, C., & Filipczak, B. (1999). *Generations at work: Managing the clash of veterans, boomers, Xers, and Nexters in your workplace.* New York: AMACOM.

Chapter 3 _____

Training, Learning, and Behavior Modification in a Knowledge Environment

In the previous chapter, we learned that the new generations of workers, Gen Xers and Generation Y, which make a large part of the workforce in knowledge organizations, are very different from past generations. Their work behavior will present a daunting challenge of unequaled proportion to psychologists, behaviorists, and organizational researchers. As we have seen previously, the growth and development of these generations have been unique. Managing them in the workplace will not be an easy task for managers who are members of generations before Gen Xers and Generation Y. These new workers have the skill and the ability to perform. There is no doubt about it. The question is will their managers have the dexterity to train and discipline them and, most importantly, make sure that their learning continues during their stay with the organization.

This chapter is devoted to answering this question. We address some important aspects of teaching, learning, and behavior modification as they have been used in traditional organizations and then decide whether they will be applicable in knowledge organizations, where the new generation of employees who have the knowledge and the skills these organizations need will be working. We present here a number of situations in which these techniques are likely to fail. Further, wherever we find them lacking the applicability, we suggest new approaches and special adaptations of existing techniques that should work in organizations operating in knowledge environments with Gen Xers and Generation Y members as their employees.

THE STANDARD LEARNING MODEL AND THE NEW GENERATION

Typically, human development has taken place through time-phased learning processes. This method of learning—what we may call organized learning—is how knowledge has been imparted from previous generations to the next. At a certain age, we went to kindergarten to learn the alphabet and arithmetic, then we joined elementary, middle, and high schools to acquire knowledge in literature, sciences, mathematics, and so on, on a step-by-step, year-by-year basis. This training has been so well programmed by time that if we know someone's age we can tell almost exactly what knowledge he has acquired, how smart he is, and how smart he will become if he continues his education up to a certain point in time. That had been true for as far back as we can go in the records of human civilization. It was true when mankind first learned how to use stone in making tools and weapons. The same was true when we entered the automobile age, about a century ago, and also when we attained the biggest feat of human spirit in the twentieth century—flying. The preceding generations had always controlled knowledge. The older generations were at the passing end and the younger were on the receiving end. That had been the mode of human learning, until now.

A similar method of human development continued in organizations when people joined the workforce. There were apprenticeship programs to induct them into the occupations and training courses to teach them new skills and refresher courses to update their knowledge as and when it became essential.

Learning and Generations X and Y

The important thing about human development is that these methods have become ineffective for the new generations in the workforce. The frontier of learning—not on the part of the young but of the old—is fast approaching. The biggest question is how to ensure effective learning of the young generation of knowledge employees—Generations X and Y.

Employees belonging to these generations, particularly those in knowledge organizations, believe that there is nothing to learn from the past. Their beliefs are based, and rightly so, on the experiences that they have had in learning. When they were very young, they learned how to play video games without help from their parents or elders. When they grew a little older, they excelled at them. In the process, they deduced that the younger a person was, the more "learned" he was. They lost respect for the members of older generations—in whatever form they knew them. Their parents failed to provide them with the leadership they needed. Generally, the parents were either not there or did not know how to be role models for them. They had to tinker with games either individually or in groups of their peers. They learned how to play and beat the video games on their own. Parents lost a chance to establish the belief that they were superior to them.

Because the young knew how to handle and overpower horrors in the form of crazy, wicked video dots and blobs, they felt grown-up, independent, confident, and able to do anything without learning from the older generation. Moreover, as we learned in the chapter on the sociology of these generations, these games gave them a sense of empowerment—that they could learn everything on their own.

However, the parents of members of Generations X and Y said, "You are wrong. Don't think that if you can learn to play video games on your own, you can learn life and work skills on your own also. It's just games; acquisition of life and marketable work skills takes place from generation to generation."

Generations X and Y members did not believe their parents. Their parents waited.

Then came the PC—personal computer—to further advance the learning concept that the young had developed. In a repeat of the past, Generations X and Y members learned computer skills without any training from their parents. Once again, their parents failed to provide learning to their young ones, as all previous generations had provided to their successor generations. In addition, this time, Generations X and Y members proved that it was not just games at which they were capable of excelling on their own. A number of them, self-trained kids, became computer whizzes and nerds who were recognized and heavily rewarded financially by society.

All this strongly reinforced a conviction in their minds that no one really has anything useful to teach them. It has become their basic fact of learning. They have discovered a new paradigm: Knowledge is technology, and you cannot learn it from experienced elders.

For members of Generation Y, this new paradigm of learning had already become a proven reality.

There is a second part to the learning experiences of Generations X and Y. It is in the form of a corollary of the above phenomenon: Generations X and Y members have not learned to respect the older generation. The reason for that lies in the fact that, as we learned in the previous chapter, those who have traditionally been the authority figures—members of the older generations—have failed to win their respect. That is why Generations X and Y members look down upon authority in general.

TEACHING, TRAINING, AND LEARNING IN KNOWLEDGE ORGANIZATIONS

Generations X and Y members do not see any difference between playing and learning. They are convinced beyond doubt that all learning is playing—playing with toys, video games, computers, and computer-based tools. Obviously, since learning is playing, learning does not require teachers or trainers or books or manuals or anything that connotes them.

This is bad news for organizational development and change. All traditional corporate learning and training techniques are bound for oblivion in the twenty-first century. The sooner an organization throws everything that gives the semblance of *organizational training and learning* out the window and adapts the newer self-help, self-teach, and support group techniques, the farther it will get in actual learning and organizational development.

Now, the next question is how to teach, and train, employees in these generations. The biggest challenge that managers will face is how to make them learn what is important to the organization and unlearn what the organization considers unimportant. The big question is: How do we modify their behavior? It's a new ball game altogether!

Because of the general aversion that these generations have developed toward training as past generations have known it, and in particular toward someone connoting the word trainer, the learning and training of the next generation of the knowledge workforce will have to be done in a subtle and unorthodox way. It may have to be subliminal and subconscious—without ever using the words teaching, learning, or training. Call it playing, partying, camping, hiking, bonding—just do not use any words starting with the letters T or L in the context of their learning and behavior modification. Put them in situations where they face real or simulated problems, and let them make their own decisions. If they get to where the organization wants them to be by themselves, then it achieved its goal by imparting to them the most effective training. However, if they do not get to the conclusion the organization desires by themselves, then the learning system, in a natural way, should lead them to the preset solutions or conclusions. Nevertheless, most of the time, they will reach a workable solution, because as we saw in Chapter 2, they are intelligent and perceptive. In most cases, just making them confront the problem might be enough to complete their training.

STRATEGIES FOR BEHAVIOR MODIFICATION

Traditional organizations have known that there are four strategies for modifying human behavior: positive reinforcement (to give the wanted outcome on reflecting a desired behavior), avoidance learning (to take away unwanted outcome on reflecting a desired behavior), extinction (to take away wanted outcome on reflecting an undesirable behavior), and punishment (to give unwanted outcome on reflecting an undesirable behavior). Of course, we do not want to provide the details on their working here in the context of learning and behavior modification of the employees of the newer generations, especially because none of the details are really usable in a knowledge organizational setting. However, we will give a working description of them as and when we would need them to show why they will or will not work effectively and also when we compare and contrast them with the new learning and behavior modification concepts applicable to the coming work generations.

Industrial psychologists and behavioral scientists preach that both extinction and punishment do not work in modifying human behavior and should be discouraged. However, it is a well-known fact that they neither mean to ask managers to discontinue their use, nor that managers believe them. Managers know that, both in social and organizational settings, extinction and punishment do work sometimes. When psychologists say that they do not work, they are simply stating the learning theories that have been developed based on animal, esoteric, and laboratory research during the early- to mid-twentieth century. As a result, both punishment and extinction strategies of behavior modification continue to impart learning to employees in traditional organizations.

Fear: Behavior Modification Strategy of Traditional Organizations

As we have seen, punishment really comes in two forms: punishment and extinction. Punishment imposes on someone something unpleasant and unwanted. Extinction, however, is the taking away of something that one being punished possesses and values and wants to retain. Both punishment and extinction do not work as behavior modification strategies because most punishments and extinctions become ineffective after they are inflicted once, or the inflicted person develops a psychological immunity against them after one or a few inflictions. Take, for example, the punishment of taking away the thing most wanted by all living beings—life—in the form of capital punishment. This is the ultimate punishment that can be imposed on anyone. The practice continues in most parts of the world, even when all know that the dead cannot modify their behavior. There is no doubt here. This fact is very direct and simple to understand. However, let us take the equivalent of capital punishment in an organization—firing—taking away the most precious thing from those employed—their jobs. Just as the dead do not learn, fired people also do not learn—definitely not for the ones who fired them. Like capital punishment, you can only inflict this punishment once, because you do not possess the power to fire the fired person *again*, so you cannot influence or modify his or her behavior. The same is also true for other punishment strategies but in a slightly different way—the one being punished becomes immune to the punishment.

In knowledge organizations, punishment takes on a special meaning. There is not enough technically qualified personnel for organizations to engage in indiscriminate hiring and firing. Moreover, they are all alike. How many of them would a knowledge organization fire? How many times?

Next, take the use of extinction as a behavior modification strategy. Consider this example of extinction: docking salary from a knowledge employee who is a habitual latecomer. After a few dockings, this person will be psychologically prepared to receive lower wages or quit and will show no improvement in his behavior.

Extinction strategy for behavior modification in the form of docking pay will probably matter less to knowledge employees anyhow given their age and financial liabilities, they are already making more money than they need to maintain their lifestyle. Moreover, there is such a great demand for the skills they possess that they can always find another assignment with a competitor and pick up the additional dollars to make up the difference, and maybe more. It is also possible that the competitor may offer an opportunity for a full-time position, which may put pressure on the current employer to improve employment conditions or lose the employee.

The Flush Toilet Approach

Both punishment and extinction as ways to modify human work behavior are *flush toilet* approaches to solving problems in general. Their use by the punisher leads to an admission that he or she has been unable to *solve* the problem and, instead of accepting this fact and the responsibility for the resultant failure, engages in the act of punishment. These are called *frustration strategies* for behavior modification. Their application emerges out of the frustration of the administrator for not having succeeded in stopping the undesirable behavior reflected by one's subordinate.

Another logic that is mostly presented in support of using these two strategies for behavior modification is that they act as deterrents—we call this the *rational model.* The assumption is that when one sees something unwanted happening to others as a result of a certain behavior, one refrains from engaging in that behavior. However, in this context, it is important to know that Gen Xers and Generation Y members have not experienced the punishments that Baby Boomers have. Some of them who did experience these punishments modified their value/desire system to suit what they could get. They modified their behavior by giving up the desire for what could have come from the missed rewards. However, they did not modify their nonwork behavior because of the fear imposed on them; they will not modify their work behavior because of punishments. Managers must always remember one thing about this generation of knowledge employees: Generations X and Y knowledge workers are smarter, more perceptive, and more apt than their predecessors with whom they still have to deal because most resources and power rest with Baby Boomers and, at least for the first couple of decades into the current century, will be controlled by them.

Managing by fear may manage employees' low-grade senses; it will not manage their higher order faculties, which are essential to attain innovation and gain productivity in knowledge organizations. If a knowledge organization manager feels that he needs to use fear for behavior modification of employees, he should reeducate himself or change professions before Generations X and Y members become more visible in the workforce.

Managers should regard punishment and extinction as unworkable in knowledge organizations; they hurt both the punisher and the punished and, in the end, do not help and may actually harm the organization. These strategies should be thrown out of knowledge organizations before they fool managers and fail the organization. They will be the prescription for knowledge organizational destruction.

Weak Behavior Modifier in Knowledge Environment: Positive Reinforcement

The behavior modification strategy most used in the knowledge environment is positive reinforcement. Managers learned that if workers behaved in the manner expected from them by the organization, they should be rewarded. Doing this will condition that behavior to the administered reward in the future. That is, to get that reward, workers will have to reflect the behavior that is conditioned to this. Psychologists call this positive reinforcement—reward as a way to make workers permanently learn to modify their behavior. Kevin Gross, of *Executive Excellence*, says to train your top managers "on the business value of recognizing accomplishments and demonstrating sincere appreciation. Ensure that they understand how feeding human esteem with something as simple as a thank-you note taps into people's intrinsic need to achieve" (Gross, 1999). Once managers understand the importance of this recognition, the tools must be available for them to carry it out, "otherwise, desired behaviors will go unrecognized—spelling the death of your [the manager's] vision" (Gross, 1999).

From the experiments on learning by Edward L. Thorndike (1898), Ivan P. Pavlov (1927/1960), and Burrhus F. Skinner (1935), we have been taught to condition human behavior. This conditioning makes use of what the American behaviorist B.F. Skinner called *operant conditioning*—a revision of the Russian physiologist Pavlov's *classical conditioning* which studied dogs' salivating behavior. In principle, operant conditioning states that when an employee reflects a behavior consistent with the management stimulus, the management should reinforce that behavior by giving the employee a reward—something the employee values—but skipping it when the reflected behavior is not desired.

In support of the technique, psychologists present examples of how animals are trained to do human acts using positive reinforcement. The popular one is as follows: a trainer commands a marine animal to do a certain act and when the animal completes the act, the trainer gives the animal a piece of fish. In this way, the animal learns to do an act (that presumably it does not like to do) through the conditioning established by giving it a fish (that presumably it likes to get).

Pavlov accomplished this with his dogs; Skinner, with his rats. Traditional managers started using this method on their employees. Conditioning became an important organizational behavior modification tool in the twentieth century.

All positive reinforcement–based behavior modification techniques make use of the principle of linearity in relationships. Since all organizational relationships by their very nature are linear for both employees and the organization, without any confusion and misgiving, positive reinforcement should work in these cases. The employee should clearly know that because the organization is paying him a good salary, it expects him to have good performance, and if he does not, the salary will be reduced accordingly. If an employee generates good increases in revenue and profit, the organization will give him or her a good raise. In organizational relationships, there is a give and a take—always in the same direction and always in equal proportions. That is how, in principle, positive reinforcement should work to modify employee behavior.

While Pavlov's and Skinner's theories of positive reinforcement may be good for setting employee and executive compensation packages or for dealing with one-shot or short-term relationships, positive reinforcement is not going to work all the time under all conditions for behavior modification of employees in knowledge organizations. Linearity will have a short-term impact on any relationship—including organizational. The ability to control rewards on a linear basis will not give a manager the power to modify employee behavior. The short-term approach to organizational relationships in knowledge organizations will not work. It will fail to lead to innovation, quality, and productivity. Positive reinforcement principles for behavior modification will not work even in the case of such knowledge organizational relationships like the ones with vendors, suppliers, and independent contractors because a short-term orientation coming from positive reinforcement will not provide the requisite outcomes for knowledge work from these relationships.

FROM PURPOSIVE BEHAVIORISM TO SUBLIMINAL LEARNING

On observing the behavior of Americans who started to work for the Japanese transplants in the United States during the 1980s, we noticed a new organizational behavior phenomenon. When these workers, even the ones with many years of experience in American plants, took jobs in the new Japanese transplants, they brought to their new employers a "clean slate" behavior, because they knew that the Japanese management style was different from the American. All work behavior patterns that they had learned and reflected on until the time they joined these Japanese transplants were forgotten. Virtually, in one stroke, the Japanese hiring of American workers erased all behaviors that they had learned for years while working for their former American employers. It was guided by the perception that behavior learned while at American companies was incompatible with their new employers.

Contiguous Conditioning

The above phenomenon makes us think of the transient nature of cognitive learning and behavior modification. That is, any behavior modification at a conscious level is temporary. It is conveniently learned and conveniently unlearned. To give it the *effect* of permanence, reinforcement on a consistent basis is essential—*contiguous conditioning*. Positive reinforcement, as we know, is at best pseudopermanent and hence not a behavior modifier. To be truly permanent, behavior modification has to be at a subconscious level, and to achieve that, behavior modification techniques have to be subliminal.

Positive reinforcement as a behavior modification strategy works at a cognitive level only. In effect, it is purposive behaviorism—a behavior that is guided by the purpose to be achieved—that is, the behavior that achieves the purpose remains in effect only for as long as the purpose is achieved. It comes and goes with the desire for achieving the purpose. It never results in permanent learning. No behavior modification at the cognitive level will ever be permanent because through cognition one will unlearn it with a minimal effort. If it cannot cause a permanent modification in behavior, then calling it a behavior modification strategy is an oxymoron. Behavior modification is complete only when it will never be unlearned. The question is how to achieve this.

Subliminal Learning: Creating Non-Contiguous Conditioning

Work behavior is a complex system of many cognitive acts and subliminal processes. During the industrial age, necessary work behavior consisted mostly of cognitive acts. The organization was less concerned about the subliminal processes that its workers went through. It was easy to understand how to make the widget, performance was derived from counting the number of them completed at the end of the day. This is very much the way most traditional organizations work today. As the shift takes place toward knowledge organizations—*intellectual organizations*—understanding work becomes very complex, and work behavior becomes very hard to comprehend, to model (especially for someone who does not actually execute the work) and, therefore, to modify using positive reinforcement techniques learned from traditional organizations.

We have to look at other methods, or devise new ones, to modify employee behavior in knowledge organizations since now we know that the techniques used in traditional organizations will not work. A few of the behavior modification methods that make use of some of the new concepts on subliminal learning and behavior modification that we have discussed above and are likely to achieve the result are given below. Knowledge organization managers should consider them carefully and apply them selectively depending on their success record with people and situations.

Anti-Classical Conditioning. At a marine park in Florida, I watched a skilled trainer make dolphins play basketball using a multicolored beach ball. She held a ring and expected the dolphins to take the ball on the tips of their noses and put it through the ring. When a dolphin did just that, she gave it a fish and patted it as an expression of her admiration. The spectators clapped.

I admired the potent application of the works of Pavlov and Skinner, and the theory of positive reinforcement for creating such a nice show.

In observing a few trips to the ring by the dolphins, I realized that the trainer gave all the dolphins who came up to her for the fish after the trick some fish and a pat even when the dolphins did not put the ball through the ring, pick up the ball, or even execute her commands. Nevertheless, the trainer showed no deviation in her behavior toward the dolphins. That did not seem consistent with the concept of operant conditioning.

"Shouldn't you be giving fish to the dolphin only when it performs what it is supposed to? Otherwise, how can you modify its behavior?" I asked her.

She said that more than getting the dolphins to obey her commands, she was interested in building a relationship of trust and closeness with them. "The learning and acting up to my commands will automatically follow," she explained. "And, to preserve and strengthen this relationship and the mutual trust," she told me, "we permit only a monogamous relationship between the dolphins and their trainers." She also said that, at times, they were tired or not in a mood to obey her commands and that she wanted them to know she understood that.

I saw it as a departure and, actually, an inconsistency from the concept of operant conditioning as applied to behavior modification in organizational settings.

Then I recalled how animal trainers in India tamed wild animals (tigers, lions, cobras, and elephants) and made them do things that went against their inherent habits. I realized that their animal-training techniques were also based on developing trust. These trainers worked to rebuild trust with their beasts, because it was shattered by their trapping and the break from their natural habitats. To reestablish this trust, a trainer who was not connected with the incident of trapping began the process of developing trust by caring for the basic needs of the beast. The trust is established to build a long-lasting relationship through the time when reinforcement could not be administered. It is not a relationship dependent on *mechanical* conditioning, which needs an ongoing reinforcement to be operative.

From our understanding of the intelligence of the knowledge workforce, we can say that a positive reinforcement system of reward, as we have learned in psychology textbooks, might partially work on some animals and may work on traditional workers. However, it is not a successful way to unleash innovation and productivity from employees in knowledge organizations because a good part of their work performance depends on skills that come from beyond cognition.

The rewards that traditional organizations use as reinforcement may be sufficient for them to sustain their employee-employer relationship. However, the basis of the knowledge organizational employee-employer relationship and behavior modification is rooted in trust. Knowledge is primarily a product of the mind, not of the body.

The Two-Way Reward Principle. For behavior modification and the learning of knowledge employees, we have to replace positive unidirectional, linear reinforcement techniques that have one giver and one taker with two-way, nonlinear, monogamous reinforcements, for which the underpinning is trust. All such behavior modification strategies that do not involve both parties in the process (the behavior administrator and the behavior reflector at a symbiotic level) will not work. Both parties should be equal in this relationship. Both should give and both should take from the relationship. Sometimes one becomes the giver and the other the taker, and at other times, the roles are reversed. That in effect means that the learner and the trainer make a monogamous relationship of switching roles. Every behavior modification exercise according to this concept will bring rewards for both, even though the rewards may be different.

These techniques do not require as intense and meaningful an involvement on the part of the one playing the behavior administrator as it does in the case of the behavior administrator in standard positive reinforcement techniques.

As an illustration of these concepts, we go back to the example of extinction to modify the behavior of an employee who is late. The management wants to correct his behavior by engaging in extinction as punishment—docking his pay. We said that it was not always going to work because it was an easy *flush toilet* approach to a complex problem that probably could be a consequence of one of several factors, such as job frustration. Now, let us consider the use of standard positive reinforcement to modify this behavior. In this case, when using positive reinforcement, the manager will institute cash rewards for those with perfect attendance but not a punishment for the occasional latecomer. In this context, however, our experience has shown that those who always came on time before the institution of such rewards—habitual on-time employees—almost always win these rewards. Essentially, the manager would be rewarding those who are always punctual, while at the same time, these rewards would fail to achieve their intended purpose—in this case, modify the behavior of the consistent latecomers. It does not redress the problem. In fact, this is a flush toilet approach to the problem. Rather than engaging in behavior modification of the latecomer (treatment of the affected), the organization, by rewarding those who come on time, is de facto engaging in the behavior modification of habitual on-time employees (treatment of the unaffected). Just as we saw happen in the case of administration of punishment, the use of rewards in modifying unacceptable behavior has a linear relationship. It does not involve the administrator in a meaningful, personal give-and-take relationship with the miscreant—the person whose behavior he needs to modify. This is because positive reinforcement is guided by the acceptance of one way to fit everyone in one perfect behavior. It is not an adaptive, flexible process that devises behavior, which accommodates the treatment of a knowledge employee as an intelligent, mature adult in a variable way by a behavior administrator who has developed trust with him.

The two-way reward principle results in a behavior modification process that should cause a reward for both: the one who engages in behavior modification and the one whose behavior he or she is modifying. The rewards could come in many forms. For example, the building of mutual trust brings rewards for both, either as being able to trust someone or having the trust of someone. In addition, behavior modification brings an additional reward to the employee in the form of the loss of the behavior that needs to be modified. The reward for the person who engaged in behavior modification is the success of the modification and a sense of satisfaction in bringing about the intended behavior in the employee.

It is this type of two-way reward system that successfully works in behavior modification in knowledge and learning environments. It is comparable to a friend modifying the behavior of a friend by working as a transient therapist or a counselor with a hope of having a payback in kind. That is how both in this relationship engage in understanding and modifying the undesirable behavior of each other.

The best way to achieve this two-way reward system of behavior modification is by creating, preferably, a two-person team, a team of equals—a symbiotic team. The manager, or whoever is doing the behavior modification, must infuse himself and the organization in the process by grouping or pairing employees who will instantaneously and on a continuous basis monitor and modify unwanted behavior. Keith Bedingham, chairman of Verax (a company that specializes in change management), says that "Dealing with people is the complete reverse of what happens in magnetism where opposites attract. The more the people are similar to each other, the easier it is to get on with each other" (Gregory, 1999). This quotation emphasizes that the manager must understand and be able to communicate with his employees if their relationship is to help the organization achieve its goals. The manager's role in the behavior modification process shifts from a behavior administrator to a behavior facilitator. This will make his role in the behavior modification process even more effective.

This method will eliminate linear behavior modification relationships in the workplace. Just as linear social relationships struggle, linear work relationships for behavior modification also do not succeed in providing innovation and productivity essential for the organizational affluence in the twenty-first century, especially for organizations operating in the knowledge environment. The two-way reward system described above is more likely to work in knowledge organizations, because no one has complete knowledge on any one topic; reward in the form of learning for both, via the process of behavior modification, can easily occur. It is for this reason that behavior modification in these organizations can result in increased knowledge through the strengthening symbiotic mentor relationships—a reward for the trainer and the trainee, the teacher and the learner, the behavior modifier and the one whose behavior is being modified.

Subliminal Behavior Modification. The best behavior modification occurs unknowingly and sits deep in the psyche of the trained for a long time. This is achieved through what we call *subliminal behavior modification.* To achieve this, the process starts at the subconscious level. At the cognitive level, in terms of the reward and reinforcement methodologies of the traditional learning techniques, this process begins with the imparting of a reward without the presence of any obvious stimulus-response relationship. It is done with a clear intent to not cause operant conditioning. Obviously, this is not reinforcement as we have known it. The presence of a reward, without a stimulus and appropriate response, creates cognitive dissonance in the person whose behavior is to be modified. This dissonance is the start of the unlearning process—the unlearning of the conditioning of a desired behavior to a reward—and also sets the stage for development of a relationship in which a new stimulus-response behavior occurs but without any clear contiguous conditioning. These behavior modification exercises have to continue until the relationship matures to a subconscious state and results in a behavior that needs no operant conditioning. At this stage, the occurrence of an unconditioned reward or vice versa—that is, its nonoccurrence when a well-accepted desired behavior occurs—will not cause dissonance. Now, the reward has no meaning. The worker has risen above it. Its presence is the confirmation of the completion of the subliminal behavior modification. In fact, its true test will show up in an almost involuntary reflection of the desired behavior when the reward is not administered—proof that the learning is deep-seated within the psyche.

Positive Punishment. Traditionally, punishment is administered when the learned behavior is either not reflected or a behavior inconsistent with the one modified is reflected—that is, the right stimulus does not generate the right response. Under the subliminal principle, we assume that an absence of a desired response for the appropriate stimulus is a failure of the behavior modification process, the responsibility for which lies with the individual modifying the behavior. To correct this flaw, we introduce the concept of *positive punishment.* Positive punishment requires administration of an even more potent reward on failure, as an investment in learning and the future desired responses. The concept of positive punishment derives from the fact that the moment a person does not give an appropriate response, and is punished for it, the bond between the behavior modifier and the one whose behavior is being modified weakens. If this occurs in the beginning of the relationship, it could result in destroying trust and decimating the relationship. Further behavior modification is unlikely to succeed. Punishment is likely to leave the trainee with an association of the correct response with a punishment, something that he will try to forget rather than remember. As a consequence, it will result in unlearning rather than learning.

The positive punishment strategy is designed to overcome this flaw in the behavior modification technique. This strategy suggests ignoring the undesirable responses in the person by (1) decoupling the wrong response and the unpleasant outcome (punishment), and (2) building a bond of trust between the trainer and the person whose behavior is being modified. Its intent is the deconditioning of the desired behavior with the reward. Once the decoupling occurs successfully, the learning will begin, and the trained person will reflect the behavior irrespective of the administration of the reward.

This strategy has to be implemented carefully. It includes setting up a front that can falsely convey that the learner gave an appropriate response in spite of the fact that he may not have done so. However, we do want to reward the person even when he gives a wrong response—positive punishment. This front is activated in the start of the behavior modification process when the bond of trust is yet to be established between the two. After that, when the learning has occurred, the behavior modifier may activate it when he feels that it will help avoid any further weakening of their eroding relationship. After the learning has taken place, there will be neither a definite link between the reward and the behavior nor any expectation of the reward on part of the trainee.

The treatment in positive punishment strategy requires giving special attention to the person who has given a wrong response by highlighting the correct behavior and the acquiescence of the mistake before administering the reward for the learning to occur. This is how a wrong behavior will not be reinforced, while at the same time, the desire to correct it next time will strengthen. In this way, the association of the correct response with a pleasant experience will last longer than its association with an unpleasant one, which people consciously strive to forget. The outcome of the positive punishment will be a strong desire in the person to reflect the correct behavior in his future attempts. He will do his best to succeed at this and most likely will succeed.

THE NEW GENERATION AND LEARNING

The concepts on teaching, learning, and behavior modification that we have developed in this chapter help us understand specific learning habits of the members of the new generations of workers—Gen Xers and Generation Y—in the knowledge environment. It is important for managers of knowledge organizations to understand these concepts because they provide the labor for these organizations. We have learned in this chapter that the deepseated learning needed to increase innovation and productivity of employees is not achieved through standard behavior modification strategies—in particular the four strategies commonly employed by traditional organizations. Behavior modification in these organizations needs subliminal methods. We have provided a number of these methods to bring about learning and behavior modification in employees.

In addition to helping managers of knowledge organizations design learning and behavior modification strategies suitable to their employees, the understanding and characteristics we have developed about members of Generations X and Y in this chapter, combined with what we have learned in previous chapters, will provide guidelines on other important management functions, such as work design, leading, motivating, and controlling. The next few chapters deal with these functions in the light of the learning and behavior modification knowledge from this chapter.

REFERENCES

Gregory, A. (1999, June). Why bullies are bad for business. *Works Management,* *52*(6), 46–49.

Gross, K.M. (1999, February). Positive reinforcement. *Executive Excellence, 16*(2), 12.

Pavlov, I.P. (1927/1960). *Conditioned reflexes* (translation). New York: Dover Press.

Skinner, B.F. (1935). The generic nature of the concepts of stimulus and response. *Journal of Genetic Psychology, 12,* 40–65.

Thorndike, E.L. (1898). Animal intelligence: An experimental study of associative processes in animals. *Psychological Review, 2* (Monograph Suppl. 8).

Section III _____

KNOWLEDGE WORK
AND ORGANIZATION

Chapter 4 ——————————————————————

Making Knowledge
Work a Pleasure

Once knowledge organization managers have understood their employees' minds, behaviors, and social surroundings, the next logical step is to check out the work that is given to them. It may require redesigning work, breaking it down into tasks, and packaging tasks into jobs, each suitable for one regularly scheduled full-time knowledge employee. This chapter addresses this function for managers of knowledge organizations. We will not address the fundamental aspects of job design in this chapter, because we assume that managers already know them. We will also not get into the mechanics of task selection and grouping. Our goal in this chapter is to discuss how best to perform the work design function with special reference to knowledge workers in organizations.

We will consider the differences between knowledge work and traditional work, particularly as they apply to Generations X and Y employees. The chapter explains how to turn all work in these organizations into knowledge work—the work that is desired by employees working in knowledge organizations—and what practices will not work in getting innovation and productivity from knowledge workers. Also included in this chapter are two instruments that may be used to understand, and map, work and work environment for their analysis and redesign to suit knowledge organizations.

TRADITIONAL WORK AND KNOWLEDGE WORK

We know that physical activity is as important to the human body as is any other physiological need—air, water, and food. When psychologists modeled their well-accepted understanding of human needs, they did not include physical activity, one of the lowest order of human needs whose fulfillment is essential for existence. On the contrary, classical management thinkers founded management theory on the basic principle that work was a disliked, unwanted activity. According to this well-practiced school, given the chance, a normal person would rather be idle than working. We know that the practice of traditional management is based on these unproven, highly presumptuous works of researchers of a bygone era. They were wrong. They did not know what technology would do to work. Playing is not as interesting as working on some knowledge applications, nor is it as challenging. Working to tame, apply, use, and develop knowledge—turn it into technology or a successful application—is not really work. It is play disguised as work. That is the nature of knowledge work.

It is important for knowledge organization managers to know what is wrong with work in traditional organizations so that they are aware of what should *not* be done.

The Evolution of Work Relationship

Certain things come naturally to all humans: to be admired, to be appreciated, to succeed, to accept challenges, to be creative and innovative, to lead and to be led, to think and to plan, to do good, and, oh yes, to work—knowledge work, in fact, to work hard—when it is knowledge work.

It is external factors that cause people to behave in ways that are contrary to their nature. The obvious question is what are these factors.

During the late nineteenth century and the earlier parts of the twentieth century (during the birth of complex organizations), a new work relationship was introduced to those seeking employment. It required normal, free, intelligent, educated adults to show up every day to work at a set time, at a set place, and to complete a set task according to the directions given by others, and to do that on machines and tools that were selected by others. These others did not undertake these tasks by themselves and, in all likelihood, had never done so in the past. It required a "boss," someone who, once again, had probably not done this job himself, to check and approve what they did, to set their break schedules and vacation schedules. This relationship was reminiscent of slavery. More importantly, the relationship of boss and employees ended at work. Outside of work, most owners and managers behaved like strangers with their workers and looked down upon them. For their socialization and nonwork activities, they associated with other people like themselves.

This new work relationship had only one positive aspect for the doer—a paycheck. Managers learned that the only way they could recruit, retain, and motivate employees was through the inducement of money paid at the end of the week. It was the paycheck that was interesting. Workers learned to focus their attention on the hours outside of work—5:00 o'clock, Friday, weekends, vacations—and on what they could do with their paycheck. They learned to ignore the work, work environment, and the dull, uninteresting process that came with it. It all came as inseparable parts of the package deal they called a "job." The job took away all the fun and satisfaction people had derived from work before the job era.

To reinforce desirable work behavior, society devised means to foster workers' dependence on money. Spiritual and other leaders preached that it was moral to work hard, be loyal to and respectful of authority, and acquire and possess goods that only money could buy. As this ambition became insatiable, organized work flourished. Workers gave their time, their independence, and their health—even their future generations' health—to acquire those "important" material possessions by holding down their jobs. Work had become a necessity. Workers had to behave in a certain prescribed way to keep their jobs. Mostly, if they did not accept the carrot, the stick was there as an alternative.

In the latter part of the twentieth century, the patterns of work behavior started to change. A paycheck by itself was no longer a sufficient motivation; managers had to use other inducements to keep employees engaged. They had to offer stock options, retirement plans, major medical policies, and share their profit, share ownership—even of closely held organizations that were previously available only to their family members or close friends.

However, knowledge organizations reveal human work behavior that is strikingly dissimilar to that of the workers in traditional organizations, members of the preceding generations. It is for this reason that it becomes imperative for us to understand the work psychology of the Generation X and Generation Y workers employed in knowledge organizations.

A number of things are different about the workers belonging to Generations X and Y. First, a large number of them have grown up without the Protestant work ethic or the influence of Christianity, as did past generations. They do not believe in hard work. They challenge authority. In fact, authority is repulsive to them. And when it comes to loyalty, Gen Xers and Generation Y members believe it to be a one-way street: the one that runs from the organization for which they work to them. Secondly, even at a young age, they are smarter than past generations. They are changing the rules of work and work behavior so drastically that it is becoming a totally new ball game of human behavior in organizations. We have to understand their psychology, to learn the modes and patterns of their behavior, to rewrite rules of work, and to discover how to productively engage them in work—not just make them work but to unleash the tremendous potential that they have to offer.

Traditional Work

A manager of a large manufacturer in South Carolina found the task of motivating his employees so frustrating that he asked for help in *CEO Sound-Off:* "how to start a business that doesn't need any employees? I am tired and fed up. Dealing with some moron whose only thought is when he or she can get home, plop in front of a TV, and get drunk or stoned is wearing me out."

That sentiment is not uncommon or untrue among employers. Some allow themselves to be frustrated by their employees' lack of work motivation, whereas others simply learn to cope with it. However, no matter what, it is there. The fact is that such behavior on the part of employees can be avoided.

To help this manager, let us pose a question:

A Question. When the clock at work strikes 5:01, who is left in the office? Other than owners and bosses, it may be someone who is working with knowledge, such as on a research project, a design, a promotion plan, a computer, the Internet, information technology, or other projects involving the use and application of knowledge.

While others are cranking their cars or cutting left and right to get through the exit door, the persons who decided to stay behind sharpen their pencils and get themselves another cup of coffee to recharge. Even though they have been working all day, they are really getting *ready* to work.

Did we say work?

What work?

Isn't it the work from which all others were running away?

The Answer. It depends! There are different "models" of work. In its more formal, better-understood, and fragmented form, these models of work are known as jobs. As far as a doer of work—worker—is concerned, work has two segments.

The first segment of work is that with which the doer establishes a relationship through his act of working. For example, a computer programmer establishes a relationship with his computer and other equipment, operating systems, computer languages, his clients, his vendors, and all other acts he engages in to fulfill his task of performing his work on computers. Collectively, we label it "work itself."

The second segment of work is what surrounds it. It is not necessary for performance of the work or to carry out the work relationships previously described, but it is essential to interconnect various similar relationships to form one organization. It is done through the creation of what is called the "work environment." Many managers know that this interconnection of works comes at a cost of loss in efficiency or even effectiveness, but they tolerate it because it is required for the organization to operate as one entity. When organizations grow too large, such costs become overpowering and, then, splitting the organization into segments, divisions, or even independent smaller organizations becomes necessary. There is a long list of business organizations that have taken such measures with exactly that motive in mind.

Work System

Work Itself. The job era (started in the late nineteenth century and projected to substantially lose its impact during the current century) saw the creation of different work packages, or jobs, dependent on the two aforementioned dimensions.

A grouping of these work packages created a smaller organization, which later came to be known as a "department," and then several groupings of them made what we today know as an "organization"—a complex of jobs, departments, divisions, and so on.

Management scientists, like Frederick W. Taylor, Frank B. Gilbreth, and others, became aware of the perils of work and realized as early as a century ago that a job was not something that people would love and admire on a long-term basis. They also knew that even money would not be able to keep people tied to their jobs. They looked for ways to make the work easier, uniform, effortless, efficient, and, maybe, more interesting. They noticed the differences that existed between the jobs that were liked and the ones that were despised, and engaged in efforts to redesign work to make it less repulsive.

Science and engineering have since continued to bridge the differences between various jobs and have tried to make all work easy and interesting. However, they have had only partial success. Unfortunately, in the process of making work easy, efficient, and uniform, they complicated work design, reduced its scope, made it too monotonous and too specific.

This new approach to designing work actually made it too mechanical, rigid, and even more disliked by the workers.

Later on, industrial psychologists came to the rescue of workers. They told managers that organized work was a mind game and that with behavioral theories they could come up with ways to modify human work behavior that would keep employees continuously motivated to perform in organizational setting. They taught managers new ways of keeping workers involved in their tasks and open to their superiors' instructions. They devised new theories on leadership. They preached the concept that asked managers to have a vision for the organization that will give meaning to working hard and excite the workers about their jobs. They also suggested a number of strategies to make the work more appealing or less dispelling.

Work Environment. Work environment is the second component of the work system. Almost anything that concerns work and its execution, but does not make a constituent of the work itself being performed, belongs to the work environment. Every job or work assignment has its own unique environment. This includes all factors, forces, and conditions that directly and/or indirectly are involved in its accomplishment. These factors, forces, and conditions affect work, working, and the worker who has little or no direct control over them. It is important to know that if a worker does have control over any part or aspect of them, then that aspect or part does not remain a part of his work environment.

Work and its environment make an integrated system. The work environment is made up of many factors, such as: What is to be done? How and where should it be done? What will be its performance and evaluation standards? How and by whom will the completed work be checked and approved? Who will schedule the start and finish of work hours, breaks, and vacations? How will the work contribute to the organization's big picture or vision? Who will have control over the doer's compensation, raises, and upward mobility?

In general, work environment hampers creativity, quality, and productivity of all work. For knowledge work, in particular, in addition to these factors, work environment creates a serious impediment to basic functioning of the work. The manager's endeavor in this regard should be to make knowledge work free of environment. At a minimum, it should be redesigned with as little environment as possible—where management wants to exercise some prerogative on all activities that occur in the organization. The new environment should be both satisfying and conducive to work and an enhancement to creativity and performance.

Understanding Knowledge Work

Knowledge work is quite different from traditional work or "operating work." Whereas operating work is structured and carried out according to a preconceived design and method, and results in "cookie cutter" output, knowledge work does not have a clear-cut method or process for its accomplishment, especially methods and processes set by persons other than the doer. Each doer has a unique way of accomplishing knowledge work. It is mostly not accomplished according to the design and method conceived by others.

Managers should accept that not all knowledge work is the same, equally meaningful, challenging, rewarding, or interesting. Sometimes it can become very abstract and confusing. Depending on the type of knowledge work, it can either draw the doer to it and make him engage in it or drive him away.

There are several ingredients that can make all knowledge work likeable and interesting. Managers can include ingredients in knowledge work, or any other work in knowledge organizations, to increase its appeal to those who perform it. Every job should be tested for the natural occurrence or absence of these ingredients before designing it. For the doer to enjoy his work, all these ingredients should be present in every knowledge job. Some of these ingredients are given below:

1. To connect the doer's work with the system outcome, end products, or services, and/or with incoming factors, inputs, services, or raw materials;
2. To have professional and social interaction within and outside the organization provided by or through the knowledge work;
3. To perform a variety of knowledge tasks and skills;
4. To know how important and visible his part is in the organization's scheme of things, or project, product, or service to come out;
5. To believe others have a high perception of this work;

6. To employ state-of-the-art technology in performance of this work;

7. To provide opportunities for new learning and personal growth.

Knowledge Work Environment. Individually or collectively, managers design most of the work environment factors, deliberately assuming that this will help them keep control of the work and the workers. Typically, the work environment manifests an organization's culture. If knowledge organizations encourage a culture of trust, freedom, and less control, the work environment will eventually disappear.

In anticipation of designing the environment for knowledge work, it is important for managers to know what does not work so they can avoid it. Based on the experiences of traditional organizations, there are a number of work system models that do not work. The next section describes them in detail.

MODELS FOR KNOWLEDGE WORK FAILURE

In most cases, the major difference between the job that is despised by workers and the one that is liked by them comes from the work environment surrounding the job. In one case, the work environment is externally set and is given to workers with little or no room for its redesign, or even its adaptation; whereas, in the other case, it is left to be designed or totally evolved by the person who performs the job. Actually, it may be more appropriate to say that in the former case, there is a tight and closely enforced work environment, whereas in the latter case, there is practically no work environment—it is purposely left without a work environment. People may find it easier to tolerate work that they do not like provided the job has no environment rather than accept a likable job with a work environment that is abhorrent to them.

Differences in organizational work environments were introduced during the twentieth century as businesses started to get bigger and jobholders assumed roles that were previously typically assigned to the owners. Various jobs in organizations, depending on their levels in the hierarchy or placement in the organizational process, had different work environments. Such differences had not existed in the pre–job era. Until that time, everyone who worked in a group to attain a common goal (an organization by the present-day definition) had practically the same work environment.

First, as a rule, managers should accept the fact that if a knowledge worker hates a particular task or avoids doing it, the work system of this task is in need of redesign. There has to be something wrong with this work—it cannot pull and retain its doer. It can be said that if this same job in the same environment, from which one worker runs away, is given to owners or bosses—the ones who stayed behind in the example from one of the previous sections—they would also run from it. In fact, they would run out even faster than the workers did. It is this kind of work that we want to redesign, and it is this kind of work environment that we want to eliminate. Knowledge organization managers' goals are to redesign knowledge work so that a worker runs to it rather than away from it. The worker should find it hard to stop working while doing this job.

Mapping Knowledge Work and Its Environment

To model a job, we first study work assignments in their environment, as a system, offered by organizations in the performance of a task. The purposes are, first, to find out how interesting the task itself is and, second, how conducive the work environment is to the completion of the task by the person who is assigned to do it.

Certain instruments have been specifically designed to perform such an assessment of knowledge work and are explained below. Complete instruments with instructions on scoring are given at the end of this chapter.

Making Employees' Work Be Like the Owner's. The aim is to so design all knowledge work that it has challenges, responsibilities, authorities, rewards, and punishments that are typically meant for the owner of the organization in which this work is located. In knowledge organizations, we do this with the help of a specifically designed instrument called *Work Harmony Instrument for Pull Measurement & Evaluation (WHIPME)* (see Instrument 4-1). With this instrument, we analyze work to measure the amount of force with which work pulls its doer toward it—the force with which it establishes a bond with its doer. It is, in fact, a measure of several work characteristics like those given previously. There are many ways to measure such an adhesion, but to make the process uniform and convenient, we introduce the 20-item instrument that operationalizes these characteristics of the work being studied.

Work assignments, as currently offered by knowledge organizations, can be scaled along a continuum, given here. At the top of this continuum is the work assignment of a sole proprietor. On the WHIPME scale, this assignment should score a 20. Since all public and most private organizations have some employees who function as owners, the work assigned to them will also have a WHIPME score that is close to 20; this will depend upon the extent to which the organization system allows these employees to replace the owner. The work assignment of a university professor should score about 17 on the WHIPME scale; corporate officers, about 15; and school teachers, about 12. At the low end of the continuum are the more regulated and controlled jobs, such as miners, assembly line workers, meat packers/processors, farmhands, and/or knitting fabric mill operators.

To get the best performance on knowledge work from Gen Xers and Generation Y members, all jobs should be designed so that they accumulate a score close to 20 on the WHIPME scale, that is, all knowledge jobs should fully replicate the work of a sole proprietor. Any knowledge work assignment that does not score close to the top has not been designed to make the highest contribution to the organization. Such changes are essential because first,

Instrument 4-1
Work Harmony Instrument for Pull Measurement & Evaluation
(WHIPME)

Job Title: _____ Department: _____ Organization: _____
Brief Job Description: _____
Analyst: _____ Date: _____ Comments: _____

Consider only the job the knowledge worker is doing and not the worker and answer the following questions.

1. How many steps away from this job is the start of the process on this product or service?

   ☐ A Not many, the worker can easily connect with the start.
   ☐ B Many, but the worker can connect with the start.
   ☐ C Too many for the worker to connect with the start.

2. How many steps away from this job is the end of the process on this product or service?

   ☐ A Not many, the worker can easily connect with the end of the product or service.
   ☐ B Many, but the worker can connect with the end product or service.
   ☐ C Too many for the worker to connect with the end product or service.

3. How many individuals depend on the output or throughput from this job?

   ☐ A Many, this is one of the jobs that feeds work to the rest of the product or service.
   ☐ B Some.
   ☐ C None, this is very much a stand-alone job.

4. How many face-to-face contacts with individuals from within the organization does this job require during a normal workday?

   ☐ A Many people from both ends of the process contact this worker.
   ☐ B Some people from both ends of the process contact this worker.
   ☐ C No one from either end of the process is likely to contact this worker.

5. How many face-to-face contacts with individuals from within the organization does this job provide opportunity for during a normal workday?

   ☐ A Many are likely to contact this worker.
   ☐ B Some are likely to contact this worker.
   ☐ C No one is likely to contact this worker.

6. How many face-to-face contacts with individuals from outside the organization does this job require during a normal workday?

   ☐ A Many are likely to contact this worker.
   ☐ B Some are likely to contact this worker.
   ☐ C No one is likely to contact this worker.   *(continued)*

Instrument 4-1 (*continued*)

7. How many face-to-face contacts with individuals from outside the organization does this job provide opportunity for during a normal workday?

  ☐ A   Many, this is our representative.
  ☐ B   Some contacts are possible.
  ☐ C   None.

8. How many machine interfaces (non–face-to-face contacts, such as the ones established via telephone calls, voice-mails, e-mails, the Internet hits, mail pieces, etc.) from within the organization are expected in performance of this job during a normal day?

  ☐ A   Many, this is an important part of this job.
  ☐ B   Some.
  ☐ C   None.

9. How many machine interfaces (non–face-to-face contacts, such as the ones established via telephone calls, voice-mails, e-mails, the Internet hits, mail pieces, etc.) from outside the organization are expected in performance of this job during a normal day?

  ☐ A   Many, this is an important part of this job.
  ☐ B   Some.
  ☐ C   None.

10. How much communication/computer technology is utilized in performing this job?

  ☐ A   A lot, it needs its own computer/work station.
  ☐ B   Some.
  ☐ C   None, no such technology is used.

11. How modern and updated are the machines, equipment and tools, etc., used in performance of this job?

  ☐ A   State-of-the-art.
  ☐ B   Run-of-the-mill.
  ☐ C   Behind-the-times.

12. How many different tasks are involved in performance of this job?

  ☐ A   Many, there is a good variety of different tasks.
  ☐ B   Some.
  ☐ C   One.

13. How many different skills are involved in performance of this job?

  ☐ A   Many, it is very much a generalized job.
  ☐ B   Some.
  ☐ C   One.

14. How much voluntary/flexible travel or opportunities to change job scenery is available in doing this job?

  ☐ A   This job is such that travel is planned by the worker.
  ☐ B   Some.
  ☐ C   None.   (*continued*)

Instrument 4-1 (*continued*)

15. What are the demands of quality, quantity, and delivery from this job?
   - ☐ A High, it is important and visible job.
   - ☐ B Medium.
   - ☐ C Low.

16. How often do the job demands (quality, quantity, delivery) expected from the doer of this job change?
   - ☐ A Frequently.
   - ☐ B Rarely.
   - ☐ C Never.

17. How good a performance rating is possible for a person who does this job?
   - ☐ A Very good if one works hard.
   - ☐ B Good is one works hard.
   - ☐ C Average even if one works hard.

18. What opportunities for promotion and/or personal growth are possible through a good performance of this job?
   - ☐ A Tremendous, this is the way up.
   - ☐ B Rare, if you are extremely good and well connected.
   - ☐ C Never has anyone doing this job been promoted.

19. How many people within the organization are qualified to replace the doer of this job?
   - ☐ A Practically no one, this job is so unique.
   - ☐ B Very few, it requires special training and experience.
   - ☐ C A lot, almost anyone can do this job.

20. How many people in the organization will be eager to replace the current doer of this job?
   - ☐ A A lot, people will love to do this job.
   - ☐ B Quite a few, there is a good enthusiasm to do this job.
   - ☐ C Very few, you will have to entice people to take this job.

SCORING THE WHIPME
Give 1.0 for each "A" box scored, 0.5 for each "B" boxed scored, and 0.0 for each "C" box scored. Add up all the points. This is the total score on work assigned to this job.

Score	Diagnosis	Recommendation
<10	911 Job	Jump in to save
10–14.5	Corporate Officers	Redesign to get higher score
≥15	Owner	Keep it up

the new requisites from knowledge work for success in this changed, global marketplace—productivity, innovation, quality, and delivery—will not be attained if the work and its environment are not conducive to them. Second, the new generations of workers would prefer not to work rather than to accept a responsibility that does not provide interesting work and an environment that they cannot control and redesign to suit their needs.

The function of management is to isolate knowledge work and its doer from extraneous forces that go against the performance of such work by its doer. The purpose of organizational knowledge work environment, in principle, should be to facilitate the most effective and efficient performance of work by its doer. In actuality, in many traditional organizations, the work environment imposes containment on the relationship between the work and its doer. The work environment, as stated previously, acts as an umbrella of forces that does not allow this performance to go beyond the limits set, many times inadvertently, by the organization. Elimination or reduction in the magnitude of these work environment forces will help performance take shape and will be determined only by the relationship between the work and its doer.

Making Employees' Work Environment Be Like the Owner's. Just as we did with knowledge work, the ideal knowledge environment is also that of the owner's. In all respects possible, we want knowledge jobs to operate as if an owner were performing them. To assess the extent to which a job does indeed meet this criterion, the *Work Environment Restriction Measurement (WERM)* has been designed specifically for knowledge work (see Instrument 4-2). With this instrument, we can analyze and assess the work environment by measuring the presence and magnitude of these forces. Again, as in the case of work, such a study can be done in several ways, but to do a standard, uniform analysis, we will use this survey instrument. WERM grasps various characteristics of the work environment, discussed previously in this chapter, in an 18-item survey instrument. A work analyst or any member of the human resource management department familiar with the situation can complete this assessment.

Work environments devised and offered by organizations can also be presented along a continuum. At the top of this continuum is the work environment surrounding the work assignments of a sole proprietor. This owner enjoys power that gives him full control over all aspects of his job. His work environment offers him all possible opportunities, challenges, responsibilities, authorities, rewards, and punishments. According to the definition of work environment developed previously, sole proprietors have practically no work environment. For them, there are not many factors, forces, or conditions in the organization that are beyond their control or that restrict their performance as owners of the organization. In other words, we can say that they, for all practical purposes, have no work environment. Nothing affects their work that they do not themselves control. Their own ambitions and abilities basically control their performance at work.

Instrument 4-2
Work Environment Restriction Measurement
(WERM)

Job Title: _____ Department: _____ Organization: _____
Brief Job Description: _____
Analyst: _____ Date: _____ Comments: _____

Consider knowledge work and the worker who is or will be doing this knowledge work and carefully answer the following questions.

1. Who decides what work will be done?
   - ☐ A The worker.
   - ☐ B According to a flexible system with the worker's input.
   - ☐ C It is decided by the organization.

2. Who decides how the work will be done?
   - ☐ A The worker.
   - ☐ B According to a set process with worker's input.
   - ☐ C It is decided by the specialists.

3. To whom does the work make sense? For example, what function does the work perform, where will it fit, who will use it, etc.?
   - ☐ A To the worker.
   - ☐ B According to a flexible system with worker input.
   - ☐ C It is decided by the organization.

4. Who sets the worker's goals for achievement, performance, and evaluation on this job?
   - ☐ A The worker.
   - ☐ B Goals are set jointly by the worker and his supervisor.
   - ☐ C The organization.

5. Who selects the machines, equipment, tools, and other ancillaries for this worker's work?
   - ☐ A The worker.
   - ☐ B The organization in frequent consultation with the worker.
   - ☐ C There are specialists in the organization who do this.

6. Who selects materials and parts used in that segment of the process for which this worker is responsible?
   - ☐ A The worker.
   - ☐ B The purchasing department with the worker's input.
   - ☐ C There is a purchasing and acquisition department to do this.

(continued)

Instrument 4-2 (*continued*)

7. Who tells the worker how he/she is doing on their quantitative output target?
   - ☐ A   The worker is able to constantly monitor and know what he/she has achieved and what is left.
   - ☐ B   A frequent review is done by the supervisor and a report is issued to the worker.
   - ☐ C   There are organizational output goals that are audited periodically.

8. Who arranges or lays out the work place for the worker?
   - ☐ A   The worker.
   - ☐ B   The worker in consultation with his department head.
   - ☐ C   There is a planning and facilities office responsible for this.

9. Who controls the worker's location of work?
   - ☐ A   The worker.
   - ☐ B   It is controlled according to a flexible system with the worker's input.
   - ☐ C   Organization's management.

10. Who decides when a worker may take a vacation or an extended absence from work?
    - ☐ A   The worker is free to plan to take it any time.
    - ☐ B   The worker has a choice but it may or may not be approved as asked.
    - ☐ C   There is a set policy on this.

11. Who decides when the work will begin and end?
    - ☐ A   The worker is free to start and finish as he pleases.
    - ☐ B   According to a flexible system but approval must be sought.
    - ☐ C   Organization has set such times in consultation with management.

12. Who decides with whom this worker will work in performing tasks that need assistance from others?
    - ☐ A   The worker is free to select his/her own team or partners.
    - ☐ B   The worker can suggest names that may or may not be approved.
    - ☐ C   Work has to be done in an organizational setting and hierarchy.

13. Who decides the timing and duration of breaks for lunch, coffee, and other?
    - ☐ A   The worker may do it whenever he/she feels like it.
    - ☐ B   According to a flexible system but approval must be sought.
    - ☐ C   The organization has set times for these.

14. Who controls how much financial remuneration the worker gets from this job?
    - ☐ A   It is based on straight value-added and output goals and measures known to and agreed upon by the worker.
    - ☐ B   There is a bonus program that supplements wages.
    - ☐ C   There are set and agreed upon aggregate time-based rates.

(*continued*)

Instrument 4-2 (*continued*)

15. Who determines whether the work is of a good quality or not?
    - ☐ A The worker has a system that constantly tells him the quality of his output and what to do in case of any deviation from the standards.
    - ☐ B Quality is the worker's responsibility and is built into his compensation plan.
    - ☐ C There is a quality assurance department for this function.

16. Who selects the benefits, like health, retirement, and others, that the worker receives?
    - ☐ A The worker has the freedom to allocate portions of his financial compensation between wages and benefits.
    - ☐ B Organization allows a set percentage of wages in a cafeteria-style system for benefits.
    - ☐ C There is a set package of benefits.

17. Who takes the credit if things go right or the blame if they go wrong?
    - ☐ A There is a system that identifies and highlights the good as well as bad done by the worker.
    - ☐ B There is a periodic recognition system to acknowledge and reward outstanding work.
    - ☐ C It is not possible to give credit for work well done or to blame for what is done wrong.

18. Who sets the overall course of the organization?
    - ☐ A There is a system in place that requires everyone to make a contribution toward the direction the organization is headed.
    - ☐ B One can submit suggestions.
    - ☐ C The management does it in concert with its board.

SCORING ON THE WERM

Give 0.0 for each "A" box scored, 0.5 for each "B" box scored, and 1.0 for each "C" box scored. Add up all the points. That is the WERM score for this job.

Score	What Type	Quality of Work Environment (QWE)
>15.5	Suicidal	Doomed to fail
13–15.5	Dying	Lot to improve
10–12.5	Crying for help	Improve for gains
7–9.5	Working	Improvement possible
4–6.5	Progressive	Satisfying
<4	Ideal	The best possible

Modeling Knowledge Work. If a task has a total absence of work environment, like that of the sole proprietor, we designate this job as a "sE work environment" (sans-Environment). On the WERM, a sole proprietor's work environment will score 0. Within the present bounds in which a business corporation operates, the work environment for the job of a chief executive officer or a chairperson of the board or any other comparable job would score between 0 and 1 on the WERM. Different corporate officers may score in the range of 0 to 3. Other occupations that have scores on the WERM close in this range would be private consultants, physicians, tenured university professors, and most other self-employed professionals.

At the other end of this continuum are jobs (such as in a meat-processing plant in Iowa or elsewhere in the United States) that are specifically designed to be taken by illegal immigrants, miners, and military. These jobs should score close to the high end on the WERM.

All other jobs and occupations will fall between these two extremes. A lawyer may score 4 and a schoolteacher 5. On the high end, a toll collector's work environment may score 18, a mass assembly line operator may score 16, a bank teller may score 14, and a school janitor will fall right in the middle with a score of 9.

Knowledge Work Environment

The only work environment that is successful in knowledge organizations is the work environment "sE," the work environment of an owner. The next generation of employees will work best in the work environment that is almost exactly sE, that is nonexistent. During the work era of the generations preceding Gen Xers and Generation Y, employees continued to work even when they were not satisfied with their work or work environment, and the employers could afford to keep them employed even when the workers were not fully effective in their work assignments. This was possible because the marketplace mechanics did not interfere with what went on in the shop. This is not the case with the knowledge organizations of the twenty-first century, which are virtually operating in a global economy. They will fail within months if this type of behavior continues unabated.

Knowledge Organization Work Matrix

Given the work and its environment as a system, we can place all organizational work into one of the four blocks of this matrix modeled in Figure 4-1. This matrix has two dimensions: The first one is the work itself, which is measured at two levels. The top level of the work is the one scoring at least a 15 on the WHIPME scale, which is the work assignment of owners. This is the work that pulls doers to it and is the ideal work design. At the low end along this dimension is the work that scores less than 15. Because this work is not the

Figure 4-1
Work Models for Knowledge Organizations

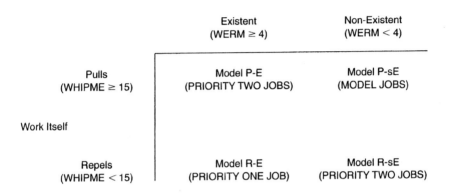

WORK ENVIRONMENT

	Existent (WERM ≥ 4)	Non-Existent (WERM < 4)
Pulls (WHIPME ≥ 15)	Model P-E (PRIORITY TWO JOBS)	Model P-sE (MODEL JOBS)
Work Itself		
Repels (WHIPME < 15)	Model R-E (PRIORITY ONE JOB)	Model R-sE (PRIORITY TWO JOBS)

work assignment of the owners, we simply discard it. Of course, the lower it is from the score of 15, the worse it becomes. We label this as work that repels.

The second dimension of this matrix, along the Y-axis, is the work environment. It also has two levels. The top level is the work environment that scores less than 4 on the WERM scale. This work environment is close to being "nonexistent." This is the work environment of owners and corporate officers. Any work environment scoring 4 or greater will be considered an "existent" work environment. Workers surrounded by this type of work environment will be totally antiinnovation and antiproductivity, and the jobs will be unworkable and not suitable for knowledge workers.

The four possible combinations of these make up the four possible work models given in the matrix and are presented in Figure 4-1.

A cursory look at the work model matrix will tell us that the worst job is Model R-E. This should be the first job set that knowledge organizations approach for analysis and redesign in order to make it suitable as knowledge work. The first endeavor should attempt to eliminate this job all together—obliteration strategy. If it cannot be eliminated, it should be redesigned so that it can be done by some machine function, computer, robot, or any other automaton. If human interaction cannot be totally eliminated, then this job should be given topmost priority for reorganization. Knowledge organization managers should label all such jobs as "Priority One" jobs.

Work models P-E and R-sE, given in Figure 4-1, present poorly designed jobs that need to be improved. Uninteresting work but no work environment (R-sE) and interesting work with a work environment (P-E) may succeed in attracting employees, but they will be hard to retain on a long-term basis due to either the lack of job satisfaction or the inability to achieve innovation and productivity at a requisite level. These employees may not frequently gripe, but they will be barely operational, with a low-to-tolerable productivity and nonexistent innovation. In most cases, owners and bosses keep employees working by using extrinsic motivation—mainly money—as a tranquilizer. This strategy worked in traditional organizations for almost one full century. However, managers should not count on it to work for too long in knowledge organizations.

The extrinsic rewards administered by the organization for these jobs take away their doers' attention from pain. Nevertheless, the pain is there—and the manager should never ignore that fact. He should also not expect high morale and motivation from knowledge employees under these conditions and, as learned previously, he can forget about expecting any innovation to come from these work conditions.

All model R-sE and model P-E jobs are candidates for knowledge work analysis. They should be labeled "Priority Two" jobs.

FROM JOBS TO WORK GROUPS

An important job of managers of knowledge workers is to ensure that their jobs are so designed that they enjoy a lot of freedom. Ideally, the work performed by these workers should have no environment—there should be no factors that they do not control. In this chapter, we found two instruments that assess both dimensions of knowledge work: work itself and work environment. For knowledge work, this chapter provided recommended scores on both these measures and also strategies to redesign or eliminate the work that does not get the recommended scores.

Once knowledge jobs have been redesigned, the next step in managing knowledge organizations is grouping them. Chapter 5 considers this function from the general to the special attention needed in knowledge organizations.

Chapter 5

Teaming and Grouping Strategies: It's a Symbiosis

In Chapter 4, it was recommended that knowledge work incorporate characteristics that attract workers to it, such as having no work environment, so that workers feel free to control work-related decisions and activities. We learned that the purpose of this approach in work design is to ensure that workers enjoy the work as much as they enjoy engaging in non–work-related activities. In the present chapter, we will learn how knowledge organization managers can use these redesigned jobs and consider methods for grouping them into teams, groups, departments, and divisions. It develops strategies for designing and organizing a firm to operate as an organization where work and work environment are designed with characteristics suited to the employees belonging to the new generations working in knowledge environments. We also present a model that takes as input certain variables relating to the firm and its industry and then devises strategies that the firm may select to follow in operating its business as a knowledge organization.

PURPOSE OF GROUPING IN KNOWLEDGE ORGANIZATIONS

Any social or business organization brings together individuals and groups with different needs—for example, employers and employees, buyers and suppliers, shoppers and merchants, and other such dyads. To be successful, the resultant grouping has to provide a forum for the fulfillment of these needs for all members in the relationship. Although the parties voluntarily enter into these relationships, there is an implied sociopsychological "contract" that gives both parties the belief that their needs will be fulfilled through this union. In knowledge organizations, a contract like this implies that the organization, for its part, will provide an environment that will facilitate the emancipation of innovation and knowledge and that employees, on their part, will engage in activities that actually cause the innovation to happen and the knowledge to emerge—resulting in applications that may be marketed immediately or later.

In an effort to create such an environment, a knowledge organization should first study and then guide collaborators in organizational endeavors to amalgamate all contributory and extraneous interactions that take place at work. The main goal is to know how to turn the organization into a mutualism.

The best design model to facilitate the functioning of a knowledge organization as a mutualism lies in a system that allows work and other relationships to evolve on their own, rather than have them set by rules from an authority. It should be a symbiosis that naturally, simultaneously, and consecutively allows all partners to emerge as contributors and later endows them with a pro portionate consequence from the symbiotic collaboration—whether it is a positive consequence or a negative one.

The organizational model presented in this chapter—*symbiosis at work*—best carries out the relationships and transactions in knowledge organizations to bring about the goals described above and to spur ubiquitous innovation. This design is also suitable to manage relationships that are not externally dictated or set. It is developed through the study and emulation of the symbiotic relationships present in nature.

Symbiotic relationships, as should be the case in successful knowledge organizations, are not molded using permanent roles of "givers" and "takers," "inferiors" and "superiors," "controllers" and "controlled," "subordinates" and "bosses," and what we *traditionally* know as "employers" and "employees." A knowledge organization, for the sake of emancipation of innovation, should allow everyone to function identically. All should be treated as participants. They are all symbionts.

Symbionts in a successful symbiosis, in spite of the presence of such a confounded mix of overlapping roles, clearly know and collectively execute their roles and work to attain the goals that are set and the roles that evolve in the organization. The symbiosis at work model closely approaches this objective. It is a management system with its own ways to perform standard management functions. Its practice will result in the creation of human symbiosis management for a knowledge organization.

Although the words "employer" and "employee" are used in the symbiotic process described here, the meaning of these words as used in the context of knowledge organizations differs from the meaning that was applied to twentieth-century operating or traditional organizations. In knowledge environments, employers and employees are both symbionts with common interests and with naturally and continuously evolving authorities and responsibilities.

EMULATION IN KNOWLEDGE ORGANIZATION: THE SELF FACTOR

The symbiosis model for knowledge organizations is designed to emulate symbiotic relationships in organizations aiming to achieve high levels of innovation and productivity essential for success. This model gives new definitions to the traditional roles of employers (or employers' agents/substitutes/managers) and employees, such that the lines between these roles thin and gradually fade away and evolve into a relationship that suits the innovative function of a knowledge organization. It gives employees the confidence to map, control, and, ideally, eliminate their environment. This model of relationship becomes systemic, and the main factor determining the boundaries on one's behavior and performance in the organization is the employee himself or herself. All others, including the employer, become nonfactors. Subsequently, everyone in the system becomes a symbiont.

For each symbiont, the symbiotic process naturally reads and understands one's conscious and subconscious needs. The symbiosis activates and satiates needs that are relevant to its functioning and success. At the same time, it deactivates and acquiesces needs that go counter to goals of the symbiosis. It facilitates the creation of environment-free, self-contained, and independently operating microsystems within the larger, organizational system, such that requisite control emerges symbiotically rather than extraneously.

Microsystems and Mutualism

A knowledge organizational symbiosis is made up of many cells called "microsystems." Each microsystem is responsible for a function of the knowledge organization, with a symbiont, an employee, at the center of each microsystem. This employee or symbiont is in control of this microsystem.

A symbiotic process naturally buoys an employee's individual innovation and talent. It brings out similar latent characteristics in other symbionts. This furthers its permeation to the whole organization. Therefore, symbiosis invigorates the whole organization to commit to the espoused goals and to work to attain them. This is how mutualism emerges.

The basis for survival and growth of knowledge organizations, like any symbiosis, lies in mutualism—optimal benefit for all symbionts (both employers and employees). In the absence of such optimization, symbiosis will evolve, apply, and, if necessary, accelerate the process to bring about optimization. Then, in case the system fails to achieve this, symbiosis will hasten its demise. It is in the self-interest of all symbionts that mutualism does exist because that is how symbiosis will survive.

Longitudinal symbiotic relationships will turn organizations into obligatory symbioses in which all symbionts require mutual interactions for their survival. A symbiosis may be stronger, as in a nuclear family, or weaker, as in a legal partnership. Stronger symbioses are obligatory where the partners cannot survive without the interaction provided by the symbiosis. To some extent, in all forms, a symbiosis is a mutualism in which every partner clearly knows that all partners exist and prosper or dwindle and perish together.

The relationships that develop through symbiosis at work will not permit the continuation of commensalism. This is how the symbiosis model ensures that the employee or the employer—a microsystem—will not be positively or negatively affected in isolation without accordingly affecting other microsystems in the symbiosis. In practice, this means that if the employer gains, employees gain, and if the employer loses, employees lose. Moreover, the proportions are also consistent.

The revolutionary change in human behavior that is taking place around the world will make the practice of symbiotic management—work symbiosis or symbiosis at work—the only surety of success in the twenty-first century. At the micro or organizational level, it will explain the difference between success and failure, and at the macro or societal level, the rise and fall of nations, because economic power will determine the fate of nations in the twenty-first century.

Human Symbiosis and the Job Era

The concept of symbiosis in human relationships such as the ones existing at work is not very new. Dependence had been an important ingredient in all meaningful human relationships—social and work-related, voluntary and biological, longitudinal and short-lived—until the concept of job evolved. Such an environment, in all organizational settings, can be conducive to intellectual independence and innovation. The work symbiosis model is specifically designed by abstracting and adapting symbiotic principles that breed, multiply, and advance knowledge, innovation, and higher productivity.

KNOWLEDGE ORGANIZATION RELATIONS

Depending on the industry to which a knowledge organization belongs and its position in that industry, a decision should be made whether and how to use symbiotic management. This decision is guided by certain information relating to the organization and the industry to which it belongs. The expected reward realized through symbiotic management may be extremely high under some conditions, while not as high under others. Although it is up to the manager to make the final choice in this regard, the process to help select a strategy for relations between employers and employees in a knowledge organization is presented here. The initial question is clear: Should the knowledge organization relations be directed by the symbiosis at work model or not?

Typically, an organization in an industry in decline is so preoccupied with its operational problems that it does not see much incentive in putting effort into planning and understanding individual and group behaviors and in applying any new management techniques. Nevertheless, this organization may have a greater need to explore the possibility of redesigning and reorganizing itself according to the human symbiosis model. The innovation and productivity that emerge from the symbiotic approach to management will help all organizations under all circumstances—even when an organization is struggling for its survival.

This strategy selection process, detailed below, employs quantitative financial performance measures of an organization and compares them to similar measures for the industry in which it belongs. These financial indicators are symptomatic of a variety of complex performance measures that go into computing them and that are translated into the health of an organization. These are potent and aggregate measures of an organization's well-being and are used to analyze and help select the right symbiotic strategy. It is safe to employ them for this purpose.

Industry Classification

The performance of a knowledge organization is determined based on its comparison with its competitors in their industry. However, the performance of an industry is determined through its comparative growth in the economy in which it operates as measured by its inflation-adjusted annual growth rate (g).

We divide any industry into three classifications based on its inflation-adjusted annual growth rate:

IN1: Growth Industry. In this classification, an industry is labeled a growth industry if it is growing at a rate substantially higher than the rate of growth of the economy in which it operates. This growth rate is compared against the GDP (i), the gross domestic product—a measure of the inflation-adjusted increase in the value of all domestically produced goods and services. The mathematical definition of a growth industry implies $g > i$.

IN2: Stable Industry. An industry that is growing at approximately the same rate as the gross domestic product of the economy in which it is operating is classified as a stable industry. The mathematical model representing this industry is $g = i$.

IN3: Declining Industry. If the growth rate of an industry is significantly less than the growth rate of the GDP of the economy in which it is operating, then that industry is classified as a declining industry. Mathematically, the model that represents this industry is $g < i$.

Organization Classification

The strength of the position that a knowledge organization holds in its industry is determined by the growth it enjoys as compared with other organizations in that industry. The measure of this growth is given by the increase in price-deflated revenue (r) of the knowledge organization. An increase in price-deflated revenue is a good indicator of the growth in the markets and product lines of an organization. This method of classifying organizations gives us the following three categories:

ORG1: Leader. A knowledge organization whose markets and product lines are growing at a rate greater than the growth rate for the industry to which it belongs is statistically in the top half of this group. Moreover, since most of the industries are economic oligopolies, the likely largest ideal size of this subgroup is two to four organizations. To belong to a leader category of this classification, the organization should have an inflation-adjusted consolidated revenue growth rate (r) that is significantly higher than that of its industry (g). This will practically limit the organizational leadership positions to one or two firms. Mathematically, we represent this condition as: $r > g$.

ORG2: Pacer. A pacer is a knowledge organization that is growing at about the same rate as the growth rate for its industry. The price-deflated revenue growth rate, r, is again a good measure: thus, if $r = g$, an organization is a pacer.

ORG3: Laggard. A knowledge organization is labeled a laggard for this strategy selection process if its markets and products (i.e., its price-deflated revenue), are growing at a rate lower than the similar rate of its industry as a whole (g). The mathematical model representing this organization is: $r < g$.

The Strategies

An industry that is growing offers an opportunity for growth to all organizations belonging to that industry, provided that they can exploit it for their growth. Similarly, an organization that has growing product lines and markets has the opportunity to manage them for its benefit and further growth. The selection of a behavioral management strategy has the potential to equip an organization to succeed through symbiosis and full involvement of every individual associated with the organization in realization of its goals.

Given the opportunity that an organization has for development and growth, there are nine possible positions in which an organization may belong, and there are three recommended behavior strategies that an organization can select to achieve them. Figure 5-1 represents the possible combinations of these conditions and the recommended relations strategies.

S1: Common and Usual. A common approach that many organizations take concerning any change is to deny its presence or arrival. In this case, an organization will adopt what we call the *common and usual* strategy. It fights and resists the changes in work and human behavior, rather than adopting new practices, such as the symbiotic management model. Under most circumstances, this behavior, on the part of management of any organization, could be extremely detrimental to the well-being and, possibly, the existence of the organization. All types of organizations benefit from symbiotic relations at work, yet some organizations decide to continue to conduct man-

Figure 5-1
Symbiotic Relations Strategy Selection Model

STAGE OF INDUSTRY

		Growth $(g > i)$	Stable $(g = i)$	Declining $(g < i)$
	Leader $(r > g)$	Support & Conduce S3	Support & Conduce S3	Adapt & Conform S2
Organization	Pacer $(r = g)$	Support & Conduce S3	Adapt & Conform S2	Adapt & Conform S2
	Laggard $(r < g)$	Support & Conduce S3	Adapt & Conform S2	Common & Usual S1

i = Gross Domestic Product (GDP); g = Inflation-Adjusted Industry's Rate of Growth; r = Inflation-Adjusted Rate of Revenue Growth for the Organization

agement as is usually done if the industry is in decline and the organization's revenue growth is below average. This is synonymous to accepting, and helplessly awaiting, an almost certain demise. This outcome corresponds to the block combining classifications of declining industries and laggard organizations in Figure 5-1.

An organization can engage in "denial behavior" in two ways. It can either discourage recruitment of people with clearly apparent traits associated with the new generation of workers or it can hire them but later put pressure on them to change. In this way, an organization forces progressive employees to concur with the traditional management style that it practices and to unlearn what they have brought to the organization. Such an organization, at the bottom of its declining industry, is going to fail almost without any recourse. This organization should not be a major concern. In fact, its selection of this strategy will expedite its demise.

S2: Adapt and Conform. This strategy suggests gradually adapting the new worker behavior and phasing in symbiotic management practices over time. It means that an organization should accept the behavior patterns of the new generation employees, consider them as the coming wave, and recruit these workers without any bias. Nevertheless, an organization that selects *adapt and conform* strategy may not actively engage in encouraging widespread symbiotic management. Figure 5-1 shows under what performance conditions, of an organization and of its industry, such a response would be appropriate.

A knowledge organization should gradually learn the behavioral patterns of its incoming employees, adapt itself to the change, and facilitate conformity of its management to symbiotic practices as needed. This strategy suggests the selective use of symbiotic management.

A knowledge organization that selects this strategy may not encourage the use of symbiotic management throughout the organization. It may select only certain divisions of the organization that thrive on innovation for the practice of symbiotic management. Such divisions may reside as separate entities or in all functional departments of the organization.

S3: Support and Conduct. The strategy of *support and conduct* requires active pursuance of the behavior patterns of new generations of workers, in particular Generation X and Generation Y. This organization should heavily recruit employees who reflect this behavior and encourage its current employees to reflect this type of behavior. This means a quick transformation of the organization to the symbiotic management practices described herein.

This strategy requires flexibility on the part of the organization to respond quickly to variations in the behavior of the incoming workforce and proceed with organization-wide practice of symbiotic management without any hindrance or reservation.

Under certain circumstances, it will be beneficial for an organization to induce and push its managers toward symbiotic management. The organization will have more to gain from changing to symbiotic management than from delaying and sticking with traditional management. Figure 5-1 indicates the industry and organization conditions that encourage this.

Once an organization has selected the appropriate strategy for the implementation of the symbiosis at work model, the next step involves designing and setting up a knowledge organization for functioning at its best. Chapter 6 covers the topic of setting up a knowledge organization as a symbiosis. The chapters after this show how to manage these organizations as a symbiosis. They consider numerous aspects particular to these organizations and recommend ways to bring teams and departments together.

Chapter 6 ⸻

Knowledge Work
Organization and Design

This chapter covers work and organization design pertaining to knowledge organizations. To caution managers, the chapter starts with work models that will not work in knowledge organizations and then moves on to those that will. It shows knowledge managers how to design and package work. It also provides various organizational design models that can successfully operate in a work relationship with diffused and confounded authority—symbiosis—such as the one we expect to exist in knowledge organizations. To generate an environment that is conducive to knowledge work, this chapter provides a methodology to schedule work for increasing employees' control of their activities.

One of the important functions that a manager has to perform on a day-to-day basis concerns work organization and design. This involves basic division of labor, assigning or loading workers, and scheduling tasks, work centers and/or workers. The purpose is to help the manager make decisions pertaining to these activities to enhance knowledge organizations' innovation and productivity. We will discuss the specifics of work and develop an understanding of how the fundamental redesign of work should be done so that work becomes an enjoyable activity, such as hobbies and play.

ORGANIZATIONAL HIERARCHY MODEL:
THE TRADITIONAL DESIGN

As we know, work design in traditional organizations is based on the central theme of cost-saving through the economy of time and effort. The principles guiding this theme were developed by the early twentieth century conceptual works of engineers and administrators such as Frederick W. Taylor (1911), Frank B. Gilbreth (1911), Harrington Emerson (1913), Lillian M. Gilbreth (1914), and Henry L. Gantt (1916) from America; the German sociologist Max Weber (1947, the original work in German was done around the turn of the century), Henri Fayol from France (1949, the original work in French was done around the turn of the century), and a number of their protégés.

This approach of work and organizational design involves keeping all work environment factors relating to the organization—such as markets, competitors, workers and their personal environments—"fixed" or "fixable," while designing a work system to respond to them. The result is presented as an "unalterable" design, implying that everything else, especially workers, has to fit into the system in order for the system to succeed. They use analysis as their main approach to understanding and designing work. To achieve this, a number of analytical techniques have been devised that enable workers to see things disjointedly and create many new smaller entities out of large, complex functions.

This technique breaks down and segregates work into tasks and jobs, which consequently separates workers according to their skills. To synthesize the whole, the procedure establishes connections with these created, smaller entities through a hierarchy, giving permanence to the system. In compliance with this hierarchy of work design, the organization formulates a parallel hierarchy of authority and control.

The management of twentieth century organized work is based on the principle of economy of scale—produce more to have efficient operations. These theories lacked the test of time. They worked then because the design used man as a peg in the work system. They ignored other economies such as of scope, psychology, creativity, and innovation—the economies of knowledge organizations. The economic race of the future is not going to be won based on the ability to mass produce identical items through an economy achieved as a result of low-paid, low-skilled workers acting as pegs in the system and as tightly negotiated vendors. The race will be won based on an organization's or a society's ability to synchronize technology and employees and provide an environment where innovation and productivity thrive.

In traditional organizations, the acts of designing, organizing, and assigning work are accomplished by isolated specialists, such as engineers and managers, based on their understanding of the work objectives, resources, and principles of economy. In these organizations, work organization is still done on the drawing board or in a laboratory setting. There is rarely concern about how well it corresponds with those who are responsible for the execution of work. In fact, it is common to find workers responsible for the execution of work achieving higher productivity by doing it in ways partly or mostly different from the work design given to them. In an attempt to avoid management's wrath, these workers tactfully keep this nonconformance from those responsible for the work design and organization. In many organizations, workers have two distinct sets of methods for designing and organizing work—one set of blueprints to show how it should be done following the organization's methods sheets and the other to give the hands-on method that is actually used to accomplish the work.

Design Mechanics and Functional Segregation

Basic work design mechanics entail dividing work that requires a variety of skills for its completion into manageable job packages. It is achieved in two main steps. First, all the work is broken into the smallest possible distinct or indistinct units, known as task elements. Next, these task elements are grouped so that each group consists of tasks requiring the same or very similar skills.

The size of this package—by definition, a "job"—is set so that it provides enough work to keep one person busy for about eight hours per day, five days per week on a rather consistent basis for a considerably long period. A person equipped with the skill required to perform this package is assigned the job, or, in the alternative, the organization trains someone to do it.

This grouping of similar tasks for designing jobs was practiced because, at the beginning of the job era, there were not many workers who possessed the skills that were demanded by a large number of growing organizations. In some cases, organizations did not want trained workers to perform more than one skill. This method had two aims: (1) to design work so that the bulk of it was suitable for execution by unskilled or semiskilled people, and (2) to separate the tasks that needed execution by a highly skilled *specialist*. This was the formula for increasing organizational economy and improving work quality.

This practice turned *trade experts*—who previously fully controlled their work and work environment, performed a family of similar skills surrounding a trade, and identified themselves with the vocation they engaged in, such as machinist, founder, carpenter, and blacksmith—into mere *operators*. Day in and day out, they performed the same package of subdivided work elements with little or no meaning or relevance to them or with any connectivity that they could understand. Effectively, it brought to a gradual end the know-how and dexterity of trades that people had mastered through learning from one generation to the next.

These newly created jobs in emerging large, complex organizations ensured that the intellectual or innovative part of doing a job was segregated from the operations part and was taken away from the person primarily responsible for transforming materials.

KNOWLEDGE WORK DESIGN MODEL: REVERSE SEGREGATION

Drawbacks of the organizational hierarchy model are that (1) it economizes the operations essential to accomplish work rather than taking a revolutionary look at work, and (2) it does not attack, manipulate, or design work to connect with its environment. The organizational hierarchy model of work created a separate class of workers—*intellectual workers*. Very simply, this design did not have the mechanism essential for innovation to occur at all levels, especially not at the grassroots level. Knowledge organizations need ubiquitous intellectual work. Employing a traditional work organization and design model is a sure way to have a knowledge organization fail.

The traditional work system deliberately disengages the well-being of all three major human constituents of modern organizations: workers, intellectual workers, and employers. The same outcome from an organizational initiative could have different consequences for these three groups.

In knowledge organizations, the primary objective should be to permit, plan, and encourage the free functioning of intellectual faculties of all people engaged in the achievement of organizational goals. The work design model presented here—*knowledge work design model*—assumes that a greater organizational well-being will result through achieving integration of intellectual and operator work assignments, and coupling the well-being of all people— workers, intellectual workers, and employers (managers included)—engaged in the accomplishment of the knowledge organization's goals. The design model presented here will provide this integration and create knowledge work. This double integration will facilitate the timely occurrence and application of relevant and acceptable innovation. To achieve this, all work in a knowledge organization must be specifically so redesigned.

The knowledge work design model requires each assignment to allow its executor the freedom to modify, change, redesign, redefine, and even partially or fully eliminate the need to do any part of an assignment. A component of performance evaluation should verify this, and there should be built-in incentives that encourage employees to take heroic steps to engage in these activities. According to Stanford University economist and founder of New Growth Theory, Paul M. Romer, even innovation, like any other productive activity, responds to incentives (Mandel, Carney, & Reinhardt).

Instead of economizing costs, the knowledge work design model will result in cost obliteration, such as the elimination of operation or the increase in work speeds and feeds as suited to the situation. This will cause cost dilution and/or absolution due to workers understanding, manipulating, and connecting various environments through innovation, like finding additional consumers for the organization's products and services, discovering new applications of its technology, and implementing innovative use of its competencies.

With the growth of technology, managers have become aware of the huge complexity and ensuing difficulty in managing knowledge organizations and have started to look for potent models in other existing systems in science and nature so that they may transfer relevant knowledge to organizational management. Drawing upon the pioneering work on understanding a system and its environment by Bertalanffy (1950) and Boulding (1956), managers developed techniques that treat organizations as systems, such as physical and biological systems. Based on the concepts of *general systems theory* (GST)

(Bertalanffy, 1950; Boulding, 1956), these works succeeded in establishing functions and linkages among various segments of the organization, but effectively extended and *naturally* legitimized hierarchy. The biggest drawback of these mid-twentieth century techniques is that, by utilizing them, a manager can only understand in physiological terms and operate a complex human social system—such as an organization—as a breathing skeleton. They cannot help a manager establish a sociology and psychology of these complex systems—both of which are essential parts of a knowledge organization, where creativity is an indispensable ingredient. These works turned organizations into a big, well-programmed robot. Later, psychologists spent decades trying (with little success) to understand the mind and behavior of this robot.

The knowledge organization work design model adds these two missing dimensions and suggests how to make the new organization work as a *holistic* dynamic system, which in effect is an amalgamation of its *motor* functions and its psychology and sociology.

Operating and Creativity Components in Knowledge Work

In every organization, especially in knowledge organizations, all workers must be made fully aware of the existence of both the operating and creativity components of their work and the differences between them. Whereas the operating component takes care of the routine and motor functions of a job, the creativity component covers the intellectual and brain functions. Workers should also know that the operating component of their work helps them to achieve short-term, quantitative objectives, whereas the creativity component allows them to engage in activities that address the *fundamental* questions surrounding their work, long-term planning, and the innovative aspects of a job that may not be visible quantitatively for a long time. We label the latter as the *creativity* component, or work assignment, in any job.

Every knowledge organization manager must analyze each job under his or her control to understand the content of both its operating and creativity components. For every knowledge job, a way should be found to increase the latter and, through automation, to decrease or, in some cases, eliminate the operating component altogether.

Creativity Component and the Symbiotic Cycle

To effectively turn creativity into innovation in knowledge organizations requires a collaborative effort on the part of all connected with the concept-to-market-to-crypt cycle of their products and services—the symbiotic cycle. A multipetal flower best represents the symbiotic model of turning creativity into innovation in knowledge organizations, where each petal represents one person responsible for each function contributing to this cycle. The symbiotic model assumes that innovation in knowledge organizations, to some extent in all organizations, is not a product of the "professional thinkers" and researchers working in large universities or corporate laboratories and R&D departments. Instead, it is a synergistic outgrowth of the combined effort of all individuals connected in any way to the end product or service. It does not require any special training or education beyond what is needed to perform the knowledge job. All it needs is creativity. In fact, in many cases, those operating functions in knowledge organizations are more likely to bring about innovation than those responsible for supervising or supporting them.

To complete the organizational setup for innovation, the symbiotic model multipetal flower has to be full—consisting of all persons directly connected with it. Creativity is like a pool to which everyone should make a contribution, eventually causing innovation to buoy. A knowledge organization has to design work and develop an environment in which every employee is equipped to contribute to this pool. A knowledge organization manager can achieve this result by reversing the work segregation policies of operating or traditional organizations that typically have assigned operating responsibilities to one group of employees and creativity to the other. It can be accomplished through increased mingling of the functions across the transformation cycle. More managers, engineers, scientists, and even salespersons in knowledge organizations should be assigned responsibilities for regular line functions that in traditional organizations are set aside for supervisors and linemen. Similarly, knowledge organizations should engage in a reversal of jobs.

It is a common practice in a number of knowledge organizations to allow workers themselves to decide transformation methods, layout their space, schedule their operations, and even select the machinery and equipment needed for their processes. This policy is credited for higher motivation, quality, and productivity. While for other organizations this practice may be a luxury, for knowledge organizations it is a condition for survival.

The token initiatives to involve everyone—like employee suggestion systems or other similar feedback systems that many organizations have adopted, or the rather more organized techniques, like Japanese quality circles—cannot achieve the innovation that is essential for the success of knowledge organizations.

Creative Work Outcomes: Integration

Work has to be designed so that everyone in the product or service value-added cycle has the ability to ask questions beyond those that concern the routine of producing and selling "knowledge widgets"—a generic name connoting knowledge organizations' products or services. Employee involvement should seek answers to questions that help knowledge organizations provide outcomes in the form of solutions to the following:

1. How can we increase the inherent value of the knowledge widget?
2. How can we design a better knowledge widget to best perform in its various roles in the concept-to-market-to-crypt cycle—in particular for the function, conversion processes, service, or disposal?

3. How can we make a better knowledge widget; for example, through better quality of conformance?

4. How can we integrate technology and develop materials and processes to produce, market, service, and dispose of the knowledge widget more economically?

5. How can we bring new and efficient vendors, suppliers, and contractors into the knowledge widget processes?

6. How can we smartly market these knowledge widgets in the present and new markets highlighting their features as they connect to the market needs and perceptions?

7. How can we better attract investors to put their capital into the knowledge widget operations?

8. How can we replace the widget with other substitutes that render as well or better the function fulfilled by the knowledge widget?

9. How can we totally eliminate the function performed by the knowledge widget?

10. How can we attract the best available talent, internally or externally, to the organization's knowledge widget operations?

11. How can we stay ahead of the competition with respect to the knowledge widget?

12. How can we best reincarnate the knowledge widget after the fulfillment of its function or expiration of its useful life?

The above questions are samples of the creativity component of work. This list is, by no means, exhaustive.

KNOWLEDGE WORK DESIGN AND ASSIGNMENT MODELS

Work design and the resulting assignments evolve from a model defining the relationship between employer and employee in conformance with the culture of the organization. Since the employer-employee relationship has been around almost as long as human civilization, there have been many models describing this relationship. With the passage of time, some of these models have died, whereas others have emerged. Those that are conducive to knowledge work are usually symbiotic in nature and are presented in the following section. A manager needs to understand them in order to design and assign work in knowledge organizations.

Symbiotic Models for Knowledge Organizations

A number of sociological models describe how humans form groups; work for mutual benefit; share responsibility, authority, and reward; and survive together. In contrast to the twentieth-century hierarchical model of human relationships, symbiotic models are derived from the examples of successful human coexistence. They have withstood the test of time. Some of the most prevalent symbiotic models that can be applied in establishing relationships in knowledge organizations are described in this section. Once we understand them, we will be more able to determine the one that best suits the needs of any particular knowledge organization.

Family/Community Model. The family/community model of organizational design can work very well in knowledge organizations because of the lack of work structure and the limited ability of the manager to provide leadership to those with direct responsibility for task accomplishment, environmental uncertainties, and frequent customer and market shifts. It can maintain high levels of creativity and productivity, especially for knowledge organizations that are in the early stages of their lives or are of smaller sizes. In general, all knowledge organizations should explore the feasibility of the family/community model for all or part of their organizations.

To understand the applicability of the family/community model to knowledge organization design, we must gain an insight into the workings of the family and community with regard to transferring this system to organizations. The family is the oldest and closest model of human symbiosis and the first institution that established humans as gregarious social beings. This institution has somehow survived and has continued to evolve standing the test of time, while all of its other competitive models fell and vanished. This makes the family organization and working model the most durable of all of the models explaining human coexistence in social organizations. Originally, this was the only way known to humans to organize relationships among themselves in any situation, including working together. From there, the family system of organization and working became modeled and transplanted to many other settings of human interaction.

It was natural for organizations that were formed by members of the same family, such as hunting cooperatives and farms, to also follow the family model for their work organization. Business organizations that became extensions of the family, such as a family store or other business enterprises run by members of a family, mimicked the family model for their work design and assignment and for making decisions relating to work. As was normal in the family-community model, persons who were responsible for the execution of work were also responsible for making decisions and other intellectual functions related to that work.

As the size of these organizations expanded and required recruitment of outside help, such as in plantations or retail operations, managers continued to uphold the family model as the way to organize and manage ventures with outside members.

The common desire to achieve the collective interests of the "family, the family model, binds all the members of knowledge organizations" because that is how any individual member can ensure his or her own interests. Even though family model knowledge organizations have a hierarchy—more correctly, perforated hierarchy—no one formally assigns or designs work for members of the family working together. In these organizations, everyone does what one feels comfortable in doing, while others who pick their tasks may later decide to select something else, following the same logic. Everyone working in this type of organization finds a niche for oneself out of the various work assignments available and makes sure that no voids are left in the accomplishment of the whole task. No one tries to overlap their niches with other members of the organization. The work design and assignment are complementary. Even though it may sound like a chaotic way to organize work, the family model naturally finds homeostasis and works well in smaller up-and-coming knowledge organizations.

In such organizations, typically, work is designed so that almost everyone in the organization is able to perform, without any concern for efficiency, any and all types of work needed to run the organization. As the workforce changes and encompasses a wider variety of employee backgrounds, it is imperative that organizations entail more flexibility and labor interchangeability so that production may be maximized. Here, flexibility is used in the same sense as Steve McMahon, senior vice president of human resources at Auto-Desk, Inc., uses it. To him, flexibility means "not just flexible in time, but flexible in all policies you have" (Prince, 2000). The gains in productivity rise not because people switch jobs frequently but because of the satisfaction people feel in having selected a job they like and the power they have to pick another task if they do not like what they are doing. There is no segregation of work, strict watertight division of labor, one definite way to do a job, or any extraneously imposed, inflexible sequence in which work must be completed.

There are several non–family-owned organizations that still follow the family model of work design and assignment. Many of them use this as strength to recruit and retain good employees. Most small-scale organizations primarily follow the family model. All volunteer organizations and armed forces in real frontline combat also follow the family-community model of work design and assignment. A significant number of Japanese organizations, large and small, in some form and size still follow the family-community model for designing and assigning work and making work-related decisions.

In emergencies, all successful organizations, to some extent, turn to the family model for work design and assignment. However, they return to their old models once the emergency is over.

In spite of the new evolution through which the family institution is going, especially in the Western industrialized nations, the basic family model dictating work design and assignment in many organizations is here to stay. This will be especially true for knowledge organizations.

Master-Slave/Stewardship Model. Even though this model of organizational relationships is not widely applicable to knowledge organizations, it is important for managers to know it because, in the few instances where it is applicable, it has no substitute.

This is the oldest symbiotic model establishing the relationship between employer and employee that is still in practice. This model extends from the time when slavery was legal and many rich people owned slaves. The British transplanted the master-slave model to modern organizations. As industrialization expanded, Britain and many former colonies and dominions of the British Empire accepted "master-slave" as a valid model for employer-employee relationships. In present times, this model exists in organizational relationships more as a *stewardship* model, in which employees assume that they are stewards of the owners or stockholders of the organization and should do whatever is in their power to preserve and maximize their investment.

Traditionally, because the master-slave relationship was expected to last a lifetime, and the slave knew that he had no possibility of leaving his master, the relationship developed an understanding in the mind of the slave that the well-being of his master really would amount to his own well-being. The master-slave relationship is clearly defined and, generally, well understood by both of its constituents. In some form, such psychological commitments became part of all social relationships, such as that of employee-employer. As a consequence, many organizations became modeled after the master-slave relationship. In organizations where this model is practiced, the employee knows that he is going to work for the employer for his entire work life and, in return, the employer knows that he has to look after the well-being of his employee to continue to receive his loyalty and commitment. Collectively, their intertwined interests make this relationship symbiotic and strong. A worker achieves this commitment through his acts. In this regard, the particular work activity in which he engages is of a lesser consequence than the fact that he does whatever he can to enhance the interests of his employer. The employee accomplishes this through completing any work that is assigned to him and, if that is not enough to keep him busy, picking other work that in his understanding will help him achieve the interests of his employer. Moreover, during the time that he works on the assigned activity, if something more important comes up, he uses his discretion to switch his assignments himself. The methods, tools, techniques, machines, and materials to be utilized in accomplishing the tasks are left to the employee. As long as the work is finished within the assigned time, the employee is free to set his own priorities and schedules. There is no close supervision, and his performance evaluation is derived from work attributes, such as conformance with specifications and deadlines.

Even though it is the oldest prevalent model for the work relationship, the master-slave model is not the worst employer-employee relationship model. There are a number of characteristics that make this an efficient organizational model. According to this model, there is no one set or specific task that is to be done. There is no job description either. The emphasis is on being responsible for completing the task at the macro level correctly and within the assigned time. The employee engages in a variety of work activities himself or gets additional help at his discretion in fulfilling that responsibility. The relationship runs more on a good understanding of each other's needs than on anything else. There are not as many rewards or punishments as there are positive or negative incentives that are extrinsically administered under this model.

In some adapted form, the master-slave model is applicable in knowledge organizations because a number of organizations constantly recruit employees from overseas. These employees, mostly because of their cultural origin, expect employers to treat them according to the British master-slave model. One example illustrating the applicability of this model comes from Maria Tray, the owner of a small Ohio-based computer consulting firm. She, out of desperation to hire qualified knowledge workers, traveled to Chennai (formerly Madras), India, and writes that, in preparing for their arrival from India, she realized that she required preparations that were not needed when she recruited domestic knowledge employees. She persuaded the superintendent of a local apartment complex to allot a row of apartments for her incoming employees without the usual screening and assigned "cultural guides" to help them find Indian grocery and sari stores.

The master-slave model provides enough latitude for knowledge organizations to engage in limited innovation, while maintaining excellent task execution. Work assignment in this case provides enough opportunity to have a creative component added to every employee's job package (Aeppel, 1999).

If a knowledge organization seeks to establish its employee-employer relationships according to this model, it should be prepared, like the Ohio-based firm, to become involved in all matters that concern its employees. Managers and their families should socialize with employees' families and provide superior and innovative benefits for their well-being.

Ethical Team Model. The ethical team model is primarily employed to design and assign work in small and upcoming knowledge organizations. A large number of Internet companies during their formative years routinely employed this model. According to this model, the suitable recommended organization size is up to 20 employees. The ethical team model will also work well where task characteristics are such that they can be accomplished only through team effort—a common practice in knowledge organizations. This model best suits cohesive teams or where members have a good understanding of each other and long-term experience working together. The success of this model for the design and assignment of work will depend on the extent to which a team is collectively an *ethical team.*

A knowledge organization can design an ethical work team by ensuring that it fulfills all or most of the following seven characteristics:

C1   All members have previously worked together or in *Ethical Team Model* environment for a long time, developed a sense of commitment for the collective interests of the team, and have given up any feelings of selfishness. In the past, members have had, and also have given to their teammates, a positive experience of working together on a team.

C2   The team is made up of members of equal or approximately equal authority without any clear domination of one member over another. This ensures that team leadership is frequently, naturally, and equally shifted.

C3   All members of the team are clearly aware of what is essential to accomplish the work assigned to the team.

C4   Almost all members of the team possess requisite skills to perform any and all functions essential to complete the work.

C5   No one person on the team, or off the team, has a greater impact on setting short-term rewards or inflicting punishment on any team member than the member does himself. Each member controls his own rewards and punishments.

C6   Division of labor is not imposed, either internally or externally. However, members have evolved and understand the division of labor process.

C7   Assignment for an ethical team must come with a clear collective charge to the whole team. It may be well-specified whole end product or service with a deadline for its general completion. The type of work given to an ethical team should not be limited by this requirement.

Because of these qualifying characteristics of ethical teams, they can achieve high productivity and innovation without engaging in any formal division of labor and assignment or loading and scheduling of work. The ethical team model develops a good understanding of division of labor and task scheduling so that work assignments and schedules turn out better than they would have coming from industrial engineering or a planning office. Each ethical team member selects a task based on his and other team members' skills and the variety and size of available tasks.

In addition to knowledge organizations, the ethical team model can be successfully applied to other organizations or to all organizations under special circumstances. Examples of these include sports teams during games, troops in action (army, police, and fire), military tactical units, professors in a university system, research and investigative teams, and advertising and promotion groups. Any organization can create ethical teams to achieve higher productivity through innovation and can successfully avoid dealing with centralized work organization and design.

Independent Contractor Model: Work Sectorization. The independent contractor model for work design and assignment is another powerful way to have employees work to their fullest potential and to help knowledge organizations achieve high productivity and innovation through the proper management of work. Any organization that can divide its total work into interconnected macro segments—sectors—should be able to adopt the independent contractor model. Strict sectorization of work is the only requirement for the implementation of this model. Organizations should break their aggregate work into smaller, identifiable sectors. We will discuss the ways to achieve this in more detail later in this chapter. Some possible work sectors may be a segment of the product or service conversion process, a program or module, a Web site, a low volume subassembly, one operation or one group of operations, or anything else an organization does that can be separated from the rest.

The term "independent contractor" is employed in a generic sense. Any individual, group of individuals, or organization can be an independent contractor. In essence, any entity accorded the responsibility for the accomplishment of a work sector is an independent contractor.

Since the primary purpose of sectorization is to divide work into smaller segments, there is always a concern that so much separation might cause sector alienation. To avoid this, sectorization is achieved through recognizing natural points in the work process, where separating the work will not be detrimental. Bounds, or defining lines of boundaries, separate as well as bring together work sectors, which are defined by the bounds. All tasks lying within certain defined bounds make one sector. All work sectors within an organization are connected through bounds but are independent for all practical purposes. These bounds facilitate integration of work sectors among themselves and connection with the rest of the work in the organization.

There are a few strings that link a work sector with the rest of the knowledge organization. These links constitute three primary bounds:

1. *Integration Bounds.* Integration bounds establish a link between the function and objectives of one work sector with the remaining work sectors in knowledge organizations. These bounds require that the work sectorization be defined by general design and specifications of the product or service, which are barely essential for the sector's integration with the rest of the work that the knowledge organization does. An example of this work sector is "0.1 hp 120 v 60 Hz Electric motor." This establishes bounds between this motor and the rest of the work performed by this organization, including other electric motors. This work sector has been defined in as broad a sense as feasible.

    Integration bounds have a tendency to create large work sectors through the lumping of as much work as possible in any one sector. Such a large sector may be further divided while planning work in it.

2. *Coordination Bounds.* These bounds are imposed by the timetable for all the work and establish time frames for splitting one sector from the whole and integrating/reintegrating it with other work sectors in its group or in the organization. Works that should be completed within one time frame will need to be put together and bounded from the rest.

    The purpose of establishing these bounds is to ensure on-time completion of the knowledge work. It should be used in preparing work schedules. An example of work grouping using these bounds is: "February 19, 2001, launch of *Enterprise* space shuttle."

3. *Outcomes Bounds.* These bounds define the outcomes for the independent contractor who assumes responsibility of accomplishing the work in a particular sector. They spell out both the positive and the negative outcomes. According to these bounds, the work is sectored according to expected outcomes from the sector. An example of these bounds is: "Five-star hotel work."

Outside of these three bounds, the independent contractor model levies nothing on the entity responsible for the accomplishments of the sector. The model permits the contractor full liberty to design his or her environment, select materials, select methods and processes, assign work, and distribute positive and negative outcomes from the accomplishments of the sector. An independent contractor enjoys full control of his or her work sector.

POSITIVE KNOWLEDGE WORK SCHEDULING

With the implementation of new concepts for work design and organization to enhance productivity and innovation in knowledge organizations, the need for organizations to engage in scheduling work, as we have known it, is going to be substantially reduced. Scheduling—setting times when employees start and complete work and take breaks, vacations, and casual time off—will become almost unnecessary if we follow the knowledge organization design presented here. Schedules will be essential only to provide links among works, individuals, and technologies.

Principles of Knowledge Work Scheduling

A clearer understanding of the reasons dictating the need for organizations to engage in scheduling can help management turn scheduling into a means of contributing to its productivity and innovation, rather than becoming an action that impedes creativity and growth. There are three principles that knowledge organizations should utilize to establish their scheduling policy.

(1) Principle of Schedule Sovereignty. The first principle guiding scheduling for innovation and productivity in knowledge organizations is very straightforward and simple. It states that each individual responsible for knowledge work should have sovereignty over his or her schedule. The principle implies that scheduling should not be done by anyone other than the person whose schedule it is. It should not be interpreted to mean that the employee who is being scheduled should be consulted or given an opportunity to offer input to schedule. It simply means that every knowledge employee should set his or her work schedule.

To implement this scheduling principle, a knowledge organization broadly identifies its needs for various skills for various time frames and, within these guidelines, employees with previously recognized skills schedule themselves to meet these needs. Positive scheduling can make this possible. Details on this scheduling technique are given later.

(2) Principle of Need Succession. The second principle guiding knowledge work scheduling requires the organizations to realize that when it comes to scheduling to enhance innovation and productivity, the employees' needs must be allowed to supersede those of the organization. The lower the placement of an employee in the hierarchical order of the knowledge organization, the more the organization has to gain by placing the needs of the employee

over those of the organization. This principle may be violated, however only with the understanding that the organization, in most likelihood, could have a losing trade-off in the net. Putting needs of the organization ahead of the employees' will not pay off in the long run.

Depending upon the hierarchical level of an employee, knowledge work or a knowledge job at that level may be somewhat standard and routine and can be accomplished by one or a few individuals in the knowledge organization. On the other hand, the employee's needs are unique and can be fulfilled only by the employee himself.

By giving knowledge employees the power to schedule their work, they can accommodate most of their needs and avoid any performance setbacks by preparing a schedule that will put them at the peak of their performance and creativity.

Almost all organizations allow their top officers flexibility in the scheduling of their activities. Moreover, owners always schedule their officers' activities to suit their ability to perform at the best level. It would be beneficial for organizational productivity and innovation if knowledge organizations allow all employees some control over their schedule and all knowledge employees total control over their schedule through positive scheduling, discussed later in the chapter.

(3) Principle of Transience. The third principle to enhance creativity and productivity in knowledge organizations comes from having transient schedules. This principle states that knowledge organizations should treat each schedule as a fully new work organization—a temporary organization that lasts the length of the schedule or the duration of the task. If the task being scheduled is temporary, the schedule will inherently be temporary, but if the task is a regular, routine task, it should be scheduled so that it gives the effect of transience. *De facto*, this principle states that knowledge organizations should treat the end of a schedule as the end of that transient organization—opening all positions. Every new schedule fills all positions anew with the only difference being a newly updated list of qualified people. This list is made up of those who have successfully completed the same or similar tasks in the past and/or are employed with the knowledge organization.

Scheduling Techniques for Knowledge Work

In application of these principles, the following are two scheduling techniques that are recommended for knowledge organizations.

Time Scheduling: Schedule Time, Not Workers. Time scheduling is recommended for routine, ongoing knowledge work and all other nontechnical work carried out in knowledge organizations. Some departments in knowledge organizations that can make most use of this technique include administrative offices, support services, customer sales and support, warehouse operations, distribution and trucking, accounting, maintenance, security, and all other services where the skills needed to perform the work are mostly standard. The scheduling objective of these operations is to have someone perform their regular routines or be present at a particular work center just in case work comes up or a customer shows up. Throughout the job era of the twentieth century, this type of scheduling was used by employers under the pretext of "needs of the organization." Of course, their definition of the organization in this understanding of "needs" did not routinely expand to include their employees' needs. Scheduling was one of the items within the responsibility basket of supervisors. It was a management prerogative that took up a good part of their time, and they executed it based on their "perception" of these needs or, many times, based on their whims.

To have every knowledge employee perform at his best ability from 9 to 5 is too much of an expectation. To make employees more creative and efficient, managers should accept their preferences for scheduling. There are certain times of the day when employees are more productive or alert. These times vary from person to person and even from day to day for the same person. This is especially true with knowledge work, since it requires more intellectual input than physical presence or manual operation. It is not possible for managers to know the specific times and days that employees will perform efficiently.

Knowledge work scheduling needs more than "flextime," a scheduling technique initiated in the late 1970s and 1980s, that gives some consideration to employees' needs in preparation of their work schedules. This technique permits organizations to have a "core" period during which all employees are present, but all times outside this core are considered flexible. Flextime achieved some success in retaining and gaining higher efficiency from certain employee categories, like homemakers, students, and young mothers. The technique was devised to accommodate the needs of these groups in the first place. Flextime is not powerful enough to address the needs of human creativity in knowledge organizations.

The time scheduling technique goes beyond flextime. It treats employees as contractors, with the only restriction being that they put in a certain number of predetermined hours per day, week, or month. "It's really moving from a focus on what schedule works for the organization to what works both for the organization and the employee, which is a significant shift," says Karol Rose, managing director of LifeCare Consulting at DCC, Inc. (Scott, 1999). The time scheduling technique creates an efficient vehicle to get optimum performance and innovation from knowledge employees through conformance with their personalities and environment, through a milieu conducive to creativity and efficiency.

Time scheduling is for regular work that is standard, or can be standardized and for every employee in a department or section who has the skills to do it. If this is not the case, employees must be put into skill groups, and time scheduling should be done within each group.

Time scheduling is performed in the following three steps.

Step 1: Reduce schedule span. First, a manager divides the total time span for each work area to be covered by this schedule—*schedule span*—into smaller time slots—*periods*, such as a monthly schedule into weeks, a weekly schedule into days, and a daily schedule into hours and maybe hours into minutes. This division is done keeping the area's workforce needs in mind. For example, Customer Support needs three Windows technicians from 7 A.M. to 3 P.M. from May 5 to May 10. The result will consist of several slots, one slot per period per worker. A period can extend over a couple of hours, a half-day, a full day, or a week, depending on the nature of the operations. It should be the smallest workable time unit.

Step 2: Workers assume slots. Once these time slots are created as per Step 1, they should be made available to the knowledge workers who are eligible to select Windows Support so that they can assign themselves to these slots, strictly on a first-come first-served basis. Since they are all qualified as "equal" and eligible for such jobs, any one of them should be able to do as good a job as anyone else, and they may pick any slot.

Step 3: Manager publishes schedules. In the third step, the manager formalizes the schedules based on the completed slots in Step 2. Except in the case of a knowledge worker who has a history of repeatedly failing at satisfactorily accomplishing an assignment, the manager should not intervene in any schedule undertaken by any worker. A worker who fails an assignment must be provided counseling on how to succeed on selected schedules and how to select schedules in which he may succeed.

This technique has worked quite successfully for scheduling volunteer work and is generally granted as a gesture of goodwill because of the voluntary nature of the workers' contribution. All types of organizations can make use of this technique without much effort and can reap rewards in the form of higher productivity and innovation.

Work Scheduling: Schedule Work, Not Workers. *Work scheduling* is devised for nonregular, nonstandard work—for example, designing and developing a Web site for XYZ Apparel retailer. The mechanics of this positive scheduling technique will require some planning. The manager should commence this process about a week or more in advance. Work scheduling is performed in the following six steps.

Step 1: Divide work into projects. The manager should convert virtually all nonroutine work into projects. For example, he can take the Web site development assignment and divide it into smaller parts, or projects. A project is any activity or group of activities that is not performed in knowledge organizations on a regular basis, or it is work or a segment of work that is organized as the manager deems fit. The term "project" may or may not be used in the same sense as it is used in project management.

Step 2: Schedule projects. Schedule the work or its parts created as projects under Step 1. This schedule should consist of the dates and times when each of the projects has to start and the duration that is allotted for its execution.

Step 3: Set qualifications. Decide qualifications essential for anyone who may satisfactorily complete this project. Include these qualifications on the schedule and any terms, including rewards, penalties, bonuses, and so forth, associated with completion of the project. Create blank slots for filling in names of those who will be willing to do this work.

Step 4: Allow a one-person project option. Next, open the projects for employee selection. The limitation at this step is that any employee who believes he is qualified can pick any project as long as he commits to complete it by himself in the time allowed by the schedule. He may simply schedule himself by filling in his name in the blank slots created in Step 3.

Step 5: Allow a team project option. By exclusion, the remaining work cannot be done by any one individual, since no one individual took it upon himself or herself to do it. It needs groups of two or more people to accomplish this work. For each of these projects, any one employee or group of employees may initiate the formation of a team to undertake its completion. These teams may then opt for the project by filling their names in the blank slots created in Step 3.

Step 6: Assign projects. Managers should finalize the assignments by selecting one employee or group who has opted to undertake each project. If there is only one person opting, he or she should be assigned to the project, unless there are severe reservations about his or her abilities to complete it. In cases where there are several employees selecting a particular project, the manager may use his own discretion. As a general rule, the manager should use a first-come first-served basis for assignment of projects. A deviation from this rule must have a good justification.

WORK DESIGN AND LOADING

For a knowledge organization to be successful, it is essential that all employees give their full commitment to the goals of the organization. That is how the organization can draw innovation and productivity. The principles of work design and loading presented here are aimed at increasing the involvement of all people directly or indirectly associated with the transformation of organizational goals. To realize this involvement, it is essential that knowledge employees are equipped with the following:

1. Specific, detailed knowledge of their own area and other areas in their vertical value chain, with greater emphasis on those that are a couple of steps away on either side of their work location in the process;
2. Broad working understanding of all areas in their horizontal chain, with greater emphasis on those closer to their work location in the process; and
3. A broad comprehension of the working of their organization in its economic and other environments in their entirety.

To make sure that all employees at all levels gain essential knowledge and understanding, it is necessary that this knowledge be created and communi-

cated at a comprehensible level. That is the only way that employees can contribute toward the achievement of organizational objectives.

Although we are recommending this procedure in the context of managing
people in knowledge organizations, it is, to some extent, a return to what
were acceptable practices before the advent of the job era. The availability of
technology in the twenty-first century has made it possible to return to the
way humans engaged in productive activity before the advent of large, complex organizations while at the same time eliminating the necessity to realize
efficiency due to the economy of scale. The complexity in these organizations
is so large that even the individual whose only job is to understand this complexity fails to make a meaningful contribution because he fails to gain a thorough understanding of all organizational processes.

The challenge of knowledge organizations is to find ways to reduce complexity throughout the organization to a point where every employee can understand all aspects of its business. Successful technologies of the future will
not be the ones that solve complex problems but those that make them simple and maybe even eliminate them. The purpose is to undo complexity,
reduce size, and eliminate obscurity in the processes of knowledge organizations. Equipping employees with this type of knowledge and understanding
will require time and effort on the part of the employees and a serious program on the part of the organization. A survey of 250 IT (Information Technology) executives, performed by InformationWeek Research, provides
support that managers are aware of the changes that must be made. Fifty-nine
percent of the executives surveyed said that business processes and functions
had to be reengineered, most notably technological skill requirements and
training (Robinson, 1999). The best way to increase employees' understanding is through training, which may begin as regular workshops for current
employees and comprehensive orientation sessions for new employees. This
orientation may last several weeks and require substantial organization resources but will probably be the best investment a knowledge organization
can make. It will convey the right tone about the role that incoming employees are expected to play and will set the stage for the continuance of such information sessions in the future. This effort will turn them into important
contributors to the organization's innovation and productivity. Extensive orientation will convey the seriousness of the new relationship and will build the
commitment essential for positive outcomes. Colgate-Palmolive followed a
similar program for its new laundry detergent manufacturing operations in
Massachusetts with great success.

To keep employees abreast of changes in an organization's work and
environment, compulsory refresher sessions should be conducted on a regular basis. Some organizations have successfully planned such sessions for
evenings and weekends to avoid taking time away from their day-to-day
operations.

Reducing Knowledge Work Complexity

Large traditional organizations have changed short transformation processes that were well understood by operators into long, complicated assembly and fabrication lines that, to many involved in the process, caused a state of confusion and helplessness. It was as if a small open bore turned into a seemingly unending, dark tunnel. That change took away the operators' vision and ability to conceive and make a meaningful contribution to improve the processes on which they were working. The complexities of the new products and services resulted in an even greater powerlessness among those engaged in the transformation process.

Even though we know that knowledge employees are intelligent and capable of handling intricate subjects, it is still important to make things less complicated to achieve greater efficiency in communication and dissemination. Without complexity reduction, it is hard to involve everyone and make him or her an important contributing member of the organization.

The goal should be to make things so simple, straightforward, and free of technical jargon that any knowledge employee with basic knowledge of the field will be able to understand and describe it to an outsider in one sentence.

That is the approach Louis V. Gerstner took in understanding operations at International Business Machines (IBM) when he became its chief executive officer. Because of his background in the consumer goods industry (not in computers or even in the knowledge field), he needed to quickly understand the complex, technical workings of IBM. It was this initiative on his part that redirected IBM culture and brought corporate communication from highly charged technical sophistication to the level of the layman.

Gerstner realized that until he and all the other individuals connected with IBM knew what was happening there, they could not solve IBM's problems. He was right. Large organizations do not fail because they are too large; they fail because managers responsible for making decisions cannot understand the problems enough to know the impact their decisions will have on them. It is simply a matter of understanding, nothing else.

Modularizing Knowledge Work

In general, a knowledge work module is a connected, live piece of the whole complex such that it is complete, independent, and simple but embodies all of the requisite details for its own completeness. Modularization is a decoupling process. It separates parts from the whole while still maintaining the context in such a way that the complexity is localized and yet the connectivity is globalized over the whole. Almost anything can be modularized keeping in view the objectives to be realized through such modularization.

Modularization of products and services is one way to cut complexity to a size that is easily comprehensible to the people responsible for their transformation. The purpose of work modularization is to restore the knowledge worker's vision of the processes and products of knowledge organizations that is lost in complex, traditional organizations. Every knowledge employee must be able to relate what he or she is doing in terms of the beginning and end of product transformation. Modularization results in the diminution of the complexity of products and services to a size that enables an operator to comprehend it. As a consequence of this diminution, transformation processes are simplified to an understandable size—cutting long, dark tunnels into small well-illuminated halls—empowering workers to be creative and efficient and making more brains work together to solve problems.

Work should be modularized into small, humanly conceivable pieces of an organization's products and services. It is important that knowledge work modules are created out of a knowledge organization's products and services and not in terms of the transformation processes or machine centers utilized in producing or distributing them. Emphasis is placed on products and services or the functions performed by them because it is through these products and services that a knowledge organization links itself with its markets and other factors in its environment. In addition, products and services are relatively more permanent in nature than their transformation processes. The latter could be a target of immediate attacks from technological innovation of which the knowledge organization is a part, which definitely would occur less frequently than drastic changes in products and services.

This diminution of products and services should continue until the module so created attains a size that restores clear understanding among all those who are connected with the transformation. This may be an optimal size for a knowledge product or service module—*work module*. Each work module should have its own well-understood function—a beginning and an ending. It should convey its place in the whole to everyone associated with the work module.

Work can follow the model of modularization of the world into continents, nations, states, counties, cities, streets, and even houses. The principle driving the modularization of work is the same.

Work modules may constitute products, subproducts, assemblies, subassemblies, and fully functional components. Some good examples of modules from day-to-day life are doors and windows of a house, automobile transmissions, and main belts, since they all meet the qualifications of a module. An operation, like making a 3-inch deep cut, is not a module.

Modularization can be done by any criteria, such as processes, geography, complexity of work, skills, revenue, and cost.

Optimizing Work Size

We learned previously that, in order to gain cost efficiency through an economy of scale, mass-producing organizations must handle large work sizes—technically known as a lot size or order size. In knowledge organizations, a large work size contributes to confusion, promotes worker apathy, and adds to the complex intricate processes for transforming integrated products and services—complexity on complexity.

As a rule, within a certain range, worker productivity is likely to linearly increase as work size decreases. This result cannot be applied universally due to the confounding between work size and human motivation to work. Work size can operate as both a motivator and a demotivator. With that qualification, there is an optimal work size that should be assigned to each worker to improve productivity and to influence innovation. In most cases, this optimal size may be what is *doable* in a manageable time slot, which would rarely be more than a day.

A large-sized job that seems to be unending does not motivate employees to push themselves harder to finish it. It adds to monotony and negative predictability, which collectively go against creativity due to the lack of fomentation. Generally, predictability dulls wits essential for knowledge work. Monotony works against productivity, thus defeating the originally intended purpose of achieving cost economy through large work size. In the short run, cost efficiency is attained, if at all, through worker intimidation, expensive, and close supervision, which are unworkable in a knowledge organization environment and go against the long-term good that comes through worker involvement. A small job size will give workers time to think of new and unique ways to do what needs to be done.

On the negative side, small size could imply a lack of work. During periods of economic slowdown, small size may convey a sense of uncertainty to workers unaware of the organization's small-size policy. Clear communication of the small work size policy by the organization to its workers, combined with a message emphasizing innovative ways to approach the work, will bring out creativity and efficiency.

WORK ASSIGNMENT FOR CREATIVITY

A knowledge organization should constantly engage in removing all impediments to the intellectual development of its employees. The occurrence of such impediments is natural as the pressures to meet deadlines and fulfill routines keep workers away from creative pursuits. It should never be forgotten that an intellectual activity that enhances productivity and culminates in innovation essential for knowledge work is caused by an assertive, concerted effort involving everyone and is facilitated by the organization. If left alone, the intellectual activity will fall by the wayside. The main purpose of every organization should be to facilitate the existence of conditions that will let workers engage their creative intellects. An organization should know specific ways to bring the whole organization to a state of intellectual alertness. In addition, there are generic job-enrichment techniques that all knowledge organizations can employ to keep workers out of monotony and predictability—the two

nemeses of creativity. Some of the many new ways that a manager can ingeniously devise to reduce monotony and predictability that dull the human
mind are described in the section below.

Work Approach

Haphazard mass production in traditional organizations brought about
widespread work predictability and monotony, causing visible effects on the
worker—notably mental and physical fatigue. The resultant battery of symptoms of the traditional organizations' malady included an increased rate of industrial accidents, a high level of worker apathy, and an erosion of
productivity gains. There was sufficient reason for alarm and for management
to begin redesigning industrial work to alleviate these symptoms. Job range
strategies aimed at reducing job monotony encompass the works of Charles
R. Walker and Robert H. Guest (1952). As a result of their efforts, the concepts of *job range* and *job depth* were introduced. *Job enlargement* is one way
that job range strategies achieve alleviation of work monotony. This concept
increases task variety by adding more tasks that add new skills to what the
worker is already doing. For example, allowing a data clerk to check errors on
his data entries, which someone else would ordinarily do, may enlarge his job.
Job rotation is a second way that work monotony is broken. In job rotation,
workers are moved from job to job to increase their perception of variety. For
example, a secretary may be moved to work as a receptionist.

Given some early decline in productivity due to unlearning and relearning,
these strategies *may* work, to some extent, for a traditional organization.
Nevertheless, they do not work for knowledge organizations. Managers
know that job range strategies do not help in the end because they simply
move the worker from one monotonous job to another or from one monotonous task to many monotonous tasks. Moreover, a knowledge organization
manager cannot afford to allow productivity declines that are associated with
these strategies.

A knowledge organization manager can employ the following strategies for
enhancing creativity through work design and assignment.

Knowledge Work Rotation. Work rotation will help knowledge workers
enjoy their jobs and rejuvenate their thought process by enhancing productivity through innovation. Work rotation reincarnates the old concept of
establishing the worker as a fully independent skilled specialist and the master of his own environment. This symbiotic functioning takes away monotony and predictability and turns employees into productive, innovative
workers. Here, a worker operates from an assigned workplace—symbiotic
system center—but the difference is that this center consists of machines,
equipment, materials, and tools selected by the worker; a layout designed
by the worker; and previously selected bounds, operating rules, and reward
system are also designed by the worker. The center is designed to allow

quick setups, loading, and unloading. The system should purposely dispatch to the worker different end-jobs requiring skills within the limits of his mastery and the establishment of the work center. The work should permit the worker to plan, quote, and accept full responsibility for execution, progress reporting, client contact, and delivery.

The manager should load the center in such a way that there is never more than one day's load on the center, even when a large number of similar jobs are to be done. The manager should create buffers of other work in between the batches of similar jobs through switching—such as the first 50 pieces of A, the next 10 pieces of B, and then 40 pieces of A, and so on. If that is not workable, the work should be assigned so that a number of work orders are released one by one—one for each day's work. The purpose is to let each day be a new day—psychologically, if not actually.

Convert the Work Center to a Work Junction. This concept can be extended to work performed along a line, like an assembly line, or a fabricating line, by converting a workstation into a pseudo–work center, merging several stations that perform a large number of small tasks previously done by all of those stations. Several workers from the workstations that comprise it should staff this new work center. This center will require a number of skills due to the expansion of work assigned to it. A manager can even add more skills to this center, turning it from a *work center* to a *work junction* by feeding several lines into it.

Location Approach

Managers know that of all work classifications, traveling salespersons, as a group, are among the most motivated. They are hyped up, feel bubbly, cut jokes, and are most optimistic. Their actions fill everyone around them with energy and life. This is because people whose jobs involve change of location, such as traveling, feel less work monotony. Many managers, as a way to allow workers to get rid of work monotony, permit them to attend workshops, information and training sessions, and off-campus activities. For the most part, it works. Monotony may not only be a function of the job that a worker is doing, it is also attributable to the location and surroundings of one's job.

Switching locations or surroundings may eliminate or reduce monotony. Take, again, the job of a traveling salesperson. Even though he or she performs the same job over and over, selling the same products or services and doing the same presentation, that person still does not get the feeling of monotony that other workers have. A good part of the traveling salesman's monotony is redressed because the audiences, the surroundings, and the settings are different.

This fact can be applied in designing and assigning routine work in knowledge organizations. Managers must shrewdly organize work with set plans, allowing for the change of location and surroundings. This can be done in conjunction with the concept of creating a *symbiotic work center*, explained above, especially when repetitive work seems to be unavoidable. Moving a worker from one work center, identified as *this worker's center*, to another symbiotic work center can reduce monotony and predictability. The idea of this technique is to allow the manager the flexibility to load the worker with the same job, or job requiring the same skill, over and over, by changing the location where the work is performed. For example, if the job requires working on the same item for a number of days, the manager should load the worker at one center for half the time and at another center for the remaining half. The worker, however, should not have prior knowledge of this scheme.

In some cases, this may require creating a few additional work centers to avoid moving two workers together at the same time. In the end, it will result in a paying trade-off for the organization.

Outcomes Approach

The manager can also reduce worker monotony and predictability by rotating his job outcomes in the form of salary, incentives, bonus, and other rewards, if any, that he draws from the successful completion of the job. In the process, this act conveys to the worker a sense of empowerment—the worker is in control of the outcomes from his job.

While discussing the symbiotic work center, we asked the manager to allow a worker, within given bounds, to play a role in setting his job outcomes. This can be achieved through the manager asking an individual worker, or a group of workers if they are working in a team, for a quotation to complete a job as if he were an independent labor contractor. The manager may then attempt outcome rotation by sometimes accepting the quotation while at other times letting the worker continue to function as an employee.

Outcome rotation can also be effected by an organization randomly attaching a bonus to some jobs and informing the worker up front of that fact. When not all jobs have a bonus attached, this random attachment will reduce monotony and predictability.

Outcome rotation may cause some problems relating to logistics and accounting, and there are questions about equity and whether an organization is getting its dollar's worth. These issues can pose some problems for the organization in the short run. If practiced often and widely, outcome rotation will work out to be extremely effective in achieving reduced monotony and predictability. It will make big strides in discovering innovative ways of approaching work and new productive ways to accomplish it.

LOOKING BACK

Even though we know that knowledge work is not as monotonous and repelling as is operational work, from our experience, we have learned that a manager can smartly organize knowledge work for higher productivity and important innovations. Work organization, as we have learned in this chapter, can help turn disliked work that is seen as a burden by employees into work that is a pleasure. This can be achieved only through eliminating the causes that take the pleasure out of work, such as a sense of helplessness, monotony, and predictability.

We have also seen that work can become exciting and fun, like playing. This can be achieved by redesigning it so that monotony, predictability, and complexity are eliminated. The redesign should enable all employees to thoroughly understand not only the work they do but also how it relates to the work others do so that they can see what they do in the larger picture, and in this way, they may help improve other jobs or make their organization more effective. We also believe that all employees like to participate in solving the organization's problems and like to share in the resulting rewards. This chapter has shown how a knowledge organization can achieve these goals.

Once the structure of knowledge organization has been put in place, the manager's next task is to see that the authority is so assigned that, instead of creating a state of helplessness and frustration, it contributes to innovation and higher productivity. All employees should have the authority and the training to make their own decisions. The following chapter will consider how can we do this in a knowledge environment.

REFERENCES

Aeppel, T. (1999, October 5). A passage to India eases a worker scarcity in Ohio: Owner of computer consultancy failed to find local talent but hit jackpot in Chennai. *Wall Street Journal*, p. B1.

Bertalanffy. L.V. (1950). The theory of open systems in physics and biology. *Science 111*, 23–29.

Boulding, K.E. (1956, April). General Systems Theory—the skeleton of science. *Management Science*, pp. 197–208.

Emerson, H. (1913). *The twelve principles of efficiency*. New York: The Engineering Magazine.

Fayol, H. (1949). *General and industrial management* (translation). London, UK: Pitman Press.

Gantt, H.L. (1916). *Industrial leadership*. New Haven, CT: Yale University Press.

Gilbreth, F.B. (1911). *Motion study*. New York: D. Van Nostrand.

Gilbreth, L.M. (1914). *The psychology of management*. New York: Sturgis & Walton.

Mandel, M.J., Carney, D., & Reinhardt, R. (2000, May 15). Antitrust for the digital age. *Business Week*, pp. 48–49.

Prince, M. (2000, April 17). Respect for employees seen as key to retention. *Business Insurance, 34*(16), 16.

Robinson, T. (1999, June 21). Reinventing the business wheel. *Information Week, 739*, 6ss–10ss.

Scott, M.B. (1999, December). Strategy is key to successful work/life initiatives. *Employee Benefit Plan Review, 54*(6), 24.

Taylor, F.W. (1911). *Principles of scientific management.* New York: Harper & Row.
Walker, C.R., & Guest, R.H. (1952). *The man on the assembly line.* Cambridge, MA: Harvard University Press.
Weber, M. (1947). *The theory of social and economic organization* (translation). Glencoe, NY: Free Press.

Section IV _____

MANAGEMENT FUNCTIONS IN KNOWLEDGE ORGANIZATIONS

Chapter 7 _____

Make Sure No One
Decides for Them

In previous chapters, we learned that managers cannot achieve maximum innovation and productivity from people responsible for knowledge assignments if they continue to apply traditional management theory and principles. The same is also true for making organizational decisions. They cannot use, in a knowledge environment, those decision-making techniques that were developed for traditional or operating companies. Such techniques will miserably fail to obtain the requisite degree of involvement from employees who matter in achieving results in a knowledge environment. While knowledge organizations are making drastic changes in their management styles, such as where to best deploy technical people in technology assignments, they are also adopting new decision-making processes and methodologies to win over their employees' commitment. Our experience suggests that managers of knowledge organizations toss out twentieth-century organizational decision-making techniques in favor of new and unique ones, in some cases very specific to their organizations.

Unlike in traditional organizations, managers operating in a knowledge environment cannot make decisions and expect others to follow, implement, and produce the results that they desire. The decisions that bring about results are the ones that are accepted by those who have to carry them out. The decisions should excite them. If managers force decisions, they will not be followed and internalized (Whetton & Delbecq, 2000).

DECISION MAKING IN ORGANIZATIONS

There are a number of important differences between decisions made in traditional organizations and those made in knowledge organizations. Decisions in traditional organizations are formulated within a well-defined, usually narrow, focus, with their scope confined to a frozen time frame. The quality of these decisions, typically, relies on the optimization of a system of models emulating well-defined, quantifiable variables into functions abstracting decision objectives and constraints that impose boundaries within which the optimization can take place. For this decision making to be effected, humans or computer software must be able to manipulate this system of models within the limitations imposed by the capabilities of available optimization techniques. Operationalization in traditional organizations of these highly abstract techniques is based on formalized processes and rule-based methodologies whose comprehension and manipulation require knowledge and skills that are not possessed by everyone in the organization connected with the decisions. Decision making in these organizations is turned into a specialized function that lies in the responsibility basket of people specifically *trained* for making decisions. Those who carry out these decisions, and those whom they affect, are typically excluded from the process. Indeed, to these people, the decisions are simply announced with instructions on how to carry them out. This type of decision-making practice has been successful in most organizations because:

1. Decisions in these organizations are straightforward,
2. Those responsible to carry them out are obedient,
3. The ones whom they concern are understanding and tolerant, and
4. Those responsible for making these decisions do not feel pressured to arrive at the best quality decisions possible.

This decision-making process suits large, traditional bureaucratic organizations and has worked successfully for them.

Survival of knowledge organizations depends on innovation—an outcome of buoyancy in human spirit—and productivity gains due to creativity, and not by the streamlining of operations or the scale of economy. Decisions, and conditions under which decisions are made, are quite different in these organizations as compared with traditional organizations. The knowledge environment is too uncertain and dynamic for professional decision makers of the type employed in traditional organizations to accurately comprehend, abstract, and model into a system of quantifiable objective functions and constraints. Because there is a lack of repetition of the same decisions, and thus a lack of a problem-solution history, objectives in knowledge organizations are not well defined. They are confounded because managers may not clearly know what exactly they are seeking to attain for the long-term good of their organizations. It is for this same reason that the scope of decisions is unrestricted. Additionally, the lack of meaningful experiences in working with the same problems over and over does not allow for the development of reliable rules and methodologies to solve them. The quality of decisions made in a traditional organization draws from—and can be proved based on—the organization of a system of models of quantifiable objective functions and a set of constraints. In contrast, the quality of decisions made for knowledge organizations depends on, first, how well the decisions will be received by those whom they impact, because without their acceptance, the whole effort would be in vain and, second, how well they will help to improve productivity and innovation from those whom they affect. Typical traditional decision-making techniques are not able to factor in the uncertainty faced by knowledge organizations and, hence, become useless for them.

The environment in which knowledge organizations operate, and the complexity of the decisions that they make, require the participation and involvement of every member directly or indirectly connected with that decision. This is the only sure way to achieve a quality decision. The use of traditional methods of decision making in these organizations results in decisions that breed a sense of helplessness among people with knowledge assignments, rather than a sense of efficacy to take initiative and work to succeed at them.

TRADITIONAL DECISION-MAKING PROCESS

In the twentieth century, the three most commonly practiced approaches to arriving at decisions were solitary, majority, or consensus. These approaches, alone or in some combination, have been used over and over in all kinds of social and economic decision-making settings. In Western-style organizations, the most common decision-making technique has been the solitary approach. Under this approach, one person, with or without any input from others whom the decision could affect, makes the decision and announces it. Through solitary decision making, a manager not only engages in but also conveys to his subordinates his acceptance of their use of this approach in making decisions. A very good example of this style of decision making is what has been practiced by Tom Siebel, CEO and cofounder of Silicon Valley sales and customer service software developer Siebel Systems. By excluding concerned employees from making decisions, Tom Siebel practiced and preached isolationism in all aspects of the management of Siebel Systems. This is how a particular, repeated behavior from a top manager becomes a model that will be replicated by all of his subordinates in the organization. A large majority of the employees would not venture out of the bounds of what is clearly communicated to them—especially when it comes to making decisions. The process will start with apathy and will end with apathy.

Nothing unexpected, good or bad, is going to come out of an organization that is "well" run, according to this technique. It may work for as long as the one superbrain running it remains super. However, rest assured, it will not be for too long. Forget individual initiative from employees in such an organization.

Except in union-related shop matters or in corporate boardrooms where policy issues are settled with a vote, decision making by winning acceptance of a majority of members is very uncommon among economic organizations. Several attempts to formalize the majority approach into a management decision-making method have occurred in the form of giving responsibility to many parallel managers with identical authorities, such as co-CEOs, presidents, and equal managing partners. Nevertheless, these methods have not been successful in organizations.

In addition to being slow and tedious, the majority decision making approach suffers from the alienation effect, quite similar to the one that we discussed earlier. Instead of creating alienation between the solitary decision maker and those whom the decision concerns, decision making by majority creates alienation between members of the majority—those who succeeded—and the minority—those who lost. In some regard, making decisions based on majority can be even worse than solitary decision making. It is for these reasons that this approach did not gain acceptance in organizations.

Of all the prevalent pre–twentieth century decision-making techniques, the one that was almost fully discarded by twentieth-century organizations is consensus decision making. In the West, it never gained much popularity for any of the decision-making situations—social or political. The rise of the Western style of government—the democratic system of majority rule—rendered consensus decision making out of vogue for almost all purposes throughout the world. Japan is the only exception, where sociopolitical organizations continue to use it in some form and evolve it for its integration with Western majority decision-making processes.

Consensus-type decision making is negotiation-based and, because of its very nature, is time consuming. To make this technique suitable for all twenty-first century organizations—in particular those in knowledge businesses—requires redesigns, reworks, modifications, and adaptations of the generic consensus decision-making technique that has not occurred yet. In consequence, these organizations have to devise their own versions and adaptations of this technique to make effective group decisions.

The *Just Do It* Syndrome Implementation

The solitary approach, the most popular organizational decision-making technique of the twentieth century, deserves a detailed study in understanding organizational decision-making processes. This *lonely* style of making decisions has been consistent with the overall management style of the typical operating organizations of this time. Managers, referring to their decision-making responsibilities, often in a vaunted manner, describe their jobs with statements like, "It's lonely up there." Through such a description, they subtly relay the lack of help or input they are offered in making "tough" decisions for their organizations. Whereas the implication is that they are forced to make these decisions on their own because no one else in the organization wants to make them, our experience and observations have shown it to be otherwise. In fact, whenever managers genuinely have asked for help in making a decision from those concerned, they have been deluged with suggestions—sometimes even fully made decisions with implementation plans—some of which were of the best quality and ready for execution. Many of the people whom these decisions concern are willing to sacrifice their time, energies, and tangible benefits to participate in decision-making processes.

Mostly, the practice of the solitary decision-making process by managers is due to a sense of insecurity they have in running their operations. They do not want to open up their decision-making process to review by anyone, especially their subordinates. Managers have engaged in solitary decision making even when those concerned have indicated their desire to participate. Such attempts typically continue deep into the decision-implementation stage. Employees ask questions in order to open up the process but are either ignored or rebuffed with empty, meaningless statements.

Managers use several defenses to keep their subordinates out of the decision-making process. The most common of these is the *I want* defense. Under this defense, a manager will avoid sharing the process, or opening up the decision to any modification, by asking his subordinates to do something with a statement that begins with "I want you to do . . ." The moment he utters these words, he tells the subordinate that "I have certain abilities and information essential to make this decision that you don't possess" and/or "I don't want you to have this" or "You can not be trusted with it." This is the most blatant way to stop someone from participating in the making of a decision, or from developing one's decision-making skills. More than anything else, it is the most demeaning way to deal with mature and intelligent adult subordinates.

In general, twentieth-century managers did not give much importance to enhancing organizational communication or increasing their subordinates' understanding of the complex work issues related to them. Standard management style dealing with subordinates of this time has been: Just do it. In other words, do not ask questions—just do it.

MATHEMATICAL COVER: THE SCIENTIFIC APPROACH

The process that has been accepted as the standard for making organizational decisions, even those that affect employee-work aspects, in large, complex firms approaches organizational decision making from a scientific angle. This "scientific approach," primarily developed during the twentieth century, has its roots in mostly archaic mathematical and economics techniques. It is for this reason that it has also been referred to as "quantitative" decision making. To be able to model this process, one must understand its essential components. The following describes what lies at its core.

Economic Objectivity Principle

According to this decision-making process, a decision is made based on the magnitude of its contribution to a particular objective to be attained. The process should begin with a clear understanding of the economic variables involved in the decision at hand. These variables are then interrelated and manipulated through simulation or observed theoretical patterns to examine their effect on each other and other important extraneous variables to learn how this total relationship affects what is of importance to the decision maker. Based on this study, the relationship is refined into a formulation that is optimized for the decision to achieve the objective set for it. Nevertheless, due to the complexity of this formulation, in practice, it becomes mandatory to reduce this relationship to writing, usually employing complicated mathematical abstractions and computer models.

All variables and interactions that have not made any direct contribution to the objective function are stopped from entering the formulation and influencing the selection process. The dependence on objectivity is so complete that it is deliberately quantified to replace all other principles, subjectivity, and intuition. Selection of one decision out of a number of alternatives depends on its ability to attain the formulated economic objective function.

Aware of the limitations of this process from their experiences with it, managers regularly correct its shortcomings by adjusting decisions derived from it. The lack of confidence in these decisions is so prevalent that many decision makers, cognizant of the deficiencies and incompleteness of the process, encourage managers to "make corrections" to these decisions based on their intuition or personal experience with the behavior of the process.

The quality of a decision, according to this methodology, is measured by how closely it gets to the "best" outcome as defined by the objective function. These functions typically are written in terms of one or more of the "generic objectives" that economic organizations work to achieve. These generic objective functions are classified into two major groups: objective functions whose *minimized* values will help achieve higher quality decisions and objective functions whose *maximized* values will help improve the quality of the decisions. Minimized objective functions incorporate a number of economies, such as a) economy of cost, b) economy of time, c) economy of people, d) economy of effort, and e) economy of space. Maximized objective functions get the maximum values on positive outcomes, such as a) profit, b) revenue, and c) unit sales.

Even though a number of managers defend the use of the objectivity principle for making "successful" organizational decisions, they do not utilize the objective-driven approach to make decisions to solve problems in their personal lives. The rationale for this behavior comes from their belief that their personal problems are more involved and too complex to be realistically abstracted by a model and solved by known decision-making techniques. In essence, they do not have faith in these techniques to model their problem-solving situations or in their ability to provide a solution that they will confidently implement. Many times, in such situations, managers are confounded by problem objectives known to them at the time of solving them.

Many managers of knowledge organizations know that the scope of problems they are attempting to solve is closer to the complex problems described above pertaining to their personal lives than to those typically encountered by traditional organizations. To some extent, the above is true for all contemporary organizations—including those we understand as traditional—however, almost all problems that knowledge organizations face belong in this category.

The "objectivity" approach may succeed in solving problems that are clearly understood, well conceived, truly abstracted, and mathematically or otherwise solvable, and when the solution derived from the decision process has a clear link to the problem. Such conditions exist only for a relatively small number of business problems. One example of this type is picking a risky investment out of a number of those offered. Nevertheless, only a few decision-making opportunities like this one exist in business organizations, especially in knowledge firms. They know neither all possible outcomes nor the probabilities associated with their occurrences. When there is so much uncertainty, making decisions based on objectivity, formulated within the confines of conceivable interrelationships among variables, is extremely risky. This will become more apparent when more and more organizations face decision-making situations in the organizational environment of the twenty-first century.

Myopic Outlook

The traditional decision-making process relies heavily on data collected on the same or similar decision-making situations that have already occurred. In fact, many decision-making techniques belonging to this process achieve reliable results by working with past data sets starting from at least 20 periods ago. These techniques become virtually ineffective and esoteric in nature if sufficient history is not built on the behavior of the model because decision making in principle is based on the projection of the past into the future. Because of this dependence on the projections from the past, these techniques fail to emulate the future beyond the immediate. At best, they can give reliable results for the near future. In case of a lack of history or workable data sets, a manager cannot rely on these techniques to make sound organizational decisions.

Result Orientation

Another problem with these decision-making techniques is their solitary focus on achieving a predetermined result. In fact, the emphasis on the result is so strong that many of these decision-making techniques start with an end in mind and continuously monitor their progress toward reaching that end. For many of them, the stop-search rule is their achievement of the result. Some of these techniques begin with conducting a "backward pass" through the progressive transformation flowchart of the problem from its end result to its origin, moving step-by-step toward preceding activities.

Knowing the desired result makes problem solving much simpler—and in many cases, it may be half the effort. However, most problems faced by managers of contemporary organizations, in particular those of knowledge firms, are not knowing exactly what to look for as a result. Additionally, with result-oriented decision making, everything is constrained to attaining that result. The process becomes limited and outcomes remain limited. At best, it may achieve this known result. Nevertheless, a manager may know too late or never know at all if a better outcome could have resulted with a better decision.

When neither the end-result nor its magnitude is known, managers can only be assured of achieving the best "unknown" outcome by stressing the process employed in arriving at decisions. This always has been true for noneconomic organizations, such as government and not-for-profit, and is becoming true for a large number of contemporary economic organizations that are operating in knowledge environments. If managers follow the right process in search of an unknown result, in these organizations, they are likely to succeed, because results can come in many shapes, forms, and magnitudes.

Narrow Scope

In this approach, decision-making techniques are closed in their operation. There is a lack of continuous interaction between the decision-making process and the problem environment—what is required in knowledge environment due to the turbulence. These decision-making techniques move in discrete steps—one step at a time. In other words, a technique of this type has formulated a problem, and its focus moves to finding an optimal solution. Furthermore, when the solution is found, the process moves to the implementation. The process steps do not operate in an integrative manner. A continuous reformulation to incorporate changes as soon as they occur is not available with these processes. In this regard, these techniques are not dynamic or open to changes that are occurring in variables affecting the search for the best solution. This reduces the scope of these techniques to only those problems that do not change, or at least do not change rapidly.

Obviously, this is not the case with knowledge organizations. The scope of these decision-making techniques for knowledge organization is further reduced due to their ability to handle only those problems that exactly fit their solution methodologies.

Dependence on Quantitative Justification

The twentieth century has created among the public a very peculiar dependence on "scientific research." There are many "scientists" who routinely engage in "research" and publicize their "facts," usually via some mass media exposure. Through their research, they tell people what they should eat, how they should behave—in public and in private—and even what is right and what is wrong. These scientists, because of their training, will refuse to admit the existence of anything they cannot prove with models, data, and other well-accepted theoretical bases. Because of the influence that these scientists have on how people think and act, many people, even when they experience something in their body and soul, refuse to accept its occurrence or existence in order to avoid any ridicule. They continue to deny it until the time that they can expect to win the acceptance of "scientists."

The above has been the general attitude of most professionals and business managers. Before they finalize any decision, they want justification founded in data, a formulation using models, and scientific/quantitative proof.

When a manager has to make a decision based on his intuition, the decision finds no support according to this decision-making process. In the knowledge environment, the complexity and uncertainty is so great that constructing justifications may be too difficult and/or time consuming to keep the firm efficient.

Need for Constant Monitoring

Since scientific decisions are made by "decision makers" rather than by those who are responsible for carrying them out, the management makes sure, through constant monitoring and control, that they are being implemented. Because of the extreme importance of this task, in many firms, it is given the status of a separate, specialized function. The magnitude of effort required to perform this activity does not permit it to be left as part of the usual management controls. In this case, the firm has personnel responsible for specialized staff functions with overtones of implementation, compliance, enforcement, follow-up, and the like. In the latter case, all these functions, in some form, are treated as a regular, integrated part of the manager's responsibilities. Managers hold regular meetings, progress sessions, and inspection rounds to ensure that their decisions are being carried out. Collectively, these activities account for the majority of the manager's time. Instead of planning, managers are busy controlling.

Historical Perspective

This decision-making approach depends heavily on historical data. It treats the future as an extension of the past. If this is in fact the case, then using decision-making techniques based on this approach may give valid results. These techniques may also be effective in making the right decisions in case the manager has a reliable understanding of the things to come. Otherwise, making decisions using these techniques would be purely an exercise in futility. Many times, the results from working according to these decisions might be more detrimental to the organization's goals than a total absence of any assumptions about the future, because an inaccurate premise about the future can effectively constrain the management's ambitions and achievements. Since there is a lack of experience with decisions relating to organizations in developing industries, such as the ones belonging to knowledge, making decisions in these industries using techniques that extend the past into the future are futile.

PRINCIPLES OF KNOWLEDGE ENVIRONMENT DECISION MAKING

Since knowledge work and work environment are different from traditional work and organizations, decision making that will succeed in these conditions is different from the techniques given above. With this in mind, and giving thought to the special nature and requirements of knowledge organizations, it is recommended that decision making be guided by a number of principles that has consideration for these. Five such principles that a suitable decision-making technique and the decision implementation process for knowledge organizations should follow are described below.

Principle 1: Train to Break the Rules

Managers in large traditional organizations, such as government, military, and politics, have always set rules of model behavior for their employees—not only for the behavior at work but for their private lives as well. However, until the advent of the twentieth century, this practice had primarily stayed in these organizations. It was the rise of large, complex business corporations during this century that standardized these rules to include all work behavior and extended them to day-to-day operations of human behavior in all organizations. There was even a design suggested to best form and run organizations for the convenience of adherence to the rules. The concepts were borrowed from ancient authoritative rulers, like the Chinese Emperor Ch'in, in designing organizations whose operations totally depended on rules. One such design, the bureaucratic model, attributed to the German manager Max Weber (1947), became a twentieth century reincarnation of managing human behavior with rules. A large number of the twentieth-century organizations chose to follow this or similar models in one form or another. These organizations have rules—written or well understood—for every conceivable aspect of their operations. Managers are trained to operate their organizations according to these rules and to ensure that everyone in their organization follows them. Moreover, in an attempt to be a good influence on others, especially their subordinates, managers are instructed to obey the rules themselves as well. The unquestioned supremacy of rules is so strong that obedience to them is important even when they have not passed the tests of common sense and internal consistency. In spite of these anomalies, a large number of managers, even at the high levels of the hierarchy, do not dare challenge or break the rules. Management feels so insecure about "breaking the rules" that doing so would be an indication of a lack of faith in them: Once people lose faith in rules, the whole system could come crashing down. Challenging the rules has been made extremely hard.

Most organizations, even the ones in the twenty-first century, are designed to follow the bureaucratic model—due to the ease of managing them with rules. To instill respect for these rules, severe punishments are inflicted on those who break them. The rules are such an important part of these organizations that the complete organizational system is designed to facilitate the enforcement of the rules. In spite of the criticism of bureaucracy from all corners, it still is probably the most applied model for organizational management and, with further minor adaptations now and then, is expected to continue into the twenty-first century.

An essential adaptation to the bureaucracy model during the second half of the twentieth century expanded the number of people in organizations with an exclusive or selective exemption from obeying the rules. Further, the number of those who could break the rules was also expanded. The work environment for success through innovation in the current century will make it essential to equip everyone in an organization with the ability to break the rules and quickly devise temporary alternatives for small frequency use or to suit the situation at hand, as the case may be. This ability is highly important for the successful functioning of groups given the knowledge assignments in organizations.

The right method for breaking a rule is the same as it is for making one. To break a rule properly, one must possess the discrete knowledge that was needed for making the rule. If one does not have that knowledge, then one will not have the ability or capability to break the rule at the crucial time or one will break it in a wrong manner, which may actually hurt the organization. In this regard, we must follow the principle that if employees do not have the experience of making a rule, then they will not have the courage to break it—and if they do break it, they will do it incorrectly.

The French sociologist Emile Durkheim used the term *anomie* to describe the confusion arising in the minds of immigrants to the United States with regard to the use of rules of behavior in their adopted homeland (Berglas, 1997). They knew that in America they could not apply the rules of behavior that they had learned back home; nevertheless, they did not know the rules of behavior that were acceptable. This anomaly (or anomie) caused confusion and pain, as well as a hindrance to growth for many. They had to know how to break the rules.

Since a knowledge work environment is volatile and has a greater need for the noncompliance of established norms and practices, an essential part of employee training for undertaking assignments in this environment should be on how to break the rules. Successful rule breaking requires a special type of discipline that should be ingrained in employees before assigning them knowledge assignments.

Principle 2: Comply with Common Sense

Sociologists have observed that people who have immigrated to the United States do better in America as compared with their counterparts in their countries of origin. They achieve success in America that they could not have achieved back home. The major difference between American culture and other cultures is obedience, which could amount to blind following. Whereas other cultures, in particular the older ones, emphasize obedience, America does not do that. In coming to America, these immigrants learn to think freely and act without the pressure to comply or obey. This free spirit eliminates the emphasis on obedience, fosters ingenious thinking, and causes innovative actions that could never have been done back in their native lands.

To create a work environment in organizations in which decision making permits the flourishing of innovation, knowledge firms should train their employees so that their common sense can overrule all decisions. They should learn to never obey a rule that, in the given time frame and situation, does not pass the test of their common sense. Complete faith in models, techniques, and specialists should be treated as a sign of a lack of confidence and, consequently, a sufficient reason for managers to train employees in the use of common sense. Employees should learn that when a decision goes against an alternative that makes intuitive sense and appeals to "common sense," they should have the courage to discard the decision (Amar, 1995).

Principle 3: Lead to Decision; Don't Decide for Others

It is important for everyone in a knowledge organization to be equipped to make correct decisions on time without any assistance. In this environment, so many decisions need to be made under time constraints that expecting assistance in making them may render them ineffective. As a first rule, managers must know that no one should make decisions for anyone else; neither for a subordinate nor a supervisor. Rather than making decisions for them, managers should give them tools, provide them with information, and teach them techniques to make correct decisions independently and quickly.

However, all should make their own decisions whether right or wrong. A manager may initiate the decision making for them but should not proceed further. The manager may present the situation as described by the decision makers to them in their own words with their own biases and prejudices. A manager should know that, with few exceptions, everyone looking for a decision from others has one's own alternative decision, which one may not accept for many reasons, such as the lack of confidence, a hesitation caused by the fear of rejection, a need for help in implementation, and a need for approval by others. In such cases, the manager may interject variables by guiding the person in recognizing these variables. He may restate the problem in terms of the recognized variables, present cases on similar situations, and let one establish linkages, draw parallels, and deduce answers.

Principle 4: *Ab initio* Thinking: Reinvent the Facts

Knowledge managers should remember the following axiom about making decisions: "It is human to seek security in the known." In essence, most people engage in known methods and knowingly or unknowingly work to achieve known results. Further, because of their own conviction in this practice, they convince others to engage in similar behavior. The innate desire in humans to engage in the unknown or the uncommon wanes with age. Because experience comes with time, it takes away the youth and makes humans seek security in the known. How wonderful it would be to enjoin youth and experience in the management of knowledge organizations. Firms try. They try by making their experienced managers engage in activities that are adventurous and exploratory, that rekindle youth in them, that change their decision-making outlook—away from the secure and traditional—and that increase their risk-taking behavior. Knowledge organizations are also trying the alternative. They are giving their young managers responsibility to run the organizations and make all decisions that require playing with the unknown and the uncertain.

In decision making, avoiding the security in the known implies approaching every decision as an opportunity to start over, doing things afresh—*ab initio*—giving a new approach to the same decisions. The *ab initio* approach does not utilize any previously known facts and assumptions in making decisions. It requires developing new facts and stating new assumptions based on the conditions and situations pertaining to the problem at hand.

Charles Wang, chairman of Computer Associates International, a $4-billion computer software firm, advocates *zero-based thinking* in his decision making.

He expects his managers to start afresh. When his employees have to make decisions, he forces them to take innovative approaches through his popular line, "Stand on your head, stand on your head" (Teitelbaum, 1997). In this way, employees are forced to think out of the preestablished set—*thinking out of the box*. He walks around the company or goes to meetings with his officers wearing rubber bands on his wrist along with expensive gold bracelets, thereby emphasizing the unique alternatives to making decisions.

Principle 5: Optimize the Principles

Traditional management has become so analysis-dependent and objective-driven that it has almost totally departed from making decisions by compliance with a set of *á priori* conditions—the principles that must be adhered to by the decisions. By adhering to these principles in making decisions, the decision maker actually is instantly assured of achieving the *optimized* objective set for the decision making. Management believes that, in the end, consistent compliance with these principles will translate into the attainment of the goals the organization has set that are more unclear, indirect, and nonquantifiable.

Typical analytical approaches contrast with this. An analytical approach makes decisions that are *á posteriori* of their making and implementation, to optimize these direct and quantifiable goals without going through the principle stage. Although this approach is likely to make efficient optimized decisions in an environment that is more stable and certain, it definitely will not work for the optimal benefit of the organization that operates in a turbulent and uncertain environment. Too much may change between developing and implementing a decision, making it useless before its implementation. Since these principles are less likely to change, the decisions are revised perpetually and automatically through full compliance with principles.

DECISION-MAKING TECHNIQUES FOR A KNOWLEDGE ENVIRONMENT

The right decision in a knowledge environment must possess the following characteristics:

1. *Acceptance:* This is the first and most important characteristic that a decision, which will prove to be good for these organizations, must possess. The decision maker must ensure that everyone connected with the implementation of this decision must accept and sincerely commit to carry it out.

2. *Promptness:* Because of the fast changing environment in which these organizations operate, a decision is only worth considering if it can be made quickly. If the best possible decision requires more time than the organization has, then it will not be of any use.

3. *Flexibility:* The third important characteristic of a good decision for these organizations is its ability to adjust and adapt to changes in surrounding conditions. A decision that is rigid and inadaptable may not be of any use in an environment that is unstable.

The decision-making techniques that meet the above requisites and should work well in knowledge environments are given in the following section.

Principled Decision Making[1]

As we have seen in the previous section, principled decision making is a simple but highly effective process-based methodology used to make decisions in organizations—both social and political. Nevertheless, it is especially suited to organizations that operate in tumultuous environments and/or do not exactly know their missions and goals. In this decision-making method, the justification that supports the selection of a decision does not draw from analysis but from its conformance with one or a few selected principles. The selection of a decision from among the available alternative decision choices is based on their adherence with the espoused principles. The decision choices are principle-based and mostly evident and, hence, so easy to select that it does not require analysis to support their selection. In addition to simplifying the decision process, the principled decision-making technique is easy to understand and gives decisions that are effectively communicated. That, in turn, can ensure quick acceptance from those whom the decisions affect and immediate compliance by those who are responsible for their implementation. Principled decisions are also timelier because they make sense and communicate this sense behind their adoption. All persons concerned with the decision who understand the principles can participate. No special skills are needed to do that.

In contrast to this, not many of the groups and individuals whom organizational decisions concern have the requisite preparation to comprehend the complicated analyses used to understand the rationale and computations utilized in making analytical decisions. This lack of comprehension deprives them of the ability to make any contribution to the decision-making process and, subsequently, to make their sincere commitment to its implementation. The consequence is a denial to the organization of a higher quality decision that has built-in acceptance of its implementers.

Similar weaknesses also exist in decision-making techniques that are pseudoanalytical—those that use pragmatism or affectivity as a major criterion in selecting a decision choice. The weakness of the pragmatism-based technique lies in the fact that emphasizing workability in selecting a decision will almost certainly result in the selection of an alternative that is neither optimal nor has the implementer's built-in acceptance. Moreover, this compromise will have to be dealt with at a time when the organization will be least able to handle it. The use of affectivity as a decision criterion meets the same fate. Additionally, hoping that the implementers will like what the decision maker did is speculative. In fact, the criteria of both pragmatism and affectivity are nothing but a simple reflection of the bias of the analyst toward a particular choice. Both are myopic.

Principled decision making can easily overcome the faults of the analytical and pseudoanalytical techniques. It can be implemented in the following three steps:

1. The first step in the principled decision-making process requires selection and communication of the right principles to which selected decisions must adhere. The principles are too specific and pointed; some examples from a sales department are: "Never lose a bid to rival X," "Don't make a sale below our cost," and "Always match advertised prices of our rivals."

2. The second step—detailed principled decision making—in the process from which a specific decision for a specific situation will emerge requires the decision maker to appropriately select the principles and actually apply them. The right decision will naturally flow out of the selected alternatives through the application of these principles.

3. Principled decision making emphasizes the *process*. The end results in more understandable terms to someone not trained in the principles are of secondary consequence. Hence, the decision maker must make sure that the process is followed thoroughly and sincerely.

Whereas analytical decision making strives to achieve optimization of a complicated, mathematical *objective function*, the adherence to principles in itself is the fulfillment of objectives to be achieved through principled decision making.

Principled decision making is potentially more effective in organizations operating in an increasingly complex, dynamic, or unpredictable environment. In this environment, each decision situation is unique, requiring a novel approach. Under such circumstances, analytical decision making cannot ensure either effective or efficient decisions. It becomes difficult for a manager to program decisions to carry out at the lower levels.

The use of principles in making decisions in organizational functions has been scant. In America, Quakers and some religious organizations used principled decision making in selecting investments that fit their beliefs. Some other investment portfolio managers practiced it to avoid investing in companies engaged in the manufacture of alcohol and tobacco. Meaningful applications of principled decision making have been tried in financial investing during the Vietnam era. The principle guiding the investment decision in that case was to negatively impact revenue and market capitalization of certain targeted firms, like Dow Chemical Company (a manufacturer of napalm), that were engaged in this unpopular war, which many labeled "immoral."

There are two different approaches in which principled decision making can be used in organizations (Amar, 1995):

In Assistance of Analytical Decision Making. With virtually unlimited investment opportunities available globally, portfolio managers set certain principles as a way to qualify investments for their investment consideration. They, then, use principles as screens to segregate these investments into groups that pass the test of principles and those that do not. This process helps define the search dimensions and/or reduce the sample space. The size problem is reduced using these principles.

Once the size of the problem becomes manageable, analytical techniques are then used to finalize the selection. This is how principled decision making works in conjunction with analytical decision making in solving highly complex problems that otherwise may not be structured. Ethical portfolios developed by Wall Street in response to investors' concerns, such as how satisfied a firm's employees are and how a firm treats the environment, are examples of the types of principles used in the assistance of analytical decision making.

As an Alternative to Analytical Decision Making. In this approach, fulfillment of a principle is the only criterion used to evaluate available decision choices (ties may be broken by other criteria). There is no follow-up analysis to justify the decision, either because the justification is too involved or because the decision maker deems it of no material consequence. An example illustrating the application of this use can be drawn from Levi Strauss & Company. The principle directing overseas investments from Levi Strauss draws upon the record of human rights. Before considering opening its operations in any country, Levi Strauss evaluates the performance based on the human rights of that country. It chooses not to invest in any country that does not respect human rights. Though quite straightforward, this principle has tremendous implications for business for a company that earns most of its revenue from the manufacture and sale of blue jeans—symbolic of Western, and especially American, culture and freedom. This Levi Strauss principle also epitomizes the sociopolitical character of a national system. A country that does not respect basic human rights will end up creating problems that will not be in the interest of operating a business there anyhow. This way of engaging in principled decision making has worked well for Levi Strauss.

To help managers make decisions, organizations can set principles that they must satisfy through their decisions rather than optimizing a certain set of criteria in the form of an objective function. One example illustrating this type of principled decision making is drawn from Sears Roebuck & Co. At Sears, all decisions are guided by the principle that the "customer is always right." Another one comes from IBM, which has its decision making guided by the principle that emphasizes "respect for the individual"—employees, vendors, customers, dealers, and others.

Principled decision making is more robust and stable. It can better cope with changes over time, shifts in leaders, fluctuating leadership styles, market conditions, and many other factors belonging to an organization's external and internal environments. In contrast, the greatest debility of analytical decision-making techniques is that a shrewd analyst could show more than one decision choice as optimal and desirable.

Consensus Decision Making

In a system that flourishes on innovation and creativity, such as a knowledge organization, it is important that everyone whose involvement is essential for the successful implementation of a decision sincerely commit to it. Such a commitment comes only when those people who make decisions are affected by them. It then instills in them a feeling of responsibility for that decision's implementation. It is achieved only through consensus decision making.

A leader may start the consensus decision-making process by recognizing key players in a decision—those whom it will involve the most—without whose commitment, successful implementation of the decision would be a struggle, if not an outright impossibility.

Many organizations during their building years treat decision making as a fundamentally rational process that is top-management centered. However, as the complexity grows, and success seems possible only by bringing everyone on board, these organizations switch to a more dispassionate style that builds consensus among all concerned employees and wins their support. Then there are those organizations that start out with the consensus decision-making process, switch to analytical techniques for quick growth through the next level, and, on further increase in complexity, switch back to consensus decision making—moving on to the next higher level upon attaining success. The San Mateo, California–based CRM (Customer Relationship Management) software developer, Siebel Systems, which was introduced in an earlier section, engaged in such a shift last year. Its CEO, Tom Siebel, mostly unemotionally and single-handedly, made all decisions for the company, whether they had to do with the dress code or color of the walls and carpets or eating habits. He expected his employees to accept these decisions unquestioningly. However, last year, when forced to loosen his grip on every detail of the company, he conveniently took a four-week vacation on his Montana ranch and passed on his managerial duties to his deputies who could connect with the employees (Warner, 2000). In contrast to Tom Siebel's management style, that was hampering further growth in this knowledge company, the new management adopted a managing process that was more democratic, open, and acceptable to all employees. It has allowed Yoga classes, which employees wanted in the past but that Tom Siebel had disallowed, and day-care centers, which he also had opposed as being inconsistent with the firm's rational goals. As a result of these changes by the new management, the annual employee turnover rate at Siebel Systems was cut to 13 percent (Silicon Valley's aggregate average rate is 15 to 20 percent) and financial performance resumed its pace, with sales from its CRM more than doubling in 2000 (http://cnnfn.com/2001/01/23/technology/wires/seibel_wg/index.htm).

Positive-Positive Decision Making

A decision that certainly will have the approval and acceptance of a person is the one made by that person himself. As a corollary, if we let all people participate in making decisions that concern them or those that they have to carry out, they will accept them. We saw previously that such decisions are arrived at by using consensus decision making. Unfortunately, the process of consensus decision making becomes so involved and stretched that, in most cases, it becomes extremely time consuming, sometimes almost impossible. Organizations in general and knowledge ones in particular do not have much time for making decisions. Knowledge organizations have to make decisions very quickly to respond to changes in their turbulent environment. It is for this reason that acceptance of decisions by all whom they concern is sacrificed for the sake of speed, which results in problems in implementing good decisions and causes their failure.

If there were a technique that would help managers make decisions as quickly as the *Just Do It* method while at the same time winning acceptance and approval from those responsible for carrying them out, we could have both *speed* and *commitment*—the two positives that make quality decisions. Positive-positive decision making achieves this. It results in what we call a *power decision*. The advantage of a power decision is its built-in acceptance, high probability of success, and timeliness. A power decision is a consensus decision made with a different approach, primarily reducing the decision-making time. The outcome of a power decision will result in a gain for everyone involved in its execution.

Power decisions can be made following the five steps described below:

Step 1: Decouple Decisions. Making consensus decisions consumes too much time when it concerns many people and therefore many people are involved in making them. In order to speed up the process, we want to reduce the number of people involved in making a decision, but we do not want to violate the basic tenet of successful decision making—that a decision must be made by those whom it concerns so that it is acceptable to them. Decoupling, the first step in power decision making, breaks down responsibility of executing a task, and the commensurate authority of making decisions relating to it, into small, self-contained parcels that have only a few links with other decisions. This may be achieved by redesigning the organization.

Decoupling will reduce decisions in size—the number of people involved in making a decision—and complexity—the number of people affected by a decision.[2] The reduction of decisions should be to the smallest size possible. The number of people involved in a decision is reduced not by leaving people out but by creating decision parcels so small that they do not concern many people. This in effect will result in a very large number of decisions, each made by only the few persons it concerns. The ultimate goal of the organization should be to reduce decisions to so small a size that each one of them concerns only one person.

If the decoupling is correctly done, each decision will have only one person whom it will concern either for its outcome or for its execution. Organizations should not stop decoupling until they attain perfect decoupling.

Step 2: Nucleic Authority. The second step in positive-positive decision making identifies the person with the authority to make a decision. It bonds the authority for making a decision with the responsibility to execute it. This authority should lie at the nucleus of the concern emerging either due to the outcome or due to the execution or both. Those carrying out a decision or affected by it—individuals or groups—should be identified and given the authority to make it.

As a rule, people who will face the consequence of a decision should make it. No one external to the boundary defined by the above should have a direct part in making the decision.

Step 3: Design Acceptance in Every Decision. In the third step, we apply the principle that a decision maker should ensure that a decision that is finally selected will be acceptable to all those whom it concerns and who are responsible for its execution. He should make sure that this decision excites and energizes them. It should release a biochemical reaction in those whom it concerns so that they get positive feelings and an intense desire to work toward its implementation. If not, then it should be revised or rejected. We have observed that almost all decision makers have a good sense of how their decisions will be received by those whom they concern. Many times, they also know why their decisions will not be well received and what should be done to overcome such resistance, but they opt not to do anything.

Those initiating a decision have to estimate the outcomes of the decision and what and how much will be gained for everyone concerned with the decision. A decision will be acceptable to all if it has a positive outcome for all— the organization and those who carry it out. These two positive outcomes make a decision a positive-positive decision. Positivism requires eliminating anything from a decision that takes away the excitement. Furthermore, it should convey the decision by using words that are exciting and energizing. The text should be free of any negative-sounding words, but it should not leave out any facts. A decision maker can analyze a decision from the perspectives of all those whom it concerns and assess how they will receive it and how to revise it if necessary to make it positive.

The words selected to convey a positive-positive decision should reflect thoughtfulness, concern, and understanding. For example, rather than using words like "cut" and "eliminate," a decision should use words that convey positives, such as "save" and "value-added." These words should be dynamically selected in a cultural context, since it is the meaning that they convey that is important.

A positive decision cares for the gain of everyone involved. An example of a thoughtless decision is not renewing a vendor—and switching to one who had a lower bid—without giving him the opportunity to review and revise. An example of a positive-positive decision in this regard would be to help a vendor realize savings in labor, materials, and overhead and asking for a share of these savings.

Step 4: Periodic Audit. To ensure that decisions are being made according to the positive-positive decision-making process and achieving positive outcomes for all those involved in making and executing them (that is, the stakeholders), it is important that management periodically makes sure that it is in fact happening by conducting a periodic audit of every decision made in the organization. An audit is also important to find out what is lacking or is misconceived and should be part of the refresher training in making positive-positive decisions for the employees.

It is important that decision audits be performed in close association with the individual(s) who made the decision. The audit itself could be a good learning experience rather than an act of intimidation.

Step 5: Training to Make Their Decision. Since everyone is making decisions in a positive-positive decision-making organization, it is important that all employees be trained to make decisions following this methodology. This training should include: (1) how to identify parties to a decision, (2) how to involve them in making it, (3) how to arrive at a consensus decision by breaking decisions into small sizes, and (4) how to ensure that the final decision results in a positive outcome for all concerned. The positive-positive decision-making training one gets may be refreshed after someone makes a decision that does not meet the approval of every stakeholder in that decision. Such a discovery may become known on an audit of the decisions made.

NEXT TO DECISION MAKING

Since it is very difficult to precisely instruct people who are operating in any uncertain environment, like the knowledge environment, on how to handle situations as they arise, it is not plausible for management to set operating rules for them without compromising innovation and productivity. In a knowledge environment, in particular the one that is also turbulent, it is important for employees to be trained in the process of decision making rather than be given a set of rules to go by. No set of rules, no matter how well thought out and exhaustive, can be sufficient to answer all questions that arise and need immediate action from those in the "heat" of things, because they are the ones who possess complete and current information to make the right decisions and then implement them.

This chapter has covered some of the techniques that work well under these circumstances. For the success of a decision, it is important that every stakeholder of the decision buys into it. All stakeholders of a decision should see something positive for them coming from the implementation of this decision in order for it to be successfully implemented. The use of positive-positive decision-making techniques given in this chapter will ensure that every knowledge organization decision receives total commitment. These techniques are an adaptation of the usual consensus decision-making technique in that the size and complexity of decisions are small enough for them to be made with the individual approval of all whom they concern and those who will be working to implement them.

NOTES

1. This section on principled decision making is adapted from an article titled "Principled Versus Analytical Decision-Making: Definitive Optimization" by A.D. Amar in *Mid-Atlantic Journal of Business, 31,* no. 2, June 1995. Readers interested in further details on this may refer to the original source.

2. For a complete definition of decision complexity or size, please refer to the glossary following Chapter 12. This discussion is in light of the definitions given there.

REFERENCES

Amar, A.D. (1995). Principled versus analytical decision-making: Definitive optimization. *Mid-Atlantic Journal of Business, 31,* 119–123.
Berglas, S. (1997, September 8). Why are you so paranoid? *Fortune*, pp. 171–172.
CNNFN. (2001, January 23). Seibel beats by a nickel: Software maker posts first quarter net income 20¢ beating street by 5¢ <http://cnnfn.com/2001/01/23/technology/wires/seibel_wg/index.htm>.
Teitelbaum, R. (1997, July 21). Tough guys finish first. *Fortune*, pp. 82–84.
Warner, M. (2000, September 4). Confessions of a control freak. *Fortune*, pp. 130–140.
Weber, M. (1947). *Theory of social and economic organization* (A.M. Henderson and T. Parson, Trans.). New York: Oxford University Press.
Whetton, D.A., & Delbecq, A.L. (2000, November). Saraide's chairman Hatim Tyabji on creating and sustaining a values-based organizational culture. *The Academy of Management Executive, 14* (4), 32–40.

Chapter 8 _____

Leading to Be a Leader

Leading in knowledge organizations is quite different from leading in traditional ones. Whereas traditional organizations lead from the base of legitimate power, this use in knowledge organizations is sure to backfire. This chapter on the leading function in knowledge organizations describes how traditional organizational leadership differs from that which is needed in knowledge organizations. This chapter conceptualizes a seven-step model for a successful leadership process in traditional organizations. Although this model seems very potent for managing any organization, this chapter pokes holes in it, provides principles of effective leadership in a knowledge environment, and gives seven steps in the knowledge organization leadership process. Through a discussion of various power sources from which a leader can draw, this chapter covers how a knowledge organization leader can get full contribution from those working for him or her. It concludes with six steps for developing effective leadership for knowledge organizations.

FUNCTIONAL LEADERSHIP

Because of the lack of either problem definition or solution methodology, or possibly both, all organizations have a number of tasks that require unique ways to be understood and accomplished. Since the number of such tasks is quite large in knowledge organizations, there is very little that senior and experienced superiors can do to assist their subordinates in the performance of these tasks. Leadership of knowledge employees gives a new meaning to the role of supervisors in these organizations. Supervisors in knowledge organizations, practically at any level of the hierarchy, cannot follow the leadership model of traditional organizations. The major difference is that task characteristics in knowledge organizations require all knowledge employees to be leaders in some form. In fact, ability to function as a leader should be a requisite skill for any person who accepts work assignments in any capacity in a knowledge organization. The challenges for managers lie in evolving practices that facilitate the functioning of every knowledge employee as a leader—a functional leader. Managers can do the following to turn employees into functional leaders:

1. They should repeatedly study and analyze their own leadership behavior toward their employees and whether it succeeds in getting right responses from the employees;
2. They should reinforce those behaviors in their employees that prove successful in inspiring others to excel at the similar abilities that they possess;
3. They should routinely review their own behavior and weed out that which works contrary to this goal; and
4. They should influence their colleagues to follow their successful behaviors and to discard those that failed in their experience.

As a rule, managers should see that all knowledge employees, in some aspect of their work assignments, encounter situations that offer them opportunities to act as leaders. Success with leadership situations can hasten lavish outcomes in more than one form for the organization. To encourage risk taking in these roles by employees, managers should increase intrinsic and extrinsic rewards from success on leadership initiatives. They should develop a desire in employees who successfully become functional leaders to draft visions for their departments and the courses to realize them.

In preparation of leading others, knowledge employees can undertake extra efforts in learning how to influence or make others work to attain organizational goals. Leadership in traditional organizations is not about leading others to attain outcomes of value to them, unless it happens to be a by-product of the firm's goals. Nevertheless, unlike these organizations, knowledge organization leadership, or the art of leading knowledge organizations, is not about using employees as "means" to attain goals that are espoused by the leader or others in the organization but is about making all knowledge employees individually form their visions relating to the tasks that they are doing and then helping others to successfully replicate their learning in similar situations such that new and unique knowledge tasks become less unique and uncertain.

KNOWLEDGE ORGANIZATION LEADERSHIP ROLE

The leadership role in traditional organizations includes leading others toward the attainment of an outcome, or realization of a vision, of direct value to, usually, a third party—someone other than either the leader or the followers. This type of leadership has become a profession and an important requisite for executives to succeed in their roles as managers in traditional organizations. This leadership is like leadership in war; it is a war of competition that is fought in the marketplace using products, technologies, services, and distribution channels as weapons. Traditional organization leadership is a refinement of the warlord-type of leadership from the pre–job era.

Knowledge organization leadership is different in both principle and practice. It is neither warlike nor politics-like—where leadership implies a successful power play. Knowledge organization leaders should not use their position of power to influence others in achieving their own or the organization's goals. There are no "generals" and there are no "soldiers" in the knowledge organization leader-led relationship. There is very little that can be transplanted from traditional leadership to knowledge organization leadership. Even though there are many theories suggesting successful leader behavior in traditional organizations, mostly in times of need, a knowledge organization manager is left to draw from his own whims and wits to lead subordinates.

A Brusque Awakening

The environment surrounding knowledge work has given rise to a large number of individuals who have to act as "real leaders" to get the work done. These real leaders do it without titles, authority, and legal controls; they are "informal" leaders. Such leaders are active in traditional organizations also, but the number of such leaders in knowledge organizations has to be much larger for it to function successfully. These leaders exercise greater influence on workers' behavior and productivity even when they do not have a legitimate power base from which to operate. Managers should know of these informal leaders, recognize their function, and harness their power for the benefit of the organization. Managers should imitate the informal leader's behavior to effectively increase their own influence on their subordinates by supplementing informal power over their subordinates with their authority from formal power bases. Typically, a knowledge organization leader without this supplemental power from informal leadership will become practically ineffective.

EVOLVING A MODEL OF KNOWLEDGE LEADERSHIP

Let us first understand the workings of leadership in traditional organizations. This will give us an idea about what *not* to do in a knowledge organization. The traditional leadership model presented here is the sum total of all successful organizational leadership behavior that we have observed from practice in operating organizations.

Traditional organization leadership highlights personage and the role of the leader in a group, such as a section, department, division, or organization. This group is organized so that its leader always appears at the center stage of its activities and is the prime mover of all workings of the group. The leader's prominence in fact, gives identification to the group. Whatever happens to the group is fully attributed to its leader. The leader takes, and everyone else gives, credit for everything good that happens to the organization. Conversely, the leader accepts, and everyone else gives, blame for all things that go wrong with the group. A group is considered as good as its leader. Because of the leader's visibility, all actions and decisions undertaken by the leader are aimed at his or her personal success.

There is a clear distinction between the leader and other members of the group in traditional organizations. It is customary to have the leader identified as the "boss," "superior," or "manager," and the rest of the group as "followers," "subordinates," "workers," or one of several other similar-sounding titles. The latter operates in the shadow of the leader. Because all activities are performed in the name of the leader, it is up to the leader to give or to not give his or her followers any recognition or credit for the achievements that may genuinely belong to them.

The traditional model of leadership is guided by the maintenance of tight control over the group by its leader. The primary source of the leader's power over his or her followers rests in the authority vested in him or her by some superior command, usually external to the leader-follower relationship dyad. It is very common for traditional leaders to further build their influence over their followers from power sources, such as charisma, expertise, or referent. This is done in an attempt to increase their acceptance. In this way, they superimpose this influence over their formal leadership role, a concept that we have described previously.

Traditional Leadership Process

Typically, knowledge organization managers should not follow the leadership process that is prevalent in traditional organizations. Nevertheless, it is important for managers to be aware of it so that they can consciously avoid falling into the trap that this process entails. We present here the process that traditional managers use for self-development into successful leaders, assimilation of their power, and fulfillment of their endeavors is accomplished by following a sequence of the seven practical steps described below.

1. Accumulation of Acquirable Leadership Traits. The traditional leadership model is rooted in the belief that leaders possess a number of physical, behavioral, and supervisory traits. Some go so far as to associate physical traits, such as height and weight, with success in leadership. Others believe that a leader should be quick, self-confident, assertive, alert, and even possess a high IQ, among many other traits. Although there is a lack of credible evidence supporting a strong correlation between leader performance and these traits, acquisition of these traits has become essential for success in landing leadership positions. Most individuals responsible for investiture of leadership responsibilities distribute such assignments based on the existence of these traits.

Prospective leaders, in an attempt to prove their suitability to be leaders, either convince important others that they possess these traits or, when they do not possess them, go and acquire whichever ones they can. The belief is that one can only become a leader through proper looks, voice, gestures, and style. There are many firms that specialize in making managers behave like leaders.

There are certain accepted ways a leader walks, waits, enters a room or an elevator, communicates, among other things. Some of these leadership traits include punctuality, conspicuity, and alertness. For example, leaders rarely carry bulky cases (they call back to their offices if any information is needed). They show gratitude for minor or unnoticeable services rendered to them. Rather than sitting back in a chair, leaders sit forward with their legs spread. They talk while maintaining eye contact with the listener but are still well aware of their surroundings. They never use qualifying or conditional sentences or make broad gestures with their hands to emphasize a point. They almost never repeat sentences because they are sure everyone is paying full attention to them. Leaders very rarely lose their temper. They are always polite. The list goes on.

2. Formation of a Vision for Organization. This step follows the notion that to be able to bring about the efforts of all their followers along a set direction, first, leaders themselves must arrive at a clear understanding of the status quo, where to go next, and how to get there. This imaginative insight into a subject or a situation that their followers find attractive as well as credibly achievable is labeled "vision." For leaders to be successful, their vision must beckon. It is a common practice for a leader to develop a vision of mass appeal. Each leader distinguishes himself through the unique vision that he develops on the subject. If the vision does not click, acceptance of the leader by the followers will not materialize. Traditional leaders are distinctly recognized by the vision that they develop—it is their vision, and everyone knows it.

Next, the leaders communicate their vision to their followers. They use unique means to convince them that their vision is superior to those being offered by competitors. It is this necessity that requires a leader to be a good communicator.

3. Coalition Building. Through this step, traditional leaders manipulate the environment that surrounds the situation to generate a coalition in support of their vision. They work for the accordance of views in an attempt to gain aggregation of effort. In the process, leaders will, as far as possible, neutralize opposition and conflicting forces, because it will help ease the task animating the vision and reduce the chance of any sabotage against its incarnation. A large number of leaders commonly engage in the practice of questionable ethics or ones that lie on the borderline of legality. Many leaders have openly justified such actions in the interests of realization of their vision. It is also common for a leader to crush the opposition that one fails to win over. Machiavellian behavior by leaders is not uncommon at this step.

4. Assembling of Means. To enable their followers to realize their vision, leaders put together an essential organization consisting of people, logistics, infrastructure, and even finances, to be used as the means necessary for this purpose. Typically, leaders should synergize their association with others whom they will use as means to attain their vision. However, a shrewd traditional leader is so focused and objective that he or she assembles people with "weaknesses" in order to easily and continuously maintain control of them. In fact, to ensure that no one will usurp the leader's influence over his followers, many leaders, in this ensemble of means, will not allow membership of the group to anyone who may have greater strength or influence on their followers than they do.

5. Aggressive Implementation and Control. With this structure in place, traditional leaders aggressively go after realizing their vision. To keep all efforts focused on the goals that they set, leaders regularly engage in cheer-up activities, motivational speeches, rewarding subordinates' replicable behavior, and ensuring that no important follower feels disheartened in moments of despair. During this phase, leaders ruthlessly curb any differences that may cause distraction from the vision and the structure leading to its consummation, irrespective of the merit of the issues being raised. Leaders will not stop short of the fulfillment of their vision because a cessation will amount to an acceptance of a lack of leadership and a certain failure of the endeavor.

6. Development of Significance of Their Outcome. Most of the outcomes in social organizations are not comparable. There are no absolutes and no standards. Unlike scientific undertakings, for social enterprises there is neither a control group nor any knowledge of the optimum against which outcome should be checked to assess the efficiency of the effort leading to the outcome. There is no set way to measure success on social endeavors. In most cases, an outcome is as good as its perception in the minds of those whose opinions matter. This is where leaders have to play their next step: They make sure that people with influence are convinced that the outcomes from their endeavors are significant. They also convince these influential people that there is nothing else that anyone could have done that they did not do and that nothing better could have come out of the initiatives that they undertook.

This phase in the traditional leadership process primarily involves public relations jobs. A traditional leader believes that it is essential to gain broad-based acceptance as a successful leader.

7. Commemoration of the Success. Even though the act of traditional leadership is not considered complete without this finale, not all leaders can gather enough power to get to this step—the last step constituting the traditional leadership process. This involves leaders having their own version of their success, as they would like the coming generations to see it, entered into records during their leadership tenure. It is done through writing about historical events, building monuments, and leaving memoirs or biographies or any other evidence that will stand the test of time.

In traditional organizations, leaders will plan to have themselves decorated for their achievements by recognized professional or other credible bodies. They may also achieve the same goal in other tangible ways, like having their portraits hung on the walls of corporate boardrooms in their organizations. They will attempt to have buildings named after them or display encased prototypes of their successful projects. The leaders' objective is to minimize the probability that anyone in the future who reinterprets the events surrounding their success may dilute their achievements. They idolize their own account of their accomplishments.

Success for a traditional leader is not really complete without giving permanence to the happenings; it is a reflection of facts of the leader's time as seen through his or her own eyes.

KNOWLEDGE ORGANIZATION LEADERSHIP: IT'S A SYMBIOSIS

The traditional model of leadership worked well for operating organizations—typical large corporations of the twentieth century. With knowledge taking the lead, business corporations redefining themselves or winding up their existence after failure, and the twentieth century job concept coming to maturity, the traditional model of leadership is not going to work too far into the twenty-first century for the success of any organization. This will be especially true for knowledge organizations that plan to grow through innovation, in particular those that plan to exploit scientific and technological knowledge in their operations or those that are in the start-up phase of their existence. These knowledge organizations require leaders, and not just leaders schooled in the traditional model. Says Peter Solvik, CIO of Cisco Systems, Inc., "Technical challenges don't tend to be the biggest challenges for companies undergoing an Internet transformation. It tends to be cultural and leadership. Knowledge without strategy, without the leadership, without the direction, without the accountability, leaves you all dressed up with no place to go" (Gollobin and Burke, 1999).

In practice, the traditional model of leadership embraces a style that is egotistic and monopolistic. These leaders succeed through the aggressive and shrewd manipulation of their environment. Nevertheless, the knowledge organization environment is not suited to this style of leadership. Knowledge organization leadership descends from a leader's individual creative initiatives, intellectual preeminence, technical expertise, and unique management abilities that involve everyone in the group, translate into the achievement of each group member's individual goals, and result in the benefit of all connected in the pursuit.

All members of a successful knowledge organization, individually, should have circumstances surrounding their work that will allow them to be leaders in some aspect. Traditional organizations do not need everyone to be a leader. In fact, too many leaders could create chaos in traditional organizations. The leadership model that they employ requires most managers to coordinate and motivate—not lead. Shrewd traditional organization leaders have coined the term "servant leader" to give managers in these organizations a semblance of being leaders, whereas, in practice it amounts to execution and realization of the will of a superior leader—usually, someone at the top who concentrates all the power without sharing.

The need for everyone to be a leader may be true to some extent for other organizations, but it is essential for the success of knowledge organizations. This is because knowledge organizations have employees who possess the desire, requisite skills, and the personality to provide this leadership. Moreover, as we have seen in previous chapters, these are the types of employees who are coming to work from Generations X and Y. The traditional leadership traits that deprived organizations of the talents of those who did not possess these traits have assumed a completely new role in knowledge organizations. The traits that they possess may not make them leaders in the sense that traditional organizations have known in the past, but they will get work done, have others learn from them, and make important contributions in the advancement of their organizations through work from others. Whether they will be leaders in the traditional sense and have followers as traditionally defined will make no difference.

Knowledge Organization Leadership Principles

Embodying the concepts of successful leadership for knowledge organizations, and the understanding of symbiosis, an ideal leadership behavior model for these organizations would be the one that suggests operating knowledge organizations as human symbiosis at work. The following leadership model for these organizations is influenced by the concepts of existence in a symbiosis, as outlined in previous sections and provided in other appropriate sections. If an organization finds that its functioning as an ideal symbiosis is not possible, it may borrow aspects of symbiotic leadership that it finds immediately applicable, apply them, and strive to eventually turn all or some parts of it into pure symbiosis. Even accepting the philosophy of symbiotic management and some initiatives in spreading its application should bring innumerable rewards for it in the form of innovation and higher productivity.

In a symbiosis, in contrast to traditional organizations, the leader power base shifts from the authoritative to the informal. Since knowledge organizations will best function as a symbiosis, leaders should draw a very small part of their power, if any (mainly for initial identification), from formal or legitimate sources. The rest should come from other sources, such as their personal influence, their capability to help others through their expertise, and their ability to win the confidence of those that they are expected to lead. In this organization, a leader's power should not be heavily based on personal charisma. It should lie in the ability to assist those who need to do better in whatever they are doing or want to do or is of importance to them. Moreover, the leader should be able to do this in subtle ways. The addition of subtlety to knowledge organization leadership takes on a special significance and urgency because a large number of Generations X and Y employees may never ask for any help. In fact, many of them will not even let it be known that they need assistance or allow themselves to be consciously led or even know themselves of their need to be led. They may have to be led latently. Knowledge organization leadership should be *incognito leadership*—a system of switching leaders and followers, all in one, without apparent distinctions or even the knowledge as to who the leader is. That is what defines knowledge organization leadership as symbiotic leadership (Amar, 2001).

Principle 1: The "I Did It On My Own" Syndrome. Knowledge organization leadership is conceived of as having a dormant existence. It should always be there, but it should not be visible. It should promptly rise to the occasion to solve a problem and quickly ebb as normalcy returns. Leadership in knowledge organizations should be pulled in by situations in need of leadership and by those who need to be led. In this regard, knowledge organization leadership is in total contrast to the traditional leadership that is pushed down from the "top" through some established hierarchy. The traditional leadership model follows a credo that states, in organizations, everyone has to have a leader—typically, externally assigned and imposed, irrespective of the leader's acceptance or lack thereof by his or her followers. However, a knowledge organization should yield a leader only when someone needs to be led. Followers—knowledge organization employees—turn their supervisors into leaders by vesting in them their acceptance of them as their leaders. It is not vested either by the leaders imposing it on them or by the organization doing it. Instead, knowledge organization employees, when they need to be led, pull in someone as their leader. Knowledge organization leadership comes from the "bottom" in the form of followship. The main long-term objective of knowledge organization leadership is to eliminate followers' dependence on continued leadership. Ideally, it is a leaderless leadership.

Knowledge organization leaders should act very much like a catalyst—both at the physical and psychological levels. At the physical level, a leader works with his followers as any one of their peers will work with them, doing what they are doing and operating in the same environment as they are operating. Such leaders create the structural conditions for future innovation from their followers and then step aside (Mandel, Carney, & Reinhardt, 2000, May 15). At the psychological level, their role is that of a catalyst. The psychological factor is the most essential ingredient of knowledge organization leadership. As a catalyst, a knowledge organization leader should make sure not only that the followers solve all their problems on their own, but that they believe that they solve all their problems *all* on their own—without any help from the leader. This is the knowledge organization leadership principle of the "I did it on my own" syndrome. In this way, leadership becomes symbiotic and operates at a subconscious level. This syndrome will achieve deep-seated learning into the psyche of the followers. This learning will become active selectively, but repeatedly, and only at the right time, and will keep doing so even long after its actual occurrence, without the person knowing that it occurred.

   Principle 2: Virtual Leadership or Leading through Psychological Followship: The Self-Learning Principle. This is a principle of learning how to self-lead in a situation at hand. Accordingly, this leadership is modeled for self-learning or *passive mentoring.* It combines psychological, mental, and metaphysical concepts in its execution. This leadership is especially suited to those who do not want to be led or the person whose leadership they desire is either not available or not willing to lead. Given our understanding from Chapter 2 and Chapter 3 on characteristics of Generations X and Y working in knowledge organizations, this leadership technique could work very well in training and leading them.

   On a psychological level, this leadership works totally in the reverse—it primarily comes from the follower end, sometimes from the follower end only. It is passive and in a passive way, mentoring is received by a "follower" from a "leader" through the process of a follower's mental alertness and concentration. Even though the follower engages in it on a conscious level, the leader does not. Because of the physical and conscious absence of the leader, this leadership is termed *virtual leadership.* In this case, the person who wants to learn—the follower—is trained to impose upon himself or herself an imaginary leadership of someone he or she wants to learn from—*virtual leader.* Not that the virtual leader does not have to be available to provide the leadership, but the leadership may go on without even the knowledge of this leader. The follower formulates this psychological leader-led relationship by the individual. In actuality, it works physically independent of the virtual leader.

   In practice, virtual leadership can be achieved in two steps. First, the follower gets as much information as possible relating to the case on which he or she needs leadership and how, in similar circumstances, the virtual leader provided the leadership. Second, the follower engages in a search for the leadership for the specific situation he or she is facing through connecting the virtual leader's known actions and the situation he is facing by concentration and meditation. He meditates specifically on: "How would the leader advise me to proceed in this case? What would the leader like me to do?" and so on. In this process, the leader contributes merely as an invisible psychological catalyst. This principle of knowledge organization leadership provides an abstraction of a leader, who does function as one in place of a real, physical entity. This person can be any individual. It does not have to be a leader or even an associate of the individual seeking leadership.

Virtual leadership is one way to attain the "I did it on my own" leadership, a learning methodology common with many Generations X and Y members. A knowledge organization should train all knowledge employees to practice this principle to seek leadership at any time, at any location, on any topic, in any situation, and from any leader of their choosing. Specific training sessions to deliver this type of leadership should be designed and practiced.

Without structured training on how to receive virtual leadership, its practice could be very difficult and could result in confusion. If done right, it could result in an efficient and effective mode of learning by leadership. It makes leadership so powerful that any person can seek any other person's leadership without acceptance from that person or contact or knowledge. This turns leadership into a metaphysical relationship with no bonds and no bounds. Simply through a juncture of a specific state of mind and cognition, one can draw upon the leadership of any individual. Through this form of leadership, one can gain guidance and motivation to achieve a goal. Virtual leadership can go beyond what is immediate or real.

Because all learning through psychological followship or virtual leadership is actually self-learning, it is never totally forgotten or unlearned. There will never be a need to seek any further leadership to learn that same skill or ability again, and it could become an unending source of motivation.

Knowledge Organization Leadership Underpinnings

Knowledge organization leadership should be so devised that there are effectively neither leaders nor followers—all operate at the same level as symbionts—coexisting in a symbiosis for mutual benefit. Collectively, they should constitute the organization to which they all belong in proportion to what they contribute to it. The success and prosperity of this organization should not disproportionately benefit the leader or any other member. Further, the level at which a member makes his contribution should be determined by the member himself and no one else.

Because all members are aware that a beneficial outcome for any one member translates into a benefit for all, and vice versa, the purpose of leadership to them is merely to increase the overall benefit for the organization. The sense of mutualism that emerges builds a lasting leader-led relationship.

For the success of knowledge organization leadership, it is essential that the factors underpinning the basis of its working be fully spelled out, clearly understood, and avowed to by all members of the group.

Knowledge Organization Leadership Process

The following seven items combine the leadership principles and characteristics that surround the evolution and development of knowledge organization leadership process and organization. It is understood that these seven items can occur without regard to any specific order. Further, it should be expected that some of the items might not occur at all.

1. Leadership Homeostasis. Leadership in organizational symbiosis is the underlined theme feature of the leadership model recommended for knowledge organizations. The model results in the occurrence and maintenance of leadership homeostasis in the group. Successful implementation of the symbiosis model will make leadership ubiquitous. It will result in a diffused presence of leadership among all members of the group, at all times. Although a strong leader of each group of knowledge workers may not be there, as is the case in a traditional organization, effective leadership will be widely present. Sometimes, in these organizations, there may be no apparent evidence of a leader; nevertheless, the leadership is there—latent but ubiquitous. In knowledge organizations, a specific member assumes leadership of a specific function, or subfunction, that suit his capabilities and the situation's need. Leadership will randomly switch from one member to another within the group and the organization. As this organization emerges and grows, relationships describing distribution of leadership among all members according to the process described above evolve and continue to do so until a homeostasis is achieved. The process of leadership homeostasis in a symbiosis establishes members as strong, undisputed, and effective functional leaders that emerge, as the need for their leadership arises, perform their roles, and dissolve into oblivion until the next time, all in a timely manner.

At the onset of symbiotic coexistence in any knowledge organization, leadership will appear to be in a state of chaos, or even totally absent or ineffective. This should simply be read as the system being in search of a balance in its leadership. The leader has to promote tolerance for ambiguity and chaos and encourage experimentation and responsibility in order for the knowledge organization to be successful (Trowbridge, 2000). While it may appear that the leadership in the knowledge organization is dysfunctional, it is only working its way toward homeostasis. Once the state of leadership homeostasis is achieved, there will be abatement in turbulence, and a state of order will arrive.

As we learned previously, skill variety and dynamism, which are essential to carry out leadership responsibilities in knowledge organizations, make it unlikely for one individual to effectively carry out leadership responsibilities. Assigning an individual as a general, permanent leader for the long-term could prove to be too risky. The system should be capable of quickly searching for a leader and allow for a quick entrance of the new and quick exit of the old. Practice of these leadership concepts ensures continued enhancement of creativity and innovation, the two essential ingredients for success of knowledge organizations, or any organization.

2. Principled Allegiance. An important characteristic of leadership in traditional organizations demands that followers or subordinates give their full, unquestioned, undivided loyalty to their leader. In effect, it amounts to followers pledging loyalty to their leader—in the business world, this translates into the workers giving loyalty to their bosses or managers. The accepted practice is that followers should work to make their leaders successful. The logic behind this edict is that because the leader understands what is good for the organization and works to achieve that, the leader's success will transform into the success of the organization. Organizations strongly reinforced this practice by vesting in traditional leader-managers all powers over their subordinates—including their organizational birth and death, that is, hiring and firing—rather than in any principle or process. It is this absolute concentration of power by the leader that puts loyalty to an individual—the leader—above everyone or everything else. For subordinates, loyalty to their leader takes precedence over ethics, principles, conscience, and even law. The concept of loyalty to the leader is so strongly rooted in the minds of subordinates that they engage in questionable, unethical, and even illegal acts. Many times these acts cover up their superiors' drawbacks, so as to protect them against external harm, help them succeed on their personal ambitions, or even to take a fall for them. There have been notorious cases of subordinates carrying out without question all of their leader's instructions. This is not the leadership practice that makes a knowledge organization successful. In contrast, it may be a formula for the failure of such organizations.

The knowledge organization system, to make the organization more successful, expects and requires every member to play a role in providing leadership for the knowledge organization. To bring the organization to full bloom and allow all employees to use their creativity in a synergistic manner, it is important that they be freed of the yoke of loyalty to any individual or group of managers. Instead, the organization should promote allegiance to something that is more stable, better defined, lucidly understood, and expected to perform more consistently for the good of the organization, such as a constitution, ethics or corporate codes, or just conscience.

3. Lax Encumbrances. With the responsibility of a leadership role in any form—formal or informal—in an innovation organization, such as a knowledge organization, there must come free reins to engage in any actions within the domain defined by one's intent to bring what is good for the organization. The leader should be free of any encumbrance. Knowledge organization leaders are driven only by their focus on outcome—outcome for the good of their organization. Their goal of a determined outcome, because of their decisions and actions, stimulates their energies and keeps them motivated to work toward the fulfillment of this outcome. Moreover, they are energized by the faith they have in their abilities to achieve that result.

There are two things that collectively serve as proxy approval for all actions of these leaders: Their perception of the utility that the outcome will provide for the incarnation of their vision drawn for the good of the organization, and the confidence they have in their abilities to bring about the outcome.

Making these leaders go through an external approval process or imposing permission encumbrances will impede their initiatives, retard innovation, and disserve the organization. The results of their endeavors will provide approval of their leadership for similar initiatives in the future.

4. *Vague Discernment.* Typical symbiotic leaders are functional and ubiquitous in the organization. A knowledge organization should be so designed that all its members function as informal leaders. Additionally, to allow this behavior to continue, it is important that the knowledge organization does not specifically reward or punish its members for their acts as leaders. In retrospect, their deeds should not be labeled successes or failures by the actions they took or the mistakes they made. They should neither be praised for their wisdom nor reprimanded for the mistakes that occurred as a result of their leadership pursuits. The leadership acts themselves should allow a leader to self-reward and self-punish. No individual should have the responsibility to reward or punish the leaders. In case they fail, they should know immediately and exactly where, why, and how they failed from the job they did and not from any individual. They should automatically become aware of their weaknesses so that, in the future, they can undertake responsibilities or endeavors similar to those that failed when they overcome the particular weaknesses that caused the failures in the past. Cues offered on their failure or weaknesses by any other individual will delay self-learning and modification. An externally administered reprimand can destroy their initiative permanently and convey a sense of discouragement to other members who are considering undertaking such ambitions in the future. Reprimands have the potential to annihilate the knowledge organization. There is a greater probability of harm than good from external reviews of knowledge organization leadership behavior.

It should be clearly accepted that knowledge organization leaders are driven by the reward they give to themselves for their successes and, similarly, are deterred by punishments they inflict on themselves for their failures. These rewards and punishments should be designed to be intrinsic. The effectiveness of rewards and punishments in controlling the leaders' behavior is far stronger than their extrinsic equivalents.

In a knowledge organization where symbiotic leadership is practiced as outlined above, eventually, success will breed success. Moreover, failure will act as a motivator for the symbiosis members to try again and succeed next time.

5. *Internalizer Behavior.* Because of the environment in which knowledge organizations operate, the leadership function should be designed to operate intrinsically. To be effective and independent, a knowledge organization leader should always have internal control orientation. Because knowledge organization leadership is an outcome of the members' individual initiatives and time, it is natural for knowledge organization leaders to always maintain a strictly internal locus of control. They should never hold others responsible

for anything that goes wrong because of their leadership initiatives. They are in full charge of the affairs of their group. Although other members of the group could have been involved in and contributed to the leader's errors, knowledge organization leaders understand that they alone had the recourse to correct or avoid errors.

Leaders with external locus of control in a knowledge organization will always feel helpless and frustrated. Under the circumstances, it will be hard for this type of leader to be effective.

6. *Apolitical Relationship.* Just as knowledge organizations should not obviously identify leaders as is done in traditional organizations, they should also not obviously identify followers. Knowledge organization leaders should not deliberately make decisions or act simply to create new followers or win the confidence of their current followers. All activities undertaken by the leaders in a knowledge organization for the primary purpose of recruiting, appeasing, or pleasing followers to bring them into the fold are wasteful, antiproductive, and antithetical to the concept of knowledge organizations. The mutualism emerging from the leaders' focus on the goal, their ability to accomplish it, and the followers' valence for the reward from its accomplishment act as the forces pulling followers to the leaders. This is how knowledge organization leaders build coalition to achieve organizational goals. This binds them together in a transient relationship. Followers flock into the newly defined relationship but only for the duration essential to accomplish the goal. In addition, as a consequence of defining the characteristics of knowledge organizations, both followers and leaders cease to continue the relationship as soon as the particular goal is achieved. At that time, a new relationship redefining their coexistence evolves.

7. *Environmental Instrumentality.* Knowledge organizations facilitate a work environment that becomes an instrument for knowledge organization leadership. Knowledge organization management should create the right structural conditions to let any member be a leader and then to step aside. It gives any member of the knowledge organization the ability to function as a leader without the necessity of external empowerment through a title, an office, an appointment, an authority figure, or even a forum or a platform. These organizations should manifest the environment that enables all knowledge workers in their organizations to function and be effective as a leader. A knowledge organization environment should be malleable enough for the leaders to mold and manipulate it so they can contribute as leaders.

A knowledge organization should be designed so that its members do not need a leadership position to function as leaders. Leadership initiatives should be feasible for anyone from anywhere in the organizational hierarchy, without having to wait for an approval, opportune time, or circumstance. The design should permit any knowledge worker to recognize a leadership opportunity, grab it, and take center stage through his or her deeds or create an opportunity that exploits his or her skills. A knowledge organization postulates that, to be able to contribute as a leader, one should not have to have technical or professional expertise, credentials, or any specialized education.

Knowledge Organization Leadership Power Base

The leadership power concept recommended for knowledge organizations follows the principle that the work environment should be such that, for any member to function as a leader, there should be no need for authority from an appointment or a title. Unlike leaders in traditional organizations, these leaders should not need legitimate power to "push" their resolves on their subordinates or followers. This leadership power should come from the "pull" of the led. As has been stated previously, knowledge organization leaders function on power bestowed on them by their followers—the influence they enjoy comes from the followers themselves. The leader does not take it—followers give it to the leader.

Knowledge organization leadership should not commence with an induction of power, which is typically endowed by some source external to the leader-led relationship. Knowledge organization leadership power is deliberately designed to avoid the use of such a power base, because this needs veneered authority to safeguard its scope, magnitude, and duration.

Instead, leaders of knowledge organizations should derive their power from the following sources. They should harness power from as many sources as possible and shift their main power base depending on the situational factors.

Uniquity Power. Typical knowledge organization leaders operate on their personal power. Even in cases where leadership initiation is derived through legitimate sources, the leader quickly shifts it to personal power before transacting any meaningful business. All members of knowledge organizations should be encouraged to enhance their personal power base by increasing the intensity of some or all components that contribute to this power base, such as expertise—professional, technical, or work—and personality, especially behavioral. The homeostasis in knowledge organization leadership will sharpen individual expertise to the point of one becoming uniquely qualified to lead the rest of the members in one area—*uniquity.* Uniquity gives an individual immense power over others. The goal of leadership in knowledge organizations is to have each member enjoy this power. A knowledge organization attains this state when everyone in the organization accepts the same person as leader in one particular functional area, such that each member in the organization becomes a unique expert and all functional areas are collectively covered within the organization. Depending on the size of a knowledge organization, this function may continue to be broken down into smaller, more specialized areas, such as subspecialties.

The purpose of willful obscurity in knowledge organizational leadership is to attain a homeostasis that, as we learned earlier, allows leadership to rest with any member for only as long as the system needs his or her expertise and then quickly shift it away to another member who can best handle the new problem. In this way, knowledge organization leadership operation results in a culmination of group expertise such that each of its members develops a unique specialized expertise, or symbiotic *uniquity*. All members are offered an opportunity to individually develop and continuously update a specialized expertise of their liking within the group constraints and thereby naturally evolve leadership responsibilities in a unique way without any gaps and overlaps. Every member becomes an unfettered leader in some aspect. Uniquity builds a power base that is very hard to challenge and allows for quick acceptance from others who may become followers. It is perhaps the biggest source of knowledge organization leadership power.

Ethics Power. All through time, in every culture, codes of ideal and moral behavior have emphasized loyalty to the system, organization, and establishment and its causes. The practice of ethics has supported leaders' positions and has strengthened their power to influence their followers' behavior. In fact, organizations can allow their leaders a greater control over their behavior by making them accept codes of ethics as a standard of organizational behavior. A leader should be able to augment his power through one's personal emphasis on ethical behavior—through precept and practice. In general, a leader becomes a model of behavior for the followers, and good leaders immensely succeed in making their followers emulate them. In particular, because knowledge organizations heavily rely on their leaders' personal power and because leaders and members switch roles frequently, ethics codes impact behavior in knowledge organizations more than they do in other traditional organizational designs. Leaders should be ethical for followers to be ethical. If leaders use a sword, their followers will soon learn to use a sword. Moreover, sooner than later, there will definitely be one follower who will learn to use it even better than the leader and will bring an end to the leadership and also the leader. It has happened repeatedly throughout human history.

Ethics has the effect of transforming leaders' legal authority into personal power—a kind of pseudocharisma. History tells us that insurrections against leaders succeeded only in organizations where there was an absence of ethics. An analysis of these happenings will tell us that a lack of ethical behavior diluted the leader's power and relinquished followers of their expected behavior toward the leader, thus rationalizing their revolt against the leader or the system.

Spiritual Power. An inscription at Harvard Law School reads: "*Non sub homine sed sub deo at edge.*" Translated, this Latin phrase means, "It is not by men but by God and the law [that we are governed]" (Reid, 1997). This ancient Roman quotation provides a source of power that can be exerted to model human conduct. Such modeling is common in many social associations, both in obligatory relationships, such as marriage and family, and in voluntary relationships, such as friendship. A spiritual power base is effectively used to lead people to stronger, healthier human bonds and exemplary behavior. (This is not a subject germane to this work and hence is left out. Interested readers may refer to other more appropriate books on this topic.)

Since the 1980s, most organizations have started to dictate work behavior through rules in the form of codes of conduct, employee handbooks, and guides, and there is an absence of effort in using spirituality in guiding human conduct. Leaders are not tapping into a spiritual power base for defining, establishing, and modeling human relationships in a work setting. The reason is the lack of research on how to harness this force for managing human conduct in organizations. An effective use of symbols, such as signs and images, and spirit, through confidence in faith, can build motivation in employees. Some examples of how to harness spiritual power come from the use of religious symbols. However, to avoid their use by some employees from offending some other employees, organizations will have to limit the use of religious symbols to a personal and private level.

Adaptation of this practice may be explored in organizations, since open practice of any spiritual concept is not going to be acceptable to American business. Knowledge organizations may adapt some subtle signs that, to members of the knowledge team, have certain meanings that lift up their spirits and give them the courage to move on in hard times. Examples depicting use of spiritual power could be in many forms, such as organizational involvement in celebration of religious holidays, company-sponsored volunteering at certain spiritual houses, and appearances at churches and temples by some leaders when other members of the knowledge team are present. We have observed a number of investment bankers commenting on spiritualism during the slow economic periods. Hospitals and church-affiliated institutions use the spiritual power in symbols to motivate employees to work and the sick to get better.

Knowledge managers should use spiritual power as a reserve or backup for when other powers fail. One of the tasks of a successful leader is to provide motivation in the face of failure and despondency, and the energy to continue on a seemingly unending organizational pursuit in spite of the failures, which may be more important for a knowledge organization than for traditional ones. The spiritual philosophy may help explain the positive side of a failure and provide the leader with a source of power at a very crucial time. Unfortunately, a lack of research on this topic leaves it up to leaders to arrive at unique ways to harness this force.

DEVELOPING KNOWLEDGE ORGANIZATION LEADERSHIP

Performance as a leader in knowledge organizations does not depend on the presence of traditional leadership traits. Knowledge organization leadership is harnessed and exercised purely through a behavioral process. This leadership behavior can be learned and perfected through training and the practice of a number of personal and behavioral characteristics. Most of these can be acquired or self-taught by a vigilant manager who is committed to gaining innovation and productivity in knowledge organizations through the flourishing of the human mind.

Knowledge organization leadership development should be based in mutualism and conceived as a dyadic relationship. It should be custom-designed to suit the partners in it—the leader and the led—and the needs of the organization. A few factors that may be considered in developing this relationship are given below.

Antitraditional Leader Traits

An important trait of the knowledge organization leader is an absence of the traits that are traditionally accepted as the essential ones for leadership, such as drive, tenacity, toughness, confidence, or cognitive ability. Their presence in the leader could be sufficiently intimidating to other members and would bring about obliteration of creativity and decimation of productivity. The leader could become an overpowering colossus who could make others inert and passive followers—a principle that is antithetical to the basis of knowledge work. If a leader naturally demonstrates a strong presence of these traits, he or she should be offered counseling and training to engage in behavior modification that would subdue and help unlearn these traits. This is how everyone in the organization can help increase organizational effectiveness. Knowledge organization leadership operates subtly and subliminally, not flamboyantly and deliberately, as does traditional leadership.

Traditional leadership traits could actually counteract the goals of knowledge organization leadership, such as the rotational, subfunctional, or ubiquitous leaderships. For example, one traditional leadership trait, a high intelligence quotient, could actually be detrimental if other members in the group do not possess it. Intelligence, like many other traits, is not something one controls. One can have control over skill and knowledge, not intelligence. Design and structure of the knowledge organization is based on employees' efficacy and sufficiency, not frustration and helplessness.

Mirror Followers' Personality

It is essential for the success of the knowledge organization that, as far as possible, its leader be exactly like the members in the group that he or she is to lead. A strong congruence between the leader and the led is very essential because that is the only way a knowledge organization leader will gain the requisite confidence of one's group and the ability to communicate effectively. Through this congruence, the leader will gain instant acceptance from the peer group and will also facilitate a quick exit from the leadership role—a necessity of knowledge organization leadership. A knowledge organization leader must be one of the members of the group. He or she should be able to function on their level in all aspects. He or she should practice the same colloquialisms and mannerisms and even espouse the same thought processes and philosophy as the rest of the group does.

In general, knowledge organization leaders should, in a subtle way, be better at doing whatever members of their groups do—preferably in every aspect relating both to work and leisure. At the minimum, they should be better at that aspect or function on which they are expected to lead the team. In practice, this is achieved by the symbiotic model of leadership that allows innumerable switches from one member to another, since it is not possible for one person to be better at every aspect of the knowledge in a group. For example, if one becomes a Web design team leader, he should be able to do better at all aspects of Web design than anyone else on the team. As soon as someone else on the team can do better, the knowledge organization system should replace him.

A corollary to this principle will recommend elimination of segregating the workers from managers/administrators or officers. This concept rejects the traditional organization leadership assignment practice that makes entry into management ranks from among workers very difficult. In such organizations, there are usually two parallel entry and advancement systems. Thus, a knowledge organization selects its members so that everyone who has skills and potential is able to serve as a leader. A knowledge organization leadership model reserves its leadership role for only those who have mastered the general and specifics of the job and have proved their excellence to their peer group. The result will be the most innovative and best productivity enhancement in the organization. To keep members motivated, knowledge organizations should not ordinarily allow nominal leadership positions to be filled laterally from outside the organization. This principle prescribes only one entry to a leadership position and only one channel to move up the administrative ranks. The practice is meant to build confidence and self-efficacy and to send similar messages through these actions to all ordinary members of the knowledge organizations. It should have little practical implication since these organizations have a flat structure.

Learn to Follow

Knowledge organization leadership and followership should be intertwined, inseparable functions. The ideal leader behavior that promotes an innovation environment is identical to the ideal follower behavior to promote innovation. This is because these roles can, and should, swiftly change—shifting responsibility to someone else in the organization: *rotational leadership*. This makes it essential for the leader to be a good follower. A person who cannot follow will not be able to lead a knowledge organization because these members learn through mimicking their leaders' behavior. Knowledge team members learn to follow from their leader. It is through the demonstration of his ability to follow others that a knowledge organization leader develops a symbiotic relationship with his followers.

Even traditional leadership recognizes that no leader can succeed without a serious commitment from followers—followers who give their undivided faith to the leader. Switching roles from follower to leader and vice versa increases empathy for the leader and increases the odds for the success of the endeavor. In preparation for knowledge organization leadership, Japanese schools teach their students followership and leadership as two integrated facets. Students, on a rotational basis, are allowed to act as class "monitors," a position of leadership that permits a student to overtake the routines of a teacher while the teacher is present (Kristof, 1997, August 17). The rotational nature of the role teaches the students not just how to lead but also how to follow. Knowledge organization leadership is successful because of ubiquity; just as it does not allow any member to be a leader longer than the least time essential to accomplish the task, it does not allow any member to be a follower longer than the least time essential.

Follower Vision Development and Realization

Rather than developing, communicating, selling, or working to realize their own vision for the organization as traditional leaders do, knowledge organization leaders work to help members develop and incarnate their vision for the organization. That is how knowledge organization leaders exploit talent and tap into the creativity of Generation X and Y members in the workplace. In the absence of a vision from the followers, knowledge organization leaders should consider it their responsibility to lead them to the formulation of a vision. They should make their followers understand their own environment, the presented problem and opportunity interrelationship, and visualization of the future. To help make the knowledge organization's future clearer to the followers, the leader may develop a strategic plan that includes a knowledge organization strategy, a 12- to 18-month knowledge organization roadmap, with an emphasis among senior management on generating a competitive advantage (Trowbridge, 2000). This is how knowledge organization leaders help their followers construct a vision for themselves and the organization. Since the success of realizing this vision will lead to the success of the group and the organization, the leader then facilitates its realization.

In case of a lack of congruence between the vision drafted by the leader and the one drafted by the follower, knowledge organization leadership should allow the follower's vision to take precedence over the leader's vision. In the knowledge organization environment, where the follower's confidence and assured behavior are considered essential for innovation, there is less to be lost by permitting a presumably "unfit" vision of a follower than external imposition of a vision by his or her leader.

Ability to Proffer

As we know, members of Generations X and Y have a unique work characteristic that knowledge organization leaders should know of when leading them, that is, members of these generations do not ask for help. Sometimes, indeed, they may not even be aware that they need help. While a sufficient number of traditional employees also reflect a similar behavior, the number of employees with this characteristic is much higher in knowledge organizations. In the future, with the new Generations X and Y members in control of the workplace, this number will increase greatly enough to force managers to set their general leadership style based on this behavior.

The first knowledge organization leadership quality this new behavior will require from managers is their ability to volunteer—volunteer assistance to employees in a latent, subdued way, with the goal to not let them know that they needed or were given assistance. Knowledge organization leaders should not forget that the motto of their leadership is to let each follower believe that "I did it on my own." To make this work, a knowledge organization leader has to build close dyadic bonds with the followers and become trustworthy enough for them to open and be willing to accept the leader's help. The leadership task will start with making them learn how to develop a focus, then bring them to a point where they will be able to assess what they have and what else they need to achieve their goals. The center of the leader's effort should be the individual employee, not the group or the organization. This will require leaders to spend most of their time with their followers doing the same things as they do. Knowledge organization leadership is not about being a leader; it is about working with followers.

While it may seem that knowledge organization leadership practice reduces the leader's span of control and may increase the burden on the organization, in actuality, it results in a more effective organization and more job-efficient leadership. The organization becomes more effective because of the reduced number of followers per leader, and more efficient because the time spent in providing leadership per follower is very low so the leader has time to produce output like a worker. With the passage of time, knowledge organization leadership will continue to become more effective and more efficient. As stated earlier, the aim of knowledge organization leadership is to sever the umbilical cord between the leader and the led.

Shared Pleasure

Generations X and Y members are guided by what is being termed the Third Law of Social Motion, which states that action and reaction are equal and opposite. Its implication in knowledge organization leadership suggests that the amount of force leaders use against their led will get from them the same amount of opposing force. Most likely, it will not come in the same form and may not come at the same instant in which the leader applies his or her force, but it will come. Moreover, as harmful to innovation would be the reaction force; exactly as harmful would be the force that the leader uses, since as we know, knowledge work is not a product of force.

In knowledge organizations, success achieved through the use of pressure is illusory and short-lived. Innovation thrives on pleasure that the relationship and the process of leadership brings to both the leader and the led. The relationship has to be exciting to both of them. If it does not bring both the intended fun, the relationship should be abandoned. Employing fighting forces to impose the relationship will hinder innovation. This result will have a special significance when dealing with Generation X and Y members. Knowledge organization leadership envisions a leader-led relationship as a natural consequence of mutualism. The relationship should bring benefit to both, and this has to be overtly understood by both. The relationship is not forced on anyone. The leadership process must ensure that everyone is free to get out of this relationship without any encumbrances. It should be, indeed, a voluntary relationship. Both sides should focus on how to make the relationship more beneficial and pleasurable to the other party.

Leadership of knowledge organizations is very different from the twentieth-century leadership that derived its mandate and authority from organizational hierarchy. In contrast, a knowledge organization leader helps his workers achieve their goals and draw on his authority from their success at making them achieve their goals. Knowledge organization leadership is specific for employees from the new generations working in knowledge organizations where success comes through innovation and growth through productivity.

REFERENCES

Amar, A.D. (2001). Leading for innovation through symbiosis. *European Journal of Innovation Management, 4*(2).
Argyris, C. (1955, June). Some characteristics of successful executives. *Personnel Journal*, 50–63.
Bennis, W. (2000). Defining moments. *Executive Excellence, 17*(4), 8.
Gollobin, K., & Burke, S. (1999, December 20–27). Dragging customers into knowledge organization. *Computer Reseller News, 874*, 6–7.
Kristof, N.D. (1997, August 17). Where children rule. *New York Times Magazine*, pp. 40–44, Section 6.

Mandel, M.J., Carney, D., & Reinhardt, R. (2000, May 15). Antitrust or the digital age. *Business Week*, pp. 48–49.

Mayo, E. (1945). *The social problems of industrial civilization*. Boston, MA: Harvard University Press.

Reid, T.R. (1997, August). The world according to Rome. *National Geographic*, pp. 55–83.

Renesch, J. (1996). *The new leader: Bringing creativity and innovation to the workplace*. Boca Raton, FL: CRC Press.

Roethlisberger, F.J., & Dickson, W.J. (1939). *Management and the worker*. Cambridge, MA: Harvard University Press.

Trowbridge, D. (2000, January). Knowledge organization success rests on four pillars of wisdom? Or folly? *Computer Knowledge Review, 20*(1), 1, 14+.

Zemke, R., Raines, C., & Filipczak, B. (1999). *Generations at work: Managing the clash of Veterans, Boomers, X'ers, Nexters in your work place*. New York: AMACOM.

Keeping Them Going: Motivation in Knowledge Environment

"It's like, 'I haven't done it before but I want to do it right away,'" says Susan Portony, a publicist in New York, describing how motivated and ambitious are Generation Y members as employees (Mui, 2001). However, at the same time, she observes that they are very impatient. Further, they say they want to make a six-figure salary in six months and have vacation time accrue in nanoseconds (Mui, 2001).

Obviously, Generation Y members are not like past generations and in some aspects not even like the early Gen Xers. Behavior modification and motivation processes of these generations are quite different from each other. Managers who have experience with Baby Boomers and early Gen Xers may have to refresh their motivation skills. In this regard, they should also know that in many respects the reward system and behavior modification processes overlap because the reward system in itself is a method of behavior modification. While going over this chapter, it is important to cover both these topics. Chapters 3 and 9 cover these topics and serve as an adjunct to each other.

Because they need the skills and knowledge of Generations X and Y members, it is important for managers of knowledge organizations to know how to motivate their Gen Xer and Generation Y employees. They should know if the traditional reward theory will or will not work. Moreover, they have to know what to do if traditional theories of motivation do not work. This chapter addresses these questions. It starts out with traditional rewards theory and suggests principles guiding the use of reward to keep knowledge employees productive; examples of rewards are also provided. Of particular importance is the use of money as a motivator in knowledge organizations. The chapter stresses the importance of transparency in reward distribution as a means to de facto shift administration of rewards from managers and the organization to employees.

In spite of offering multimillion dollar options designed to attract and retain qualified employees, knowledge organizations in the technology sector, like Yahoo and Netscape, are failing miserably. They are losing employees—many times not to another employer but to the dreams that the employees have. Why should anyone be surprised? Knowledge organizations are places to dream and where, employees' experience has shown them, all dreams come true. To them, knowledge organizations themselves are examples of the fulfillment of dreams. Many employees join them to learn how to dream and realize these dreams. There should be no surprise when one reads stories, such as the one in *The New York Times Magazine*, describing how a number of young employees in these and other companies quit to form their own company, Epinion.com, to pursue their vision. They did not want to wait for their options to mature (Bronson, 1999).

Organizations can design attractive jobs. The question is can they design dreams. Employees that make knowledge organizations successful are visionaries, dreamers. They may be weird or borderline crazy, and the organizations will have to accept them to keep them motivated to innovate and produce. Successful knowledge organizations are designing dreams, and others will have to do that uniquely and ingeniously to attract and retain employees. Founders and officers of these organizations should recall their own dreams and use them as metaphors in framing strategies to motivate employees.

We know that a large number of current and potential employees of knowledge organizations belong to Generations X and Y. Moreover, even those employees who do not belong to these generations reflect a work behavior that they learned from the successful maneuvers of these two generations. Motivation theories commonly designed and tested for use in traditional organizations may not apply to them. Their personalities have been formed during the 1970s and 1980s when the rules governing business management were being rewritten—for the corporation. These generations shrewdly watched how business treated past generations and they thought out and modeled their own behavior for dealing smartly with employers. They have learned new lessons. No knowledge organization will be able to motivate Generations X and Y employees by using reward strategies, such as wages, job security, and benefits, the way traditional organizations did to motivate their parents. A study by professors in the management and marketing departments at Christopher Newport University (VA) suggests that organizations expand their repertoire of rewards to include nonfinancial incentives, such as work/life benefits, training opportunities, and flexible work schedules (Karp, Sirias, and Arnold, 1999). More recently, a number of knowledge organizations have added parent and elderly care to the list of benefits they are offering their employees. Then there are others who are providing employees home cleaning services, laundry services, and even grocery shopping services. This begins an evolution of new rules in employment in general and on motivating and rewarding desirable behavior at jobs in knowledge organizations in particular.

Rather than employers continuing to devise tactics to force employees out as in traditional organizations, Generations X and Y employees in knowledge organizations are expediting the extinction of their jobs, as we have known, to their benefit. The biggest challenge for knowledge organizations is to devise strategies to keep employees in their jobs. Their employees are taking every job as a transition to something else. They may not give their best for just the reward of a paycheck. They will hold back their skills, loyalties, and initiatives. They will behave like monopolists—in no hurry to cut deals. They will transact their skills, loyalties, and initiatives only if they get the right price—their asking price.

THEORY OF REWARD AND KNOWLEDGE WORK BEHAVIOR

Reward Fundamentals

The basic theory of rewarding acceptable behavior in traditional organizations is derived from observing animal behavior. Psychologists established, and these organizations agreed, that if animals were presented with something that they found pleasant when they reflected a desired behavior, they tended to repeat that behavior in hope of receiving that pleasant feeling again. The big assumption in its transference from animals to employees in traditional organizations is that because it worked for animals it will work to get the best from adult, rational humans. The practice of rewarding desired behavior from employees started without proving that the underlining conditions that held true for animals will hold true for humans.

In spite of the lack of research supporting validity of this reward theory for humans, for the most part, the practice described above worked to motivate and modify employee behavior in traditional organizations, especially employees within certain sociopsychological environments.

Despite full or conditional success of this reward theory to motivate employees in traditional organizations, relying on it to help create a work environment conducive to innovation in knowledge organizations is too presumptuous. Given the intellectual level of knowledge employees, its use as a real motivator will be too simplistic. Typical knowledge employees associate traditional reward administration with a tool for extracting desired work behavior through manipulation and with an action that lacks maturity. Gen Xers and Generation Y members connect this practice to motivate them with one of their early exposures to reward—the one that they experienced at their pediatrician's or dentist's office, or from their nursery school teacher.

Reward Principles for Knowledge Organizations

Share in Success—and in Failure. Until the 1980s, when it came to sharing in their firm's success or failure, executives at the topmost levels of American corporations behaved like monopolists. They kept all the rewards for themselves. During the 1980s, this behavior started to proliferate to levels below that of the top executive's. Nevertheless, in most traditional corporations, success, failure, reward, and punishment trickled down from the top two, three, four, or five levels of the hierarchy and then stopped. For employees working at any level in a knowledge organization, this is a standard way to reward performance—good or bad. Reward is good for good performance and bad for bad performance. Knowledge organizations that accept this notion, quickly adapt to the new reality and devise and negotiate a reward and punishment system with all their employees that will attract, retain, and motivate workers of the highest caliber. Those organizations that decide to fight this reality by sticking to a traditional reward system will harm the organization and will waste their energies confronting and repelling those who would genuinely want to "share" their abilities in making the organization succeed. Knowledge organizations that do not share the fruits of their organizational successes and the consequences of their failures with all employees will suffer setbacks in innovation and productivity because the practice causes disengagement.

The medium that a knowledge organization uses to divide its outcomes with its employees is less important; what is of prime importance is that *everyone* associated with it should have a part in it. The greater the reliance employees have on this reward, the greater will be their effort in devising innovative ways to enhance performance of the knowledge organization. As a preference, the guaranteed part of their compensation should be close to their subsistence needs.

Reinvent the Reward System: Rewards Á *Priori*

There is another feature of the reward process employed in traditional organizations that hinders efficient working of knowledge organizations. These organizations should understand the concept of rewards a posteriori and rewards *á priori* as given below. In knowledge organizations, the reward system most likely to produce the desired effect will come from rewards that are administered *á priori*.

Typically, rewards in traditional organizations are administered *á posteriori*, that is, they are given for a previously exhibited desired behavior. The practice is founded in the *belief* that rewarding occurrence of a desired behavior of the past will encourage employees to reflect the same behavior in the future *and* that they will continue to value that reward with the same valence and intensity. Success of this linkage is dependent on following four assumptions.

1. The first assumption states that the same set of conditions for which rewarded behavior was the appropriate behavior will continue to occur in the future.

2. Moreover, given that these conditions do indeed recur, it is assumed that appropriate behavior under these same conditions will still be the behavior that was reinforced through the reward.

3. Third, employees perfectly, positively correlate reflection of the same behavior with occurrence of the same reward in the future.

4. Fourth, at their will, employees will actually be able to reflect that behavior in the future.

If these conditions are validly applied in designing a reward system for practice in traditional organizations, they could be quite useful. However, the story is different in knowledge organizations. The first two of these four assumptions are too presumptuous to be applied to knowledge organizations because most employees and employers do not precisely know the behavior that is rewardable. When either employees or employers do not have a past, what should employers like to have replicated? Given the complexity and uncertainty of the knowledge organizations' future, this practice of rewarding behavior will be too risky a way to manage them. The third assumption is antithetical to the concept of reward. If a reward system does in fact operate consistently with this assumption, then it will defeat the basic purpose expected from reward. The fourth assumption is very unlikely to take hold in knowledge organizations because it involves too many events that will almost never simultaneously occur enabling employees to replicate rewarded behavior. It is these weaknesses of *á posteriori* rewards, as they are currently being administered in traditional organizations, that makes them ineffective in ensuring repetition of the desired behavior among employees.

The better use of reward in eliciting desired behavior from knowledge workers who are intelligent, rational, mature adults is to administer the reward in anticipation of the outcome—*á priori* to the reflection of a desired behavior. *Á priori* rewards will *pull* knowledge employees toward appropriate behavior. They may feel in control of the events surrounding the desired outcome. It will be especially potent because uncertainty, as is common in knowledge organizations, is so great that no one may know what behavior is the desired behavior. The basic premise of these rewards is to psych-up the performer to successfully select and reflect a behavior appropriate for the conditions that may occur in the turbulent environments of these organizations. *Á priori* rewards are likely to work at the subconscious level and make the employee exhibit the best behavior one can possibly give. It changes the basis of the reward process in knowledge organizations from being manipulative to one that conveys the employer's commitment to have the employee reflecting desired behavior.

These anticipatory rewards work far better than traditionally administered rewards—posthumously to the reflection of a desired behavior.

Examples of *Á Priori* Rewards

A number of organizations are already making use of *á priori* rewards for their top executives. Traditionally, these rewards have names such as investiture, inauguration, invocation, initiation, induction, and so forth. An offering of stock options to come on board is also an example of such a reward. Many Wall Street firms have engaged in *á priori* rewards by offering their incoming employees sign-up bonuses, relocation purses, nonrepayable loans, and other unique incentives to get them started. An intense, well-publicized selection process, well-publicized charge, and visible assignments can also work as *á priori* rewards. All rewards that make a person feel important and special through the exhibition of a certain behavior *before* the behavior is performed will be *á priori* rewards. These rewards are effective for all employees at all levels of knowledge organizations just as they have been effective for those at the top in traditional organizations. Industrial psychologists and human resource managers can design specific *á priori* rewards for their knowledge organizations based on the principles we have discussed here.

One of the biggest accounting firms in the world, Ernst and Young, engages in *á priori* rewards by notifying employees in advance of the rewards that are available by completing a certain assignment within defined constraints.

As a first step in implementing an *á priori* rewards system, a firm should clearly define the objectives to be achieved through the completion of a task. Then, the firm should clarify how the employee doing the job can control its execution through efficiently operating within the constraints given by the objectives. Thirdly, the firm should establish the rewards, and announce it to the employee. Two well-understood objectives are cost and schedule. For a reduction in cost, there should be a reward, and for completion before the deadline, there should be another reward.

INNOVATIVE REWARDS

Sociological Rewards

Sociology has always been important in all organizations for understanding human behavior. In fact, an individual's physiology, sociology, and psychology are interdependent and play an important role in successful human functioning at work. Understanding the sociology of workers has taken on a special meaning in knowledge organizations because its line employees are, and will be so more predominantly in the future, products of the changes that have occurred in society in the last few decades. We cannot learn management of knowledge organizations without being aware of sociological implications.

It is instinctive in people to want to be loved, liked, and admired. This is one evident weakness in all humans but even more so in Gen Xers and Generation Y members. They go to great lengths to engage in activities that will result in getting love and admiration from special people in their lives. This observation can be applied as a motivation tool in knowledge organizations. Selective sociology can function like a reward, just like any other material reward. In fact, love, liking, and admiration could even be potent rewards in knowledge organizations, because they enhance buoyancy in the human spirit, which frees human intellect and gives birth to innovation. The Internet retailer Amazon.com holds periodic mask and costume parties, allowing employees to mingle freely with those whom they admire. To some employees, these rewards have such a great importance that they would be willing to trade other tangible outcomes, like money, to attain these rewards. People seek appreciation—especially public appreciation—for work well done. Managers can exploit this type of recognition, done in front of those whose relationships these employees value.

To use sociology as a reward, a manager has to know that both love and admiration are transitive. One cannot complete the transaction of love by oneself. This belongs in a group of rewards that motivation psychologists call "extrinsic"—controlled externally. Someone has to give this reward. One cannot get it by oneself. To administer these rewards, a knowledge organization manager should first understand the sociology of each employee and, then, combine it with each worker's psychology and design specific sociological rewards applicable to each one. First-line managers do it best.

Examples of Sociological Rewards

Reward of Affiliation. A reward of affiliation is one of the most common sociological rewards in nature and can be rather easily administered.

Let us understand the sociological revolution that has occurred during the upbringing of Gen Xers and Generation Y, the big part of knowledge organizations' present and future workforce. During this period, the value system that defined the structure of and roles in a traditional family were tossed out. In fact, the definition of the word "family" itself was rewritten. More than one-third of Generation Y has been brought up, at least for some time, in a household headed by a single parent. Many of them have spent more time with their babysitters or friends than with their parents or siblings. To a large number of them, first-order biological relationships may not be as important as are the voluntarily established sociological relationships or other affiliations that they have formed. Many have not even had a sibling. In the first decade of the next century, human sociology and relationships will become even more complicated. We will have a substantial number of knowledge employees that may not know two parents. Many may not even know who their other parent is, and some will be brought up by parents of the same gender.

This evolving sociology is making relationships that knowledge employees develop at work very important to them—the equivalent of parents and siblings. Similar to the way the second half of the twentieth century diminished the role of extended family in human development, the role of the nuclear family will be substantially reduced during the twenty-first century. Managers should make use of this knowledge for effectively using rewards to encourage desired behavior from their employees. Letting knowledge employees form their own work groups, work with people whom they like, and switch groups or partners or colleagues as and when they please will make for stronger rewards than other material rewards that are extrinsically administered. Gen Xers and Generation Y members will continue to work at lower wages simply because they like working with the people there.

Recognition Rewards: Eliminate the Dead End

During the 1980s and 1990s, managers have used recognition in different forms to reward requisite behavior on the part of their employees. The premise on which these rewards are based is that if employees are made to feel important, they will act accordingly and continue to be productive for their organization. Recognition should give an employee all the tools and environment essential for success: visibility, prestige, personal pride, and self-esteem. Most organizational attempts utilize recognition rewards that are rare, limited, insignificant, ends-in-themselves, and primarily designed for employees at certain levels. Some examples of these rewards are a temporary special parking spot, an employee-of-the-month award, a spotlight in a company newsletter, a service pin, a certificate of recognition, a plaque, or a trophy. In an effort to give these rewards their due importance, some organizations create euphoric excitement and nostalgia such as at the Oscar Awards organized by the National Academy of Motion Picture Arts and Sciences (Amar, 1994).

Like other rewards, recognition, to be effective, has to be timely, relevant, fair, and make all employees feel in control of the criteria of the rewards—both those who win the recognition and those who do not. Those who do not win must be excited about winning in the future. One such rather criticized reward—the service pin—effectively satisfies these conditions. Since it is simply recognition for time with the organization, it makes the criteria clear and puts everyone in control of achieving this recognition. The flaw with this recognition, as with most others, is that it is a dead-end reward. The worth of these rewards stops at their inherent value. If the "10-Year Pin" awarded to the employee does not convert into something more tangible, it is not likely to be very effective in motivating knowledge employees.

The military and other uniformed services use another example of successful recognition. Meaningful rewards are derived through wearing uniforms, insignias, and decorations. These rewards symbolize something substantial. They are not dead-end rewards. Not only do they signify a certain statutory recognition, they also translate into higher salary, benefits, and increased authority. Other examples of successful rewards, that are not dead-end rewards, are winning the Nobel Prize, an Olympic medal, the Oscar, the Pulitzer Prize, and other performing arts awards and beauty pageants. They go beyond the value contained in them. They translate into much greater value than what is inherent in them.

To make the recognition they bestow on their employees effective, knowledge organizations must add value to them as with some of the successful recognition rewards described above. A 10-year service pin should not only tell an onlooker that its wearer has spent 10 years with the organization but also should communicate what the organization does for those who have worked for it for 10 years. For example, the organization may guarantee special privileges commensurate with it, such as some aspect of job security, special stock options, increased benefits, enhanced facilities, or special retirement packages. Without these privileges, recognition would not have any meaningful role in motivating employees to reflect productive behavior.

Reward of Ethical Fulfillment

A very potent reward in knowledge organizations that is intrinsic and controlled by the doers is deriving satisfaction from doing the right thing. The reward is administered through the ability one has to engage in the act that one considers *ethical*. Just like other process rewards discussed previously, ethical fulfillment is very effective. It is administered by the doer, has clearly set administering criteria, and is administered as frequently as the appropriate behavior is reflected. One important aspect of this reward is that there is no loss of time between the appropriate behavior and the reward administration. This reward is instantaneous, because it comes through the engagement in action that the doer sees to be ethical. It is internalized because the doer rewards himself.

A proper use of and emphasis on ethics in organizations can result in a source of unending rewards for managers and employees at all levels. Top managers and owners have always felt rewarded by the satisfaction they derive through making decisions and taking actions, even when unpopular, based on their ethical strength. Administration can practice the same type of reward at all levels. The reward system must filter down to other levels because it will be as effective at those lower levels as it has been at the top levels of a knowledge organization.

Management can very well implement this type of reward system through a policy and training that emphasizes ethics in actions and decision making. It can be achieved without much cost. The only cost may be training and infrequent short-term setbacks because of practicing this ethics policy.

MONEY AND MOTIVATION IN KNOWLEDGE ORGANIZATIONS

Money has a different meaning for employees in knowledge organizations—Gen Xers and Generation Y—than it did for the Baby Boomers. While growing up, they saw an increased role of money in control and management of society. They observed and felt the power of money that their parents had never known when they were growing up. This new meaning of money came directly from their own experiences with money. They noticed money replacing the roles that previously, during their parents' time, were in the realms of family, community, religious institutions, and other similar organizations. They felt all the power of money. Money, they saw, could get them anything. It got them play and fun in the form of organized sports, friends through camping and parties organized in party arcades, and even parents in the role of paid babysitters. The babysitter took care of their needs in exchange for money. They knew that money is what motivated the babysitter. She did not take care of them or give them company because of any ethical commitment to the community or an emotional bond with them. The monetary compensation kept her going. Moreover, and ironically, they learned that money was the reason why their parents left them with the babysitter and went to work. The potency of money became especially great for them because they noticed that both their parents had to work hard to maintain a reasonable lifestyle. To them, everything somehow translated into money.

This was not the case when their parents were being reared. In fact, during most of the early to mid-twentieth century, industrial psychologists preached the inability of money to act as a motivator. They stressed replacement of monetary rewards, which inherently are externally controlled, as a motivator with nonmonetary rewards that are internally controlled, such as "job enrichment." Psychologists told employers that if they let their employees make important decisions then they would feel motivated and more willing to work with less money. Some employers implemented this belief system and did achieve some positive results while working with the Baby Boomer generation during the second half of the twentieth century. It might have been true for a large number of people then, but it is not going to be so in the future. Business executives of the 1990s, the models that most employees liked to follow, did not allow a reduction in their present and future financial incentives because their jobs were "enriched."

The work environment of the twentieth century gave employees job descriptions that did not come with authority to make decisions or to take part in the management of their organizations. For them, the motivators could have been the job "enrichments." In knowledge organizations, these enrichments are an essential part of knowledge jobs. If not part of their jobs, they are definitely part of the "psychological contract" of employment in a knowledge organization. These enrichments are not the motivators that knowledge employees need to achieve to make a trade-off. In fact, knowledge employees will want compensation for the "enrichments" of their jobs since those are an essential part of their job description. Knowledge jobs do not contain a large component of physical work as their parents' jobs did.

The biggest motivator of Gen Xers and Generation Y employees is giving them the ability to control their own rewards—to be able to make as much or as little money as they may want. Money has different meanings to different knowledge employees. The ability to trade off money with something more important will play a big role in motivating knowledge employees. Heather Neely, a California-based consultant who specializes in the working styles of

Gen Xers, and is a Gen Xer herself, points out, "We're going to have different expectations in the workplace. We're not expecting long-term employment anymore. Rather, we're looking for daily proof that our work matters. It's about creating a new type of security. Of course, we want to make a good living. But if managers reward performance with only money, in many ways they've lost the war because we also want freedom and flexibility in the workplace" (Hays, 1999).

Money as the Third Factor in Knowledge Organizations: The Innovator Factor

The theory of motivation that controls work behavior in traditional organizations came from a team of psychologists during the 1950s, headed by Frederick Herzberg of Harvard University who studied motivation and advanced a rather credible theory of motivation, better known as the "Two Factor Theory" (Herzberg, Mausner, & Snyderman, 1959). This theory states that in any work setting, the presence of certain conditions, called dissatisfiers or hygiene factor, is essential to let employees *not* feel dissatisfied. The dissatisfiers include the lack of such things as proper salary, job security, working conditions, status, company procedures, and quality of interpersonal relations. The presence of the hygiene factor in an organization does not guarantee that its employees will be satisfied. To make employees feel satisfied an organization has to have the presence of a second set of conditions called satisfiers, or motivators. Motivators include a sense of achievement, recognition, responsibility, advancement, attractiveness of the work itself, and the possibility of growth. Herzberg and associates state that while the presence of this factor in any work package will satisfy, its absence may not necessarily dissatisfy.

In some parts, the essence of Herzberg's two-factor theory might still hold in knowledge organizations. As given earlier, absence of the first factor is expected to continue to be a dissatisfier with Gen Xers and members of Generation Y. At the minimum, knowledge organizations will have to offer the hygiene factor for knowledge employees to allow them the subjugation of their "senses"—but, of course, probably nothing more than that. The presence of the second factor may satisfy and let knowledge workers lend their "mind" to their job, but it is not going to be valid for attaining the level of commitment necessary for innovation and high levels of productivity essential for the success of knowledge organizations.

Existence of a third factor in the study of motivation in knowledge organization work environment was noticed in the behavior of corporate executives during the 1990s. Let us name it the *innovator factor*. The presence of this factor will make employees engage in acts that are innovative and productive, whereas their absence may not necessarily make them *uninnovative*. Nevertheless, its presence will essentially make employees innovators.

Let us try to explain this with the behavior of executives of the 1990s. They enjoyed complete control of their environment, took whatever decisions or actions they thought were essential to respond to the needs of their work environment, and were given full credit for the outcome. There was only one measure of success—a common denominator across assignments, divisions, organizations, and even professions—money. The purpose of money made this way is mostly not to fulfill an economic need. It is to fulfill a psychological need—a symbol of the success attained with its full magnitude. It worked well for Wall Street firms, banks, insurance companies, manufacturing firms, entertainment, communication corporations, and knowledge organizations, among others. The only thing that acted as an innovator to motivate them was money. It is true that, beyond a certain level, the economic utility of money declines. It stops being a major motivator, but by connecting money with one's performance, moves money to a higher, psychological level, and the psychological utility of money still has not attained a saturation point at any level.

The New Old Method of Payment to Motivate

Knowledge organizations do not use payment as a productivity generator in the same manner as the most powerful industry of the twentieth century—the automotive industry—did. When it started to grow, the automotive industry hired large numbers of employees to work on assembly lines and other jobs on a piecemeal payment system—not an hourly wage rate—as a standard method of payment. According to this system, workers were paid by a simple multiple of the pieces they made with the agreed upon average payment rate per piece, very much like work done by an independent contractor. When the work decreased, workers made less, but when the work increased, they made more. Many times, they worked fast and finished their pieces sooner while still making good money. Because of the unaccounted technological enhancements or the tremendous growth in automotive production, workers started to make more money, sometimes making substantially more than their supervisors, engineers, or managers. In return, these salaried employees grew resentful, and the industry, rather than allowing them a share in the growth the same way the workers did, devised hourly wage rates for workers to limit their earning. Workers started getting a fixed amount of pay like the supervisors, engineers, and managers did. Everyone was paid for just being present at work. Workers were paid for their presence as given by the hours punched on their time cards and the rest were paid based on their "assumed" presence, not by any other criterion.

Probably the worst legacy of twentieth-century organizations is the practice of paying employees not by services performed, or pieces of widgets made, but by the time spent at place of work. That is like paying workers based on John Million's philosophy—"they also serve those who only stand and wait." It may be all right for a security guard, whose job is to keep an eye on a certain building, however it is improper to manage organizations by this mode.

Knowledge organizations use innovative methods to directly or indirectly tie all payments to all employees to the output from them. In knowledge organizations, paying workers by time card or by a time-based salary is not going to ensure the achievement of organizational goals. Typically, a knowledge organization does not want to have "people at work," it wants them to attain some progress toward completion of the organization's goals—work done. Work enhances knowledge organizational revenues and profits, not the mere presence of people. Then why pay people on a time-based system?

The second big drawback of paying people by time is that it adds a dimension of determinism to outcome from work and thus fails to excite and energize—the two essential components of innovation and productivity in knowledge organizations. The absence of payment like this, then, can demotivate, whereas its presence may not motivate.

Knowledge organizations have to be very innovative in designing schemes to pay employees so that this payment becomes a motivator. Here is a case from a suburban restaurant in New Jersey. Its management noticed that to increase the bill per guest it had to make guests order more drinks, appetizers, and desserts. The management decided to push waiters to ask guests specifically for these items at the appropriate time. Every evening, management held a brief meeting with the waiters, which resulted in yelling and screaming because of low sales and pushed them to do more the next day. Nothing helped. One day, on a suggestion, management agreed to an experiment: Increase prices on all drinks, appetizers, and desserts by 20 percent and give that 20 percent to waiters. The sales took off and management never looked back.

Transparency and Equity

It may be correct to say that the content of rewards from the work that knowledge employees get is just one part—an essential part, though—of the outcomes from work behavior that motivates them. Another part of this process that also has an important, maybe even more important, impact on knowledge employees' motivation is the perceived fairness in distribution of these rewards. When knowledge employees complain about the way their organization treats them, they really convey their discontent with the process that distributes rewards from work.

Most knowledge organizations are aware of this fact and engage in extensive efforts to see that the distribution process is equitable and fair. Whether employees actually perceive it that way is a different question. Whatever methods, formulae, and models an organization's job analysts may come up with for paying employees fairly and equitably for the work they do, they will rarely be able to perfectly link the rewards from work with the employees' work inputs and outputs. Given work, work environment, and the employee executing the work, no two jobs done in a knowledge organization are ever identical, even for identically described jobs. By realizing that it is indeed hard for an organization to pay employees fairly and equitably, we see that winning their "perception" of fairness and equity is almost an impossible goal to achieve.

Gen Xers enter work partnerships with their e-employers on an understood sociopsychological contract. This contract implies that the knowledge organization will treat them fairly and equitably. This is true for both those who have already entered and those who will enter this type of work relationship with this knowledge organization or, sometimes, even with other knowledge organizations that somehow are grouped with it. To develop into a long-lasting, rewarding relationship for both the knowledge employee and the knowledge organization, the employer has to honor this implied contract.

Equity—Real and Perceived

In this context of equity and transparency, it is important to understand the impact on knowledge organizations of the concept of equity developed for traditional organizations primarily by a management researcher J. Stacy Adams. In November 1963, Adams wrote on this problem in the *Journal of Abnormal and Social Psychology* (Adams, 1963). In effect, Adams states that if outputs to each employee from the work system are not relatively equitable to the inputs the employee gives to the system, the employee will be dissatisfied. In case of an inequity, the worker will first attempt to have the work system increase his or her outputs to the level of his or her inputs. If that does not happen, then the employee will try to end the relationship, and if that falls through, then the employee will reduce inputs to the level of the outputs from the system. If this event ends in the last scenario, the system has alienated this employee and lost his motivation for innovation and productivity.

The effect of perceived equity is also the same. Its lack can be a big demotivator. When an employee perceives that another employee who brings in as much, or even less, is being compensated better, either through pay or through other combined sources, this employee becomes dissatisfied.

Knowledge organizations need employees' intellectual engagement and creative thinking, which come with high morale and motivation. They cannot afford to let their employees have a perception of inequity because it affects both of them. A definite means of keeping employees' high morale and motivation is to make sure that there is no inequity—perceived or real. The only way to ensure this is to eliminate all sources of inequity, which can be some individual or system that controls what should be the knowledge employee's work outputs. Because the employee is the one who controls the inputs that go into his work system, it is obvious that the control of outputs should rest with the employee. J. Stacy Adams's research helps us understand the mechanics of equity in inputs and outputs. If knowledge employees realize that their outputs from work are not equitable to the inputs, they will attempt to make them equitable. Moreover, since the employees control inputs, they will reduce them to a lower level, comparable to the real or perceived lower level of outputs. If this perception is not dispelled, many times it will create a spiral effect that will result in outcomes that are not pleasant for the employer and outputs that are not consistent with the employees' abilities and capabilities. Adams's theory may apply in other organizations also; nevertheless, it seems to work in high-innovation organizations, such as knowledge organizations. These organizations have to combat inequity and pay attention to the perception among employees.

Knowledge Work Inputs, Outcomes, Outputs, and Transparency

To communicate a sense of equity regularly and to keep employees motivated, as was stated previously, a knowledge organization work system must allow the control of outputs to rest where the control of inputs does—with the employee. The system must be designed to allow inputs, outcomes, and outputs from work to congregate. Clearly, right from the time the job relationship begins, the employer is interested in outcomes, whereas the employee's main interest is in the outputs. The inputs the employee brings to the system are essential for the achievement of both outcomes and outputs.

To let employees control the most *fundamental* output from their work relationship—wages—knowledge organizations should pay the employees through work outcomes, without any condition or resistance. There should be no hurdle to pass or quota to fulfill before directly linking outputs to outcomes. Setting a minimum wage guarantee, or any such payment that resembles it, creates resistance to establishing a positive and directly proportionate relationship between outcomes and outputs. All norms controlling pay should be spelled out clearly and made known to all involved so that employees understand how to set their levels of outputs from the work. Alternatively, if employees fail to achieve that, then they should automatically be able to explain to themselves why they made less than their expectations.

This kind of control and transparency is essential to excite knowledge employees about their work, make them intellectually productive, and put them back in control of their outcomes. Money earned in this way becomes a measure of outcomes from one's work inputs. From the first unit until the last unit, each person who contributes to the completion of outputs should have a direct and immediate stake in the rewards that come from them.

Corporate officers whose performance is tied to the price of the company's common stock regularly monitor stock market moves relative to it and know how they are doing. If this type of control makes them excited and motivated, why not allow the concept to proliferate. Let it be replicated for everyone connected with the organization. It will motivate everyone to perform well and to find the means to improve performance further. If performance decreases, all employees, just like the top executives of the organization, will try whatever they can to stop its erosion. The system should provide the same kind of feedback and monitoring ability to all employees. There should be a clearly described link between outcomes and outputs with a complexity at or below the intellectual level of the person providing inputs to this work system. The measure of outputs for each employee should be instantaneous so that the employee knows without any extraneous assistance, on a real-time basis, what his or her outputs are. The Universal Card, formerly a unit of AT&T, designed such a real-time–based system that instantly provided the workers with their bonus amounts. It worked wonders for the company's productivity and profits and, in the process, won the company a Malcolm Baldrige Award from the U.S. government.

Pseudohurdles

Certain managers of knowledge organizations, especially those who have spent extensive time managing employees of traditional organizations, leave some measures in the reward system that in effect create pseudocontrol of outputs. They genuinely do not want to relinquish control of outcomes to those who control inputs. This pseudocontrol will allow employees' supervisors, department heads, or the organization to maintain real control of employees' outputs. Two examples of these are the bonus system and commission system with a base salary. All bonus systems are somehow flawed. First, they are designed to kick in only after crossing a set quota—the large hurdle. Second, they allow increases in bonus in steps—the small hurdles. Third, they are given in addition to a guaranteed salary. One requisite of management by objectives (MBO) that renders it less effective, is its bonus system. MBO organizations give bonuses to managers who exceed the objectives laid out in their MBO contracts. That means that objectives act as a hurdle that has to be crossed to gain reward in the form of bonus. For this reason, employees set their objectives realistically—that is, low.

All effective reward systems in knowledge organizations must operate in a linear fashion with a zero base and infinite top.

Relevant Standards

For the rewards from a job to act as motivators for knowledge employees, it is important that they are relevant to the organization's mission and objectives and are so clear and straightforward that anyone whom they concern can understand them. Confusing, detailed reward standards that are not easily communicated or need to be constantly explained do not effectively motivate employees and hence do not do their job. Easily communicated and simple standards that sink in without extra effort always stay in employees' minds and perpetually motivate them while they are working.

A vivid example of how standards might conflict with the basic goals of the organization is drawn from the way the medical system operates in the United States. The basic purpose of the medical system is to keep the population healthy. If the service providers keep people healthy, they are considered to be doing a good job and the system rewards them accordingly. However, that is not what actually happens. Health service providers are actually rewarded contingent upon the number of people falling sick. The Chinese medical system inspired the concept of the Health Maintenance Organization, or HMO, in America. In the Chinese medical system, the health service provider was paid a monthly fee for keeping patients healthy. These payments stopped during the periods the patient became sick, effectively doubling punishment on the provider for not keeping his patient healthy. The system had an incentive for the provider to keep patients healthy. In America, HMOs decided to correct this anomaly by paying primary physicians a fixed amount to maintain the health of their insured. In effect, if the insured fell sick, the provider had to spend time and effort to make the insured healthy. It is actually better to penalize the provider by cutting off the payment for that period, as the Chinese did.

EXTRINSIC INTRINSIC REWARDS IN KNOWLEDGE ORGANIZATIONS

The most effective motivator of knowledge employees in general, and Gen Xers and Generation Y members in particular, which should work on a long-term basis, comes from rewards we classify as extrinsic intrinsic rewards. All intrinsic rewards come from the employee's work environment and are controlled intrinsically—that is, the person doing the job gives these rewards to himself/herself. One is not dependent on someone else giving these rewards to the person. These rewards come from the job itself in the form of accomplishment, learning something new, and the pleasure of doing something one enjoys doing. Rewards such as these are sought after by Gen Xers who like to decide on their own how to accomplish something. In this regard, managers can help by allowing Gen Xers "a little flexibility and creativity," says Deborah Masten, human resources development director for JCPenney. Masten adds that a manager should be a resource, not someone who details everything for the employee (Hays, 1999).

Extrinsic intrinsic rewards are a subcategory of these rewards that meet an additional condition. This condition is that rewards are intrinsic only in the short term and have the potential of conversion to extrinsic rewards—money, upward mobility, recognition—if not from their current employer, then from a new employer or someone important to the person receiving the reward. The efficacy of extrinsic intrinsic rewards as a motivator depends on the probability of their turning into an extrinsic reward and the worth of that reward. To be an effective long-term motivator, these rewards must turn into extrinsic rewards.

An example of extrinsic intrinsic rewards is an artist who is rewarded by working on a piece of art—his or her creation. This motivates the artist to complete the work. In this way, one can continuously get this reward and be motivated, for as long as the work is being completed. Once the work is completed, this intrinsic reward, and subsequently the motivation, ends. For this reward to motivate the artist on a long-term basis, and to let him or her continue to engage in this activity, this intrinsic reward must turn into an extrinsic reward. It may be praise from others—especially from those of importance to the person—a meaningful formal recognition, its display in an exhibition or museum, or purchase of the art work by someone at a good price.

Second, let us take an example from the computer industry. A computer microchip designer is highly motivated to successfully complete the design of a new, powerful chip that the designer envisioned and the company allowed him to undertake. The source of this motivation is intrinsic and will continue until the project is completed and the designer sees this new chip perform much faster and much better, exactly as envisioned. For this to be a long-term motivator for the designer, this intrinsic reward must translate into an extrinsic reward, such as a share in the profit from the sale of the new chip, a promotion, or a plaque at the company's annual picnic.

The third example comes from another industry where employees are motivated through intrinsic rewards and employers turn it into a long-term motivator through extrinsic rewards. A stock analyst conducts research for a company to forecast the direction and size of change in its common stock price on the stock exchange in the next 30 to 90 days. This analyst's intrinsic motivation comes from completing the research, coming up with a price target, and later finding the stock price actually hit the forecast that was projected. This motivation will continue if the employer allows this intrinsic reward to turn into an extrinsic reward. For example, the employer allows the analyst to take a percentage of the profit that the employer makes because of the correct forecast on the price of this equity security.

Every knowledge organization can redesign its reward system to fuse intrinsic rewards into extrinsic rewards. A basketball league may turn the intrinsic reward that players get from playing and winning their games into an intrinsic extrinsic reward by allowing them to bet on their team winning.

Knowledge organizations must redesign the reward system so that it works to help the organization achieve its goals while at the same time it stimulates employees to put in effort to help the organization attain its objectives.

REFERENCES

Adams, J.S. (1963, November). Toward an understanding of equity. *Journal of Abnormal and Social Psychology*, 422–436.

Amar, A.D. (1994). Motivating employees in the 1990s: Reward and recognition. *Mid-Atlantic Journal of Business, 30*, 129–131.

Bronson, P. (1999, January 11). Instant company. *New York Times Magazine*, pp. 44–48.

Hays, S. (1999, November). Generations X and Y and the art of the reward. *Workforce, 78*(11), 44–48.

Herzberg, F., Mausner, B., & Snyderman, B. (1959). *The motivation to work.* New York: John Wiley & Son.

Karp, H., Sirias, D., & Arnold, K. (1999, July/August). Teams: Why Generations X and Y marks the spot. *The Journal for Quality and Participation, 22*(4), 30–33.

Mui, N. (2001, February 4). Here come the kids: Generation Y invades the workplace. *New York Times,* p. 1, Section 9.

Chapter 10

Putting Them in Control

Like other management functions, controlling in knowledge organizations is different from controlling in traditional organizations. Managers have to find a delicate balance between creativity and control, as the two complement each other routinely. Control in knowledge organizations covers important management functions of controlling for knowledge firms. It begins with making the reader aware of the purposes of controls and what is likely to go wrong with traditional management controls when employed in knowledge organizations. It portrays traditional management controls in two categories and suggests that both of them go against the spirit of innovation and productivity in a knowledge environment. It stresses the need to turn knowledge employees from "controlled" to a state of "in control." This chapter gives four principles of effective controls for a knowledge organization and provides new and refined controls that may work under conditions prevalent in knowledge organizations. The chapter also gives three tests that must be applied before accepting any controls for knowledge organizations. For managers who may be interested in designing controls for knowledge organizations, an instrument is given at the end of this chapter that should be used to avoid designing and installing controls that may stifle innovation and productivity in knowledge organizations. In addition, also appended with this chapter, there is a work on controls and creativity that throws further light on how to balance the two, reproduced from *The Mid-Atlantic Journal of Business.*

In effect, traditional management is centered on control. Typically, managers of these organizations use control as a way to consolidate and exert power over their employees to influence their behavior and restrain their actions. To management in traditional organizations, the presence of controls signifies success and effectiveness. Many managers focus more on control function and controls than on the achievement of organizational objectives or excellence. Their basic assumption is that without control, they will not attain anything. In an effort to maintain control, they sometimes accept sacrifice of innovation, creativity, and even productivity. Many managers argue in defense of these actions exerting controls: "There cannot be growth and success if there are no controls." They also make sure that if controls are delegated, they are only put in the hands of those whom they can control so that they effectively maintain these controls with them also. Traditional management treats control as an indispensable management "right" or "privilege."

On the contrary, insistence on controls is a formula for failure in a knowledge work environment, where control takes a new dimension. By reviewing some basics of the control theory, we can discover how to best adapt controls available from management literature or design new controls for success in knowledge organizations with the new workforce, working in the changed labor market.

CONTROLS AND THEIR PURPOSE

Control signifies constraint, restraint, or regulation. All controls designed for humans are aimed at behavioral conformity—to make the individuals act in accordance with the norms established by others, who individually or as part of a group are more powerful than those for whom they have designed these controls. In all human relationships, voluntary as well as socially or biologically dictated, control is truly an indicator and consequence of some type of power. Control, in effect, is a constant reminder, to both the one controlling and the one being controlled, of the distribution and direction of power in their relationship.

Historically, control has been an essential requisite in defining and establishing all human relationships. It can be confidently said that, in some form and in some magnitude, control has been used forever and, over time, has been allowed to steadily grow with the evolution and development of human civilization.

Typically, organizations increase controls as they grow in size. The usual argument for doing so is that controls are introduced to bring discipline and regularity to the organization. In a stable and defined environment it may work well, but it will not allow full potential exploitation in an environment of relentless growth and turbulence. In spite of this, it is not likely to cause survival problems for organizations during periods of prosperity—when there is enough room to make mistakes and still come out unscathed. Nevertheless, control will rein in creativity—a worker's ability to think outside the box. Take, for example, Intel Corporation, an icon of the knowledge industry—a company for whom science and technology are its bread-and-butter. The company that had been known in the industry for its "disciplined management" stumbled miserably when faced with a meaningful test of its ability to operate in a tight environment. Its controls, that had brought about the disciplined management, did not allow all brains to function in understanding the dynamics of the marketplace due to the changes in demand for personal computers (PC) and the strength that its arch rival Advanced Micro Devices (AMD) had been gaining. First, it failed to grow capacity in response to the growth of the PC market in 2000, and then, in a rush to match AMD, it misunderstood its capability and marketed a faulty version of its flagship processor Pentium III (Reinhardt, 2000). The discipline and controls that worked wonders for it in a stable environment failed miserably in the turbulent one.

Physical Controls

We know from the evolution of controls that physical controls have been conceptualized and implemented mainly in engineering, where there is a need for humans to control a machine or any of its mechanical or automatic functions; if not controlled, they would follow a course unacceptable to the engineering system. Let us take, for example, the controlling of one of the most common of all machines known to human beings—the automobile. It is with the help of the physical controls, which are specifically designed to manage the motion of a car, that the car is actually overpowered by its driver. Without these controls, it may wander off the course charted for it. In the same way, other controls perform other important automobile-constraining functions. The controls give the driver the ability to keep the car from engaging in motions or actions that are undesirable to him.

Based on the same basic principle, humans have designed and used controls for restraining or constraining forces in all spheres of life that they believe can change their magnitude or direction and move along a path that they believe will be contrary to their plans. The main goal of controls is to harness the power necessary to carry out certain functions.

Management Controls

From human relationships, control grew into other social relationships, such as those that have emerged in the work environment. To manage the large and complex social organizations of the twentieth century, a group of techniques and tools was devised to dictate and monitor human behavior. These collectively came to be known as *management controls*. They multiplied and prospered during the job era. Over time, controlling became one of the four major functions of management. Managers advocated its use as essential to restrain and regulate acts of those who helped them attain organizational goals. Since management acts in proxy for its owners, it is the control of employees by the employer. Managers have used controls to compel their employees to behave in a certain manner or to abide by certain standards and codes, to monitor their progress along these lines, and to see that outcomes are in compliance with their plans. Their basic function has been to ensure that the events brought about by employees are constrained to follow the organizational plans.

All traditional organization management thrives on control. Its basic tenet is to make others work without giving them any control over the environment surrounding their work. They practice the well-known principle: "Delegate responsibility and centralize authority" or, in other words: Get the help of people at hierarchical levels below you but control all the strings. The consequence of this principle had been that everyone at the next higher level wanted to pull the strings—maintain the control.

INEFFECTIVE KNOWLEDGE ORGANIZATION CONTROLS

Traditional management imposes controls on employees in many ways and spends a good part of its resources in administering these controls. There has rarely been an audit or a study undertaken by organizations to assess the effectiveness of the controls that they have instituted. Whenever I asked any manager about the usefulness of a control, I was told that because it has been an established practice for a long time, it must have a purpose and an effect. They further added that either they had no authority to abolish it or they did not have an alternative practice available that could replace the control.

Controls in traditional organizations come in many forms, from the obvious ones, such as budgets and audits, routings and methods, inspection and quality control, inventory and materials controls, schedules and deadlines, goals and plans, periodic performance evaluations, to the subtle ones, such as promotions, raises and bonuses, and the ability to exercise employment at will. Most of these controls become ineffective or counterproductive in knowledge organizations because they are inconsistent with the work demands of these organizations and the new type of workers that are entrusted with the responsibility to execute the work.

Keeping in mind the operations of knowledge organizations, we can analyze management controls for their usefulness, or lack thereof, by assigning them to one of the following groups.

Nuisance Controls for Knowledge Work

In a knowledge organization, nuisance controls are the most ineffective controls because they either do not achieve their intended purpose or are performed at a time when the intended purpose is lost and the result derived from the control is rendered useless to its attainment. Because these controls are mostly a nuisance to knowledge workers and the knowledge work system, they are labeled *nuisance controls*. The goal is to eliminate them from knowledge organizations and thereby enhance creativity in their employees without causing any collateral damage. Some examples of these controls are given below.

Set Work-Time Schedules. Studies have shown that biological clocks of Generations X and Y members are set quite differently from past generations. A large number of them function at a higher level of efficiency during the nighttime than during the day. Accordingly, if an organization wants them to be alert, creative, and at the peak of their productivity, it will have to schedule them for work at this time—a time only they know. An organization cannot use one work schedule for all. By setting a time when a knowledge worker should start, interrupt, and conclude his work, managers make a naive and simplistic assumption based on a generalization of human psychology and physiology—that all people perform at the same level of efficiency at the same time. The controlling of knowledge workers' physical presence at their place of work is too shortsighted for innovation and productivity.

By the late 1980s and early 1990s, a good number of American organizations had relaxed control of work timings. At the Metropolitan Mortgage and Securities Company, managers are allowed to work with employees to develop individual schedules in which workers can set their own daily starting and finishing times. The company's manager of compensation and benefits, Mike Schelstrate, says "As long as the work gets done, the number of hours and when those hours are worked is flexible" (Burke, 2000). Most of these organizations have flexible schedules except for a few hours a day—the core time—during which period all employees should be present.

Other time controls, such as break times and vacation times, are even greater nuisances and contribute negatively to the efficiency of a knowledge workplace.

Bell Labs, the brain powerhouse behind the emergence of American Telephone & Telegraph Company as the world's leader in communication, did not exercise any of these controls because it did not want to hinder the creativity of its technicians and scientists. It is policies like these at Bell Labs that have brought about so many lucrative inventions and patents for AT&T.

Most of the time, the reason given for the imposition of work time controls in any organization is that the work demands are such that the simultaneous presence of employees in their work groups at certain times is unavoidable. This is supported by a work design concept known as "dependence" or process dependence. This dependence dictates the simultaneous need for the presence of those doing these jobs.

For higher levels of innovation and productivity in knowledge organizations, managers have to eliminate, or at least tremendously reduce, this dependence to allow knowledge employees the freedom to choose work times when they are most creative and energetic. Knowledge work design can easily allow for work *decoupling*, which is not so for other organizational assignments. Those parts of the knowledge work for which dependence cannot be eliminated should be redesigned to function with the available communication knowledge and without the requirement of the physical simultaneity of more than one employee. Managers should be on the lookout for the technologies that will help them achieve this, because much research is going on in this area. Sometime during the current decade, communication knowledge will make it possible for management to fully eliminate work time controls. The innovative use of the Internet, video-conferencing, and other electronic media can make it possible, even now, to reduce the need to have long and/or frequent departmental or divisional core times, as many organizations currently have. If managers commit to eliminating core time, they will be able to fully achieve it.

The chapter on redesigning knowledge work in this book spelled out strategies that managers of knowledge organizations can adopt to eliminate or reduce work dependence.

Periodic Performance Evaluations. A common routine that all supervisors working for traditional organizations have to go through periodically—typically once a year—is to write performance evaluations for their subordinates. In most organizations, by the time these evaluations come out, the period is over, the scene has changed, the players are different, and even the person who is being evaluated has forgotten what he did wrong or right and might even have already adopted a new mode of behavior. The likelihood of an evaluation done following this methodology achieving its stated purpose is very low. Its use either as a behavior modifier or as a control device is insignificant. Many organizations do it simply because they believe that it is an essential part of managing the human element. Managers accept it because that is how they retain control of their subordinates.

Since knowledge employees and demands on them from their organization are quite different from that of their counterparts in traditional organizations, engaging in similar performance evaluations of their work may be meaningless and a waste of the organizations' scarce resources. As a rule, performance evaluation techniques of traditional organizations should simply be discarded in knowledge organizations. Knowledge organizations can control employee performance by building self-feedback devices into the work process. It has to be instant, continuous, relevant, fair, and a vehicle for learning and behavior modification. It should not be a control in the traditional sense but still provide its essence and the benefit.

Chapter 12 on the future of the knowledge organizations gives some importance to achieving it through research on knowledge work and the workers.

Corporate Plans. Another way organizations control their employees is through plans. The corporate or strategic planning department of an organization understands the vision of the chief executive officer or the board of directors and then turns this vision into goals for each division or department. The divisions or departments then chalk out goals for regions, districts, and sections under them, much like a chain reaction. The heads of these units start to work toward achievng these goals. If these plans suit the abilities and capabilities of the employees—meaning they are achievable by them—they succeed. If these plans do not fit the predisposition of those who have to carry them out, then they do not succeed. In that case, the planners learn and for the next time set plans at a "more realistic" level to ensure that they "succeed."

Corporate plans relating to knowledge work, due to its nature and scope, may never fully succeed in exploiting the potential of all those involved in the organization. This may be due to the lack of understanding of the opportunities that are available and the lack of employees who are best qualified to "own" part of the plan. Another question in this regard pertains to the commitment that employees might give or be able to give. In a knowledge organization, if it is not the plan of the employees who are engaged in its accomplishment, it is not going to be effective in making employees innovative and productive.

The same type of logic can be presented about an organization's vision regarding its ambitions and projects. A typical knowledge employee's, especially of those belonging to Generations X and Y, approach is: "If it's your vision for the organization, you work to achieve it. I have my own vision for the organization and my own plan to achieve it." In fact, employees who truly believe in this adage and behave accordingly are the ones who are best suited for the job. They will achieve what they espouse and contribute to what they accept and will not need to be motivated or controlled.

To be able to successfully use plans to embody visions and to control their achievement, it is essential that every knowledge employee sees himself in the organization's vision and contributes to the plan. This is the only way employees will feel excited and empowered to work toward their realization. In a knowledge organization, traditional managers will not be able to achieve anything on their own—including thinking—and to achieve something meaningful for the organization, you need everyone in the knowledge organization to contribute. Let the knowledge workers plan for their individual functions and connect with others at their levels, above them, and then eventually the organizational planning team.

De Minimis Controls for Knowledge Workers

Some enlightened contemporary knowledge organizations substituted their usual controls with the newer diluted versions for dealing with certain segments of their firm. These practices became visible during the late 1980s and became more prevalent during the 1990s. Such diluted versions of standard controls are called *de minimis* controls because they do allow a good amount of freedom to employees. Most of these controls, with some adaptations, may work efficiently to enhance the organizational productivity of Generations X and Y workers in knowledge organizations. Nevertheless, these are not expected to work in enhancing innovation—the most important ingredient for success under the new work demands of the knowledge organization. Some of the more common *de minimis* controls and their applications are described below.

Deadlines. In an attempt to control load and activities of employees, managers commonly assess content of the work to be assigned to them by using one of two techniques. For most engineering or technical organizations, the work is scientifically measured using methods sheets or work measurement standards. In other organizations, especially service operations—the majority of contemporary organizations—the assessment starts with an assumption about how long the work will take to complete and then explicitly or implicitly allows employees that much time in the form of a deadline. A manager feels relaxed and leaves the employee alone until that time. This deadline becomes a loose, controlling device that managers believe works well in most cases. The problem is they do not know the amount of risk in assessing the work content in time units. If work content is assessed on the high side, it begins with built-in waste. If it is assessed on the low side, the worker will take at least as long as the work *actually* needs to get done, which usually is more than the time allowed. However, the chances are that the worker will take even longer, since the standard became meaningless and loses its credibility, effectively making the employee lose faith in the estimate and the courage to take as long as he or she needs.

With regard to deadlines—the time allowed to complete a job—the wisdom of management thinker C. Northcote Parkinson, whose works became popular among business and engineering students of the 1960s and early 1970s, becomes relevant. Parkinson says, "Work expands to fill the time (allowed)." The simple interpretation is that whatever time you give to do a job, it will be filled. That means if you set a deadline with pessimistic time estimates, according to Parkinson, it will be fully utilized and will be considered the right amount. Conversely, if you set a deadline using realistic or optimistic estimates, then the work will be delayed. You will have to allow for more time for and will learn to set deadlines that allow for these increased times in the future. The cycle goes on. Inefficiency builds on itself and the organization gets closer and closer to failure.

The only time a deadline will become an effective control measure is when the manager exactly assesses the work content. Now what is the probability of that happening? It is the probability that setting deadlines as a way to control employees will be an effective way to have high productivity.

What happened to the organizational goal to enhance innovation? Controls, by their very nature, do not foster innovation, no matter how they are done. To foster innovation in knowledge organizations, managers have to discard deadlines as a control device. Simply let knowledge employees accept the responsibility to execute a task with very loose description and limitations. The rest should be left up to them. The synergistic innovation that the employees generate will lower the time to complete the job, enhance their performance in the job, and produce learning usable for a long time to come.

Management by Objectives. Another *de minimis* control that knowledge organizations should reject is management by objectives (MBO). It was introduced during the 1960s. Credit for its introduction goes primarily to an American management author and thinker, Peter Drucker (1954), and caught on in the organizational world during the 1970s and 1980s. It preaches control through the setting and achieving of customized, individualized organizational objectives negotiated between the employee and his or her superior. These objectives operate like a contract between the employer and the employee and everything—allocation of resources, performance evaluations, and so on—for the employee is based on these objectives. This management control is definitely better than other management controls imposed through schedules and deadlines. It has worked well for traditional organizations and, for that reason, is very likely to be considered effective in knowledge organizations.

Because of the basic concept driving MBO, it becomes unsuitable for exploiting or containing uncertainties in the work environment of knowledge organizations. MBO starts with a major assumption, which is invalid for knowledge organizations, that implies good understanding of the work and organizational environment by both the employee and his or her negotiating supervisor. This assumption further implies that both parties have the requisite ability to make these two environments interact with each other for the attainment of the desired organizational objective.

The constraining of thought processes and initiatives of knowledge employees by any means, such as MBO, inhibits innovation. Another problem with MBO is that its objectives are usually set for a period of one year, which is too long for any knowledge organization. Some knowledge organizations belonging to the investment industry live by as short a time span as a fraction of a day. Many of these have thrown MBO out the corporate window.

Organizations that must use MBO, and for the sake of uniformity do so in the case of their knowledge employees too, need to make certain adaptations to suit MBO to the creativity requirements of knowledge work. The first adaptation that a knowledge organization should make is to define and write a broad-based mission statement as it relates to the knowledge segment of its business. The mission statement should be straightforward and publicized so that all knowledge employees and their managers are able to translate it into the expectations from them and the roles they should play in its attainment. Individual knowledge employee objectives should then be written in terms of the mission statement. These objectives should specifically be kept flexible so that they may be molded, redefined, and maneuvered to accommodate eventualities of the knowledge environment. Attainment and evaluation of these objectives should be measured in light of the changes occurring in the environment.

Second, to allow for the fast pace in knowledge organizations, MBO should be modified to handle objectives covering shorter time spans, preferably shorter than one year—maybe a quarter, a month, or even a day. One year is too long in the life of knowledge organizations. Even a quarter may be too long for some of them.

Financial Budgets. The use of budgeting as a way to control is based on the fact that accomplishment of all activities requires some resources and that, if there are no resources to do a certain activity, that activity will not take place. Since the most potent and flexible resource that exists in a metamorphic state is capital, all organizations use financial budgets as a method of control. In some form, all organizations—many times even the smallest ones, like the mom and pop operations—make some use of budget as a planning and control tool. Government organizations at all levels—local, county, state, and federal—most prominently make use of budget as a way to plan and control. The rationale for their use of this tool stems from the lack of any other control tool that can replace budgets.

Our knowledge of how the governmental budget process works and how it is implemented should be more than enough to make us lose all faith in budgeting.

A budget is probably the worst way to monitor and control activities of any knowledge organization or knowledge employee. Understanding both the budgeting process and the working of a knowledge organization will show us why this is true. One obvious reason is that most budgets are annual—too long a period to do anything in the turbulent environment of knowledge organizations. On top of that, a budget is a culmination of a long and strenuous process that covers a number of steps. First, it is customary that a budget must be in place before the year for which it is begins. Second, the budgeting process is usually so long and so cumbersome that it has to be initiated many months to years ahead of the period for which the budget is planned. In essence, the process starts with planners making assumptions about the future state of affairs and estimating figures that have relevance to things that may actually happen during the planning period. They have to make estimates about both the revenues and the expenses. Thinking up numbers for the sake of completing budget requirements is common practice in all organizations. There is just no other way to engage in budgeting. It is a process that is inherently flawed. Therefore, using it to monitor and control activities of knowledge organizations simply aggravates the problem because of the nature of the knowledge work and its environment.

Budgeting gives departments and their heads the right to engage in budgeted activities. The criterion for validity of an activity is not whether it actually contributes to the organizational goals but whether or not it is budgeted. As we have discussed, the probability that an activity is budgeted inaccurately is greater than the probability that it is accurately forecasted. Budgeting makes it extremely hard, if not impossible, to change the course of an activity or a unit until the next budget period. It imposes a constraint on management, which is detrimental to innovation.

Budgeting is in many ways comparable to deadlines. They both connote a sense of contract. There are other ways the two are similar. While deadlines set time limits on activities, budgets lay financial limits on them—a deadline of another sort, on resource. All the drawbacks we previously observed with deadlines apply here.

In case budgeting has to be used in knowledge organizations, there are two ways to attack budgets. The first comes from the desire to put a stop to the wrongs of the past budgets. An example of this comes from Colorado. It practiced a budgeting concept that came to be known as zero-based budgeting with the explicit goal to eliminate the right of automatic continuity of activities, offices, or departments. At the end of a budget period, each budget item went to zero. To be rebudgeted, an activity had to be rejustified and rebudgeted from the base of zero rather than from the base where it was last budgeted (Bort, 1999). Zero-based budgeting very effectively corrected budgeting errors of the past, the kind of errors we discussed under deadlines. The technique is old, and it entered the business and organizational world during the 1970s and 1980s. However, most managers did not like it because it increased uncertainty and made them work harder in justifying each budget item. No doubt, the technique would work for knowledge organizations and all others that value innovation.

The second attack on budgets is aimed at giving the knowledge organization manager immediate power to make corrections to the errors made in the funding of the activities. As we know, all budgets—including zero-based budgets—do not allow for any corrections or changes during the budget period. These corrections/changes are doable in the future only if zero-based budgeting is used. Traditional budgets may not allow for changes, even after the period is over, without a political fight. Ideally, for knowledge organizations, the only way immediacy in changes/corrections in expense errors can be gained is when there are no budgeted activities. Financial and other resources should be allocated as needed to enhance the prospect for revenues or profits of the knowledge organization. In practice, this can be achieved by reducing the budget period. Just as we learned in the case of MBO, periods covered by budgets in knowledge organizations must also be very small.

The best way to control knowledge activities will be to have no budget for them. The manager may constantly keep reminding the knowledge workers that the work they are engaged in is not budgeted and has to earn its continuation through its progress in achieving knowledge organizational goals.

KNOWLEDGE ORGANIZATION CONTROLS: TURNING CONTROLLED TO IN-CONTROL

We have shown that to successfully work in a knowledge environment, one needs an unbounded mind and the empowerment to do what one believes will work—in other words, feeling and being "in control." We know that controls, as known in traditional organizations, are antiexcellence, antagonistic to creativity and innovation, and an indirect impediment to productivity. Think of people who have made meaningful contributions to their organizations. Were they controlled? Would you have liked to control them? What would have happened had you controlled them? Would they have succeeded in making the contributions to the organization if they were controlled?

Nevertheless, they were *controlled* of course, but without controls. What were the controls that worked for them? It is these controls that we want to emulate or adapt as effective knowledge organization controls for the future. Organizational success will depend on how managers do this.

Many talented knowledge workers will not accept certain assignments because they will not allow themselves to be controlled by the traditional methods. Let us present a scenario: Ask the CEOs of large, successful organizations if they will subject themselves to the controls their companies have devised for their employees. For the same reason, ask all those who have devised control systems for employees if they themselves would like to work under those controls. They will give you a circular answer. It will be a rationalization justifying an exemption for themselves. The fact is, controls impede everyone at every level of the knowledge organization.

A basic assumption about controls for knowledge work environment is that an organization is better off without controls even when its managers think that they are essential. To excel in an uncertain environment, all organizations need different controls from those we have already known and exercised. Firms need to devise ways to remove traditional controls and let employees feel that they are not being controlled. Take, for example, Great Harvest Bread Company, a Montana-based bakery franchiser that rejects the concept of command-and-control and turns controls into what it calls "handrails" (Hopkins, 2000). This means that there is help if it is wanted, but there are no constraints.

The new controls proposed here should turn an externally controlled worker into one who is in control of his work and work environment. While designing the new controls, we should make sure that the control does not set any one course as the right course for knowledge employees to take—or even convey the feeling that there is one recommended course. The new control should emphasize that only the employee knows the right course to take under the circumstances. In addition, only the employee knows exactly what to do and how to provide close supervision or guidance in securing solutions to the problem.

The management's sense of insecurity and/or its distrust of its knowledge employees should not guide the design of controls. In case such a situation does exist, it should assume that the problem lies with management and should be addressed before designing any controls.

If there is a person who cannot function without being controlled (there would not be many in a knowledge organization), it may be that he or she is unfit for a knowledge organization. In fact, an individual who requires to be controlled and the one who has the will to engage in control of others are misfits in a knowledge organization and become a hindrance to its development and growth and should be sent for behavior modification.

In designing new controls for knowledge organizations, managers should make use of the rather loose, time-tested generic controls that already exist in the form of social or societal norms, religious/moral and ethical codes, professional standards, and legal controls, among others.

Principles of Knowledge Work Control Design

Principle of Vesting Power to Control. The first principle that guides the design and implementation of effective knowledge work controls is based in vesting power to control where it will be most effective—that is, with the person who is being controlled. It should be operated within the smallest work system, called the *nuclear work system*. The nuclear work system keeps work and its doer at the nucleus of the system and surrounds it only by the work environment relevant to this nucleus. The environment of the nuclear work system consists of forces and factors that can be influenced and manipulated by the worker whose work environment it is—de facto, its aim is to eliminate the work environment.

Principle of Independent Functionality. The second principle guiding knowledge work controls requires that after initial monitoring, mainly to ensure design relevance of control and its proper implementation, there should be no need for the management to be involved in the process of controlling. In fact, a control's ability to function independently of the management is the true test of its effectiveness. Management should reenter the realm of control or the process of controlling only when new controls have to be designed and/or installed.

Principle of Control-System Integratability. The third control principle states that an effective control should be an integral, internal part of the system. It should neither exist nor function extraneous to the nuclear work system consisting of the work being done and the worker doing it. It should not need to be monitored by anyone or any system outside this nuclear work system. In case a control system needs to be monitored or guided for its functioning outside the nuclear work system, it should be considered not suitable or ready for controlling behavior in knowledge organizations.

Principle of Target Zero Control

For systemwide proliferation of innovation in knowledge organizations, the goal should be to eliminate all controls, or to achieve *zero control*. It may be a hard goal to attain but that should be the target for management success. By setting this as a target, management will reduce controls and, at the least, not impose new controls if it cannot eliminate them all.

Problems of traditional organizations are simple to define, structure, solve, implement, and monitor. The solution space is known and easy to confine. Problems in knowledge organizations are too complex, obscure, dynamic, and abstract for one person, such as a supervisor, or one group, such as a committee, to manage them practically, technically, or economically. It is difficult, even impossible, for anyone to understand the importance of the work that people in this environment do. A successful contribution from these people is clear only in hindsight. Stories about science and knowledge are filled with this illustration. Take for example the case of the integrated circuit (IC). Today, life runs on it; however, in 1958, when Jack Kilby at Texas Instruments created a hive of transistors and circuits in a single block of a semiconductor—among the world's first ICs—other engineers did not see much use for it (Appenzeller, 2000/2001). This is the way knowledge work is in a technology and knowledge environment. It is searching for solutions in an unknown, multidimensional, constantly changing and overlapping space. Under these circumstances, management would not know *what* to control. On the other hand, if they did know what, they definitely would not know *how* to control it. It may be strategically more beneficial to such organizations to create a work system that can function without any external control and to set a target that will eventually lift all controls.

EFFECTIVE GENERIC CONTROLS

Self-Controls

All controls that are self-imposed by the person being controlled are classed as self-controls. Such controls are regulated by one's personality. We should not assume that we are talking about the "you-got-it-or-you-don't" approach; this type of control is a part of one's acquired, rather than innate, traits. A personality diagnosis should be performed on workers coming onboard for knowledge work. In case there is a need to provide behavioral training to bring them in line with what will be needed for the control in the organization, the organization should do it before giving them any knowledge assignments. There are certain assessment tools available that can be used to do such an analysis. One important factor that can be reliably measured is known as *locus of control.* The locus of control of an individual tells us the degree to which an individual attributes the cause of his behavior to environmental factors (*external locus of control*) or to his own decisions (*internal locus of control*). In the June 1971 issue of *Psychology Today*, an American psychologist, J.R. Rotter, wrote on external and internal loci of control of individuals and devised an assessment instrument (Rotter's Scale) to measure this outlook. Self-control requires an internal locus of control to a large degree and, if not, employees may be trained on how to engage in controlling their environment.

Self-controls will automatically appear if there is a good fit between the work and the person assigned to do the work. The questions here are: Does the worker love what he or she is doing? Is he or she having fun? For those workers who are not, give them something they love and have fun doing, otherwise allow them to redesign their work and work environment to allow them to have fun and enjoyment when performing their knowledge assignments. That will be the single biggest control.

Cybernetics Management Controls

Cybernetics controls are designed to make use of reflexive, predictable human behavior and, depending on its desirability, allow for its recurrence or elimination. In engineering, cybernetics science is widely used in the design of optimal controls. For example, to prevent an operator's hand from being caught in the running blade, most lawn mowers have a deductive/built-in control that will automatically shut off the engine when the operator releases the handle. Similarly, to avoid losing control, most automobiles are designed so that the engine will not start unless the gearshift is in the "park" or "neutral" position. Such controls are reliable because they predict and react to human behavior. The probability of their failure is minimal, and the detection of their failure is quick. Such controls require a substantial initial design investment.

These concepts are also employed in designing social controls. For example, inner city youth leagues are organized and sports facilities constructed to deter adolescents from engaging in antisocial activities. Many organizations also use similar controls to build in punctuality, such as calling all meetings at 8:00 A.M.—the time the work company starts. Company softball and other leagues are organized to breed organizational loyalty and team spirit.

Based on cybernetics principles, individual management controls are designed either to arrest human activities that the knowledge organization wants to discourage or to superimpose them in congruence with desirable human responses. We can draw upon the occurrence or lack of occurrence of one activity as a way to control another. In management, these may also be designed as intrinsic or built-in controls. In that case, no individual outside the system will have to engage in the exercise of these controls. Just as each cybernetics control is individually designed to meet a particular application in engineering design, each knowledge work assignment should be studied for a natural presence of activities in the process from where these controls could be derived. In the case of activities that do not naturally occur in the process, activities suitable for such controls may be designed and built into the knowledge work itself. Take, for example, the quality control of customer service work. Control of this activity can be deduced from the work itself by building into the process a requirement that asks every customer service representative to have his/her customers check out the work performed and sign for it. The piecemeal wage system of payment is another example of such a control. When you pay an employee on a piecemeal basis, you need not control his start and finish times through the punching of a timecard. By setting a piecemeal rate with employees that depends on the completion in accordance with the expected delivery date, management can turn one from being controlled into one who is in control.

Unique, specific controls require a particular knowledge of work operations and an understanding of the process for design and implementation of cybernetics management controls. It may require additional resources from knowledge organizations, but it is worth the effort.

Ethical Controls

A large number of controls emanate straight from the conscious part of human behavior. Such behaviors, in general, have a direct or indirect bearing on organizational operations and performance. If employees engage in ethical behavior, there may be no need for designing and enforcing management controls on which organizations spend billions of dollars. For control of human behavior, organizations can make use of a potential power that rests inside every employee. In some employees, this power may already be active, in others it is dormant and needs to be awakened. This power, ethical power, can be utilized to influence humans to reflect the right behavior at the right time—eliminating the need for any external controls.

It requires an overall training in ethics and an emphasis on moral behavior in general. Management can stress ethics only if it practices ethics itself, both in organizational and individual matters. In traditional twentieth-century organizations, employers and managers successfully created, and employees simply accepted, a power distance between themselves and their superiors. As a result, two groups of primary behavior patterns in organizations emerged: one for management and one for workers. The workers would not be expected to, and actually did not, behave like managers, and managers did not behave like workers. Generations X and Y employees of the twenty-first century are not permitting multiplicity in organizational behavior. There is just one emerging pattern of behavior—the behavior of the managers. All employees will replicate this behavior, good or bad. If managers do not allow themselves to be controlled by their organizational, ethical, or other codes that they expect workers to abide by, they will find their efforts to regulate employees' behavior a frustrating experience. The best control of employees of these generations is through precept.

Social Controls as Informal Knowledge Organization Controls

Because humans are social animals, they value social acceptance and work to achieve it. In return, society makes use of this weakness and establishes its own dicta on behavior that people abide by. In this way, society has successfully prescribed behavioral norms. In the past, when the legal code was weak and the enforcement system basically nonexistent, a social code was the only way to control human behavior. In many societies where social existence had more value, social controls worked more effectively than legal controls. The fact that humans still aspire for social approval can be turned into a powerful source of control in knowledge organizations where other controls, do not work.

In the workplace, this phenomenon was first observed when a team of researchers, led by Elton Mayo and his associates of Harvard University, conducted a study to learn correlates of productivity at Western Electric's Hawthorne plant outside Chicago—popularly known as the Hawthorne Studies (Mayo, 1945). It brought to the attention of management the power of informal social relationships at work and guided management on how to use them in attaining productivity gains. In fact, the team concluded that controls emerging from these relationships were more powerful than formal management controls (Kennedy, 1998). Moreover, since these controls came from the informal work groups that management indirectly controls through group formation and membership, management can play an important part in setting acceptable behavior standards. Managers should select a behavior that they want a particular worker to emulate and then put him or her in a group that reflects that behavior. For example, if an employee reflects a lack of punctuality, he may be put in a group that practices extreme punctuality. In management, we name them *informal controls.*

Informal groups are exerting more influence on the new generation of employees working for knowledge organizations than they did on employees of traditional twentieth-century operating organizations.

Extended Social Controls

In Eastern societies in general and the Japanese in particular, organizations control the behavior of their employees with what can be roughly named *extended controls.* These controls emanate from those who are more important to employees than their employers or managers—their family members. The Japanese prudently allow this hierarchy to thrive, and even strengthen, because they use it as a ploy in their management controls. They involve their employees' families in their workplace, effectively turning work into a family affair.

Employment of several members of an extended family is a common employment practice in Japan. Companies prefer to employ members of a present employee's family and extended family in preference to other new people with whom the management has no experience. This builds and/or increases the forces of loyalty among these employees whose common employment increases the bond between members of the family and the organization. Those family members who bring other members into employment control their behavior. By teaching a new control to one person, the management can ensure that many others will learn it without much effort on its part.

We know that there have been pronounced social and familial differences between Japan and the United States. Many management researchers say that

U.S. corporations cannot successfully emulate Japanese practices. In particular, researchers say that while family is first in the East, the job comes first in America. The new reality of work life with Generations X and Y weakens this argument. To them, family *is* very important. They define family differently. It is not an outgrowth of biology, which they belittle, but a social group of their choice. This family will exert the same control on these employees that the biological family did in Japan during the twentieth century.

In the United States, extended controls can become powerful substitutes for the reward-based controls practiced during the twentieth century. Companies can use employment as a way to bond those who are important to the employee—members of the extended or immediate family—with the company's goals. This will automatically start to exert controls favoring management practices and can take the form of activities that involve employees and their family. For example, frequent spousal/mate involvement, children's activities, picnics where employees can bring their parents or even siblings or any other people who are important to them. The result will be effective and efficient management controls.

TESTS FOR EFFECTIVE CONTROLS

Test for Acquiescence

It is a common practice in ergonomics to consider the ease of operation on the part of the user of any human control as a condition of its approval for implementation. For management controls, the concern should be how the control will be taken by those who are to be controlled or are going to be affected by a particular control. We definitely do not want a control that will be disliked by those whom it most concerns—people who are supposed to be controlled by it. No control will serve any good purpose if these people oppose it.

The only effective control for knowledge organizations will be the one that is acquiesced to by those whom it affects. Lack of acceptance of a control should be seen as a design flaw rather than any implementation problem. A control that is not accepted should not be imposed. It should be redesigned. As a strategy for designing acceptable controls, it may be prudent to let the person whom it affects devise the control oneself or, if that is not possible, the person should have a meaningful contribution to its design and should feel a real excitement about it. Externally imposed controls will have a worse effect than a total absence of controls.

Test for Pragmatism

Before designing and implementing a control for a knowledge organization, management must know the exact purpose of the control and how it contributes or relates to the organizational mission and goals. It is not uncommon to come across controls that go against the basic objectives of the organization or the system for which the particular control is devised. These are called here the *oxymoron controls*. This test ensures that such controls are weeded out before they are allowed to go into the operation of a knowledge organization, or should be abolished if they already are in operation.

Social organizations, in particular governmental, are full of such oxymoron controls. The reason may be that, because of the nature of such organizations, the controls were devised to handle the problems of a different time that are not applicable or are different from what is happening in knowledge and other contemporary organizations.

Test for Creativity

As we stated in the beginning of this chapter, controls are constraints that can easily hinder creativity. A deliberate test on all controls, before their installation in knowledge organizations, must be done to make sure that they do not asphyxiate creativity and that there is enough room for deviation from controls.

In general, management in knowledge organizations has to give up the notion that management controls are essential to get work done by knowledge employees. In the changed environment, organizational success will require that controls be minimized or altogether lifted. The goal should be zero control because all knowledge jobs need the essential ingredient of innovation. The man-machine interaction will become so intense and complicated that even productivity gains will be tied with the extent to which controls allow operators to have discretion with processes and the ability to apply their judgment in innovative ways. The core value of MindSpring Enterprises reads, "We respect the individual and believe that individuals who are treated with respect and given responsibility respond to giving their best" (Jablonsky & Barsky, 1999). This illustrates that respect, not any form of control, is what brings out the best in employees at this organization.

Additionally, we should know that controls should not be used for behavior modification. If behavior modification is the goal, the manager should use other venues for that. Use of controls for disciplining will be a misuse.

The greater the number of controls, the greater the need for additional and new controls; they feed off each other. Eventually the controls will spread and replace excellence as the goal of the organization.

REFERENCES

Appenzeller, T. (2000/2001, December 25/January 1). Innovators 2001. *U.S. News & World Report*, pp. 46–48.

Bort, J. (1999, November 15). Great plays. *Network World, 16*(46), 66–67.

Burke, A. (2000, March 9). Flexible work schedule gives wholeness to people. *Journal of Business, 15*(6), A14.

Drucker, P. (1954). *The practice of management.* New York: Harper & Row.

Hopkins, M. (2000, November). Zen and the art of self-managing company. *Inc.,* pp. 54–63.

Jablonsky, S.F., & Barsky, N.P. (1999, November). Core values from fad to fact. *Strategic Finance, 81*(5), 50–54.

Kennedy, C. (1998, May). Great minds think alike. *Director, 51*(10), 52–56.

Mayo, E. (1945). *The social problems of industrial organization.* Boston, MA: Harvard University Press.

Reinhardt, A. (2000, December 4). Intel inside out. *Business Week,* pp. 116–120.

Instrument 10-1
Guidelines for Designing Controls for Knowledge Organizations
(GDCKO)

Job Title: _____ Department: _____

Supervisor: _____ Organization: _____

Brief Job Description: _____

Analyst: _____ Date: _____ Comments: _____

Consider the management, the job, the worker who is doing or will be doing this job,
the supervisor of this job, and answer the following questions.

1. How clear are the objectives of the organization or department of which this job is a part?

   ☐ A Management has only a generic knowledge of these objectives.
   ☐ B We know what we should be doing but don't know how it connects with other units of the organization.
   ☐ C We know exactly what our objectives are and how they connect with other units of the organization.

2. How sure is management that the course it wants this job to take is the right course that will result in the achievement of organizational goals?

   ☐ A It is not exactly possible to establish such a relationship.
   ☐ B Management has a fairly good idea.
   ☐ C The management knows it exactly.

3. Is this a well-defined, structured job in the organizational objective hierarchy?

   ☐ A No, we are still working on some parts of this.
   ☐ B Management has a fairly good idea about what to do.
   ☐ C Management knows exactly what to do.

4. How exactly does management know how to do this job the best way possible?

   ☐ A Not much.
   ☐ B Management has some idea.
   ☐ C Management exactly knows the course to be taken to best do this job.

5. How much scientific or technical knowledge is required in performance of this job?

   ☐ A This job requires highly scientific or technical knowledge.
   ☐ B This job requires low level of scientific or technical knowledge.
   ☐ C The job requires no scientific or technical knowledge.

(continued)

Instrument 10-1 (*continued*)

6. How many individuals depend on the output or throughput from this job?
   - ☐ A We have succeeded in making this job independent of others.
   - ☐ B There is meaningful dependence between this and other jobs.
   - ☐ C There is a total dependence between this and other jobs and in spite of all our efforts we have totally failed in making this job independent.

7. In your understanding, to what extent does the person performing this job not know the right course to take in the execution of this job?
   - ☐ A He/she is well trained to do this job.
   - ☐ B With a little guidance, he/she can do it.
   - ☐ C He/she has no idea. Constantly needs help.

8. How would you rate the ethical and moral character of the person performing this job?
   - ☐ A Everyone knows this person is an ethical, moral person.
   - ☐ B He/she has a spotty record in this regard.
   - ☐ C We have had consistent problems with him/her whenever he/she is left alone.

9. How frequently does the job demand change?
   - ☐ A Quite frequently.
   - ☐ B Often, but not too much.
   - ☐ C Not expected to change at all.

10. How available is the supervisor to meet the control and supervision expectations of this job?
   - ☐ A Supervisor is too busy with many other jobs.
   - ☐ B The supervisor has other meaningful, time-consuming responsibilities.
   - ☐ C It is a close team relationship between the supervisor and the worker.

SCORING THE GDCKO
Give 1.0 for each "A" box scored, 0.5 for each "B" box scored, and 0.0 for each "C" box scored. Add up all the points. This is the total score on this scale for the job.

Score	Diagnosis	Recommendation
< 6	Hot Potato	You will be better off not controlling this job at all.
3–5.5	Deck of Cards	Selectively control and back off at first sign of doubt.
> 2.5	Archaic	Control it for now but redesign to move it up.

Controls and Creativity in Organization

A.D. Amar

To excel one needs freedom—an unbounded mind—and efficacy to do whatever one commits to do. The same is also true in an organizational setting. However, because management wants to ensure that employees' ambitions concur with the organization's goals, it introduces checks and corrective actions, which are known as management controls. With the basic function of ensuring compliance of work activity with the set goals, management controls are built into all stages of the firm's processes. Further, as an organization grows, management enhances and adds controls in an attempt to increase its sense of understanding of the organization. This is how, eventually, every aspect of the organization comes under control. The emphasis on compliance takes priority over creativity and innovation. It results in an environment that impedes change, becomes antagonistic to productivity, and becomes a ubiquitous obstacle to excellence. A large part of the organizational effort is allocated to taking care of the mundane—that is the organization continues to transact its business in the usual way and operates in control of all subfunctions. Performance criteria are set based on how well one works within constraints of the control. There is little emphasis on how efficiently or effectively the organization is executing its underlined function and, more than anything else, how well it is working to enhance these functions for the future.

Corporate organizational theory accepts that control is a management function, but for the greater good of encouraging innovation in contemporary organizations, it needs to be evaluated very carefully. It is somewhat ironic that organizations that thrive on innovation are more likely to fail in the presence of most of the traditional management controls than due to their lack. Theory has simply not kept pace with the practicalities of organizational change.

The obvious question is how to control or manage organizations while permitting growth and creativity. The answer to the question may lie in understanding work ethics and controls regulating those who are accomplished innovators. How were they controlled? What kinds of controls were most successful? How can we emulate these controls in an organization that hopes to germinate innovation?

In pursuit of an answer to the above, we may start with transformational leaders. In an organization, these leaders include the top officers, such as the chief executive officer, chief operating officer, and other top corporate managers. We should study the controls that regulated their behavior and gave them their work ethic, which resulted in organizational creativity, not at the expense of, but to the credit of, the organization.

If is often said that, typically, organizations exempt their top officers from general management controls. Organizations have one set of controls regulating top management and another regulating the rest of the employees. Organizations defend such a practice because they believe that imposition of general controls on top managers will impede effective functioning in their positions. However, the fact remains that controls hinder creativity at all levels. The difference may be dictated by what a corporation has determined to be more important, innovation or control.

It is not that the work behavior of top managers is not controlled at all. Without some type of control, they would not be able to attain the successes they do. However, the source of these controls is different. Understanding these controls and their underpinnings may unlock the secret to turning any organization into an innovation organization. These innovation controls may be then emulated by everyone. These are the controls that actually work. All organizations will require them since success in the future will only come through innovation emanating from all levels of the organization. The future will require creative approaches to solving all kinds of problems that organizations will face. In fact, organizations will need each member of their workforce—not just the leaders—to be innovators. This was the conundrum that Eastern European governments failed to recognize and was the chief flaw of the command-and-control system.

The new controls should focus on turning ordinarily *externally controlled* workers into those who feel that they are *in control* of their work and their work environment. The source of the new controls should be shifted from externally imposed to the internally directed. Organizations should make sure that management controls do not set any one course as the course to be taken, or even convey the notion that there is one best or recommended course to be taken. The new controls should be designed based on the theme that the correct response, given a time and a situation, could be best determined only by the person who is handling the situation. Its corollary is that no one else knows exactly what to do in this case or can provide close supervision or guidance in securing effective solutions to problems. Management's sense of insecurity and/or its distrust of its employees should not be used as a guide in designing controls. If such a situation actually does exist, then that may signal a different problem that management must address separately.

The basic assumption about controls for the new work environment is that an organization will be better off without any of the management controls practiced during the twentieth century. Requirements to excel in the uncertain future environment will require totally different kinds of controls than those we have already known and which have been exercised. The challenge will be to find ways to gain operational effect of the controls without actually having to impose them overtly on employees. Any control that employees find hindering their functioning should be considered unfit for anyone in an innovation organization. The key will be to meet the desire for organizational control and function with the absolute necessity of innovation.

Source: Reproduced in original from *The Mid-Atlantic Journal of Business*, 34, no. 2, June 1998. Published by Division of Business Research, W. Paul Stillman School of Business, Seton Hall University. Reprinted with permission.

Chapter 11 _____

Lifting Them Up: Combating Low Morale in Knowledge Organizations

Organizations operating in a knowledge environment face vicissitudes of a more severe magnitude than those commonly experienced in traditional organizations. Direct reflections of these swings affect all those associated with these organizations. Their morale tends to fluctuate exactly as do the vicissitudes. The management of morale is an important issue in knowledge organizations. If not regularly monitored and improved as soon as it sags, low morale can result in significant drops in creativity and productivity and also increase the employee turnover rate—severely aggravating the problem of recruiting and retaining valuable employees, which itself causes a ripple effect in the morale problem.

This chapter is devoted to understanding the morale problem in knowledge organizations. We will learn how to assess morale, look clearly for warning signals, and examine how to keep it high. Since a low morale problem is not a problem in itself but a compendium of symptoms brought on by other problems that may not be obvious, a study of morale in organizations should reveal what must be done to fix these underlying problems. With this in mind, a number of topics subsequently covered in this book are based on important cues for keeping employee morale high in organizations operating in a knowledge environment.

Study after study has shown that high morale gives people a buoyancy that makes them feel free, think unconventionally and out-of-the-box, and makes them engage in acts that contribute positively to human knowledge and well-being. It gives them a sense of efficacy that translates into creativity—innovation and high productivity. High morale and a high work contribution are positively correlated because morale is the state of a relationship between an employee and his or her organization (Zemke, 2000). High morale implies the functioning of this relationship at a higher level and, consequently, a higher effort strengthens this relationship.

Morale is an individual thing, but mainly it is a sense of overall satisfaction with the present and a confidence in the future. Morale works on a subtle level, and managing morale requires doing so individually with each employee. However, since it is hard to measure, it is not possible to make statements regarding morale in any organization—whether it is low or how, if at all, it can be mended—with any precision. For this reason, many managers tend to ignore it. The helplessness that it entails tends to be so powerful that managers consider facing the consequence of low morale as inevitable and fail to work to lift it. They forget that the way people feel about their work and the organization determines not only how hard they work, how long they stay, and how much they produce, but also how much initiative they take, how much they sacrifice for their job and the company, and how much psychic energy they contribute to improve their job and the organization.

Nevertheless, managers do know that morale is something that can fluctuate both in themselves and in their subordinates. However, they do nothing to help themselves or their subordinates to redress it. In fact, a number of organizations, many of them in the technology sector, have taken an approach that the problem of managing morale is the employees' responsibility. Employees should learn on their own how to maintain their morale at a level high enough that it does not negatively affect their performance at work. Of course, taking this approach signals helplessness in understanding and combating the problem and, under the circumstances, yields minimal improvements at best. While it is possible that minimal improvements may actually be sufficient for most traditional organizations, it is definitely not sufficient for organizations that are operating in highly volatile environments, such as those in the knowledge environment.

LOW MORALE IN KNOWLEDGE FIRMS

Low morale localized in some areas of a company or widespread throughout it is quite a common occurrence in firms of all kinds. However, in some industry groups, because of their operating and environmental characteristics, the problem could be prevalent throughout all organizations. Some of them show a worsening of the problem due to other contributing factors, whereas, in other organizations, with different readings on the same class of factors, low morale may come and go. Similar observations can also be made about individual organizations. Some segments of an organization, irrespective of what industry the organization is in, could show signs of more severe kinds of low employee morale, whereas others may not show any infliction. Sometimes the problem may afflict the whole organization.

Turnover Rate and Morale

One of the primary reasons for the high occurrence of low morale among employees is a high rate of turnover. When people see one of their colleagues fired, they garner a confounded sense of fear and guilt, which turns into a decline in morale. Surprising as it may seem, the consequence of a coworker voluntarily leaving is not very different in terms of employee morale. This voluntary severance gives the remaining employees a sense of rejection, and they feel left behind—two important causes of low morale. They conclude that the departing employee left the organization for better opportunities—a promotion, a higher salary, or maybe a venture of one's own—of which they will not avail.

The phenomenon explained above occurs more in organizations operating in the knowledge environment, since the presence of the reasons that cause the problem is more prevalent there. For example, there is a greater environmental turbulence in knowledge environments, which contributes heavily to the uncertainty in these firms. Factually, there is no escaping it. For the management of these companies, the challenge lies in managing the low morale problem among their employees such that a long-term or widespread affliction due to its presence is avoided.

Employee morale also suffers during the mid-growth period in the life of an organization. It is during this stage that companies become attractive to other mature firms in their industry and are acquired or end up merging with them. The cultural shock and future uncertainty make a number of employees quit, and a number of those who are left behind continue to have low morale. Take for example the linkup of Paris-based Cap Gemini, an IT (information technology) consulting firm, with the Ernst & Young consulting arm. The uncertainty and ensuing decline in morale caused its attrition rate to jump to 25 percent and forced it to seek special remediation (Ellison & Delaney, 2000).

Knowledge and Technology Employment Patterns

In general, ups and downs in employment are a common phenomenon in free market economies and cannot be avoided. Managers know how to best manage necessary shifts in employment. In the United States, the unemployment rate during the last decade has been the lowest in almost a half-century, and it has been difficult to fill empty spots in organizations. However, it is also important that this fact not be looked at in isolation of its adjunct, that employers have eliminated positions at record levels during this period. Moreover, this rate has accelerated toward the end of this period. In 1998 and 1999, organizations eliminated 677,795 and 675,132 positions, respectively—the largest increase in any year in the 90s (Smith, 2000). This phenomenon is even truer for jobs in the technology sector where, even though there has been a great demand for technology talent, the jobs have been most insecure. Because of the pressures of this environment, the rate of employee turnover in high-technology firms has been much higher than in other firms. Moreover, it is expected to continue at these higher levels for the near future.

The second reason for the high rate of employee turnover in high-tech industry is its rate of growth. The pressure from its environment to regularly recycle talent and constantly search for new talent to stay competitive is expected to continue. The U.S. economy as a whole is going to further exacerbate the problem. For example, the forecast from the U.S. Bureau of Labor Statistics indicates a continuation of similar patterns in the U.S. economy as a whole—there will be 6.2 million more jobs than the number of people that will be available to fill them in 2008. The problem will be more pronounced in the technology sector. The number of jobs in the high-tech industry will jump from 5 million to 7 million in 2008, with software and computer-related jobs almost doubling.

Environmental Volatility and Pressure on Resources

Environmental volatility is the third important factor that contributes to the high turnover rate in technology and knowledge industries and the subsequent decline in employee morale. It comes from not only the market and constantly changing technology but also from the behavior of the investment community—its expectations from organizations in these industries are much higher than from traditional organizations. As long as this volatility is there, the rate of turnover will remain high. For the near future, there seem to be no signs indicating any letup in volatility and, therefore, the rate of turnover. New knowledge firms touting the most up-to-date technology will continue to emerge based mainly on the prospects that they offer and will pull away resources from those that had gone into business only a few years earlier, threatening their independent existence. Short-cycle times in technology are likely to get even shorter and, in return, this problem even more severe.

The push to recruit the best talent from around the world is putting pressure on organizations to make themselves more attractive to employees. Growth firms, such as those operating in the knowledge environments, have a history of paying ultrahigh salaries and hiring more people than necessary to run efficient operations. These companies find it cheaper to steal away talent than to pay astronomical costs to acquire firms and see employees quit (Thornton & Timmons, 2000). That is what VerticalNet did. Joseph Galli, president of Amazon.com, quit to join VerticalNet in return for a $5 million signing bonus, beause the incentive he was expecting from the appreciation in Amazon.com stock was disappearing due to the decline in its price. Out of fear of losing more executives for the same reason—stock options losing prestige among new recruits—Amazon.com paid a number of its executives a bonus of a million dollars each in an attempt to retain them. Many other companies had to do the same. Whether the revenue is up or down, organizations in the technology and knowledge businesses will have to provide attractive compensation packages to recruit and retain qualified employees. Employee costs in these firms will continue to be higher than average in the private sector. According to the American Electronics Association, the average salary in high-tech industries is 82 percent higher than the average salary in the private sector. When employers pay high salaries, they expect higher commitment and output. Working long hours and sacrificing going to kids' ballgames and family events becomes a norm to their employees. While the conscious mind of employees understands and acquiesces to this trade-off, the subconscious one does not. The blues set in, morale goes down, the turnover rate becomes high, and human resources cost even more. It costs 125 percent of the annual salary of an information technology professional to replace him or her, according to a study by Walker Information (Smith, 2000). In addition to other costs, this includes costs due to the lower morale of those who experience this departure.

When firms are under pressure, their employees will not be able to escape the stress and other problems that make their morale low.

ASSESSING AND CURING

Knowledge organizations should seriously consider an assessment of their employee morale when there is a high rate of turnover of newly hired employees. If that bright programmer you stole away from your competitor is handing in his marching papers after only six months at work, then in all probability your company could be suffering from a serious morale problem and every other problem that comes with it. The intensity of a low morale problem could be as severe as the rate of turnover among newly hired recruits. Consider that as the single most important indicator of low morale in any organization.

The commitment of effort and resources to combat and reverse low employee morale, and in fact working to continuously enhance morale, would be the best investment a knowledge organization could make. This way, it would be able to retain employees who might otherwise defect to other companies. Such efforts can build a pool of the most valuable employees that an organization could have—employees who are both talented and loyal.

Successful high-tech organizations are working to devise many ingenious ways to bring their employees' morale high and keep it high. The main theme of this effort has been that, since employees spend more time at work than at home, their workplace should be turned into a sort of surrogate home. These organizations are making the work environment more casual, letting them bring their children along to work, and, in some cases, letting them take work home so that they do not have to even go to work during regularly scheduled work hours.

UNDERSTANDING AND MENDING

Knowledge organizations, particularly those in the technology sector, need to focus on groups of issues that relate to low employee morale, those belonging to behavioral, organizational, and communication matters. A knowledge organization manager should consider all of these in assessing and designing programs for uplifting employee morale.

COMMUNICATION FACTORS

Ignore No Cues

The first thing a manager should do to assess and mend employee morale is to study formal and informal communications that come across to him. He should heed messages—rumors are definitely included herein—pertaining to what is going on in the organization at all levels, make sense from them and, as the situation calls for, intervene by sending out his own formal or informal communications. He should pay keen attention to what he sees and hears, and he should extract the meaning of what these messages are intended to convey—more important, the subtle meaning that they suggest. The morale problem has a very subtle existence and needs to be assessed with that fact in mind.

Knowledge organization managers should distinguish between what is called "baseline bitching" (borrowing from Zemke [2000]) that goes on in any organization and meaningful informal communications that have subtle messages. Managers should heed and attend to above-the-baseline griping. They should pay special attention to organizational grapevines when they convey that the company or a particular department is going down the tubes and nobody gives a damn. It is this kind of message that, if not heeded, will surely bring morale down further.

Make Symbiotic Communications

When organizations operate in tumultuous environments, as most knowledge firms do, then their managers have to be ever prepared to handle all kinds of communications. They should be regularly taking steps to squelch or clarify messages that come through various communication channels—grapevines included. The manager either squelches or clarifies a message, which will reduce uncertainty in the minds of workers and help improve their morale. Most people can handle bad news better than the uncertainty that surrounds it. As a rule, as soon as a rumor spreads, it should be either turned into news or quashed ruthlessly but credibly. Allowing a rumor to hang on will continue to make employee morale sag when it is negative. On the other hand, it would be a cliff-hanger on an issue that is positive. The net effect will be the same.

Because people who work on knowledge assignments are usually more intellectual, managers should communicate with them as if communicating with people on their level—more symbiotic, more open.

Don't Be Concerned about Communication

Available communication technology makes it easy for any organization to eliminate rumors; however, it is even easier for knowledge organizations. They possess cutting-edge technology. Frequent electronic communications clearly addressing the rumors and outlining their progress can be used efficiently to improve communication and help alleviate the rumor mill. Waiting for the company's newsletter to come out in print form for clarification would prove to be too costly.

Management should use frequent communication as a way to share information and consult with employees before making decisions. If nothing else, over time, it will build a trust between the management and the employees.

BEHAVIORAL FACTORS

The assessment and management of morale also needs to be measured against the state of employees' work psychology. The psychological dimension serves a dual function in this regard. First, because morale affects work behavior, an employee with low morale is not going to fully engage in work and will not perform at the same level as those not suffering from low morale. Second, because work behavior affects morale, a conscientious employee with consistently low performance could very well develop low morale. There is a very important association between morale and work behavior and performance.

Involvement and Concern

Morale will take a nosedive if there is a common feeling among employees that their organization really does not care much about them. This feeling is mostly embedded in the thought that the company cares only for those at the top and that only they count and no one else does (Turpin, 2000). Such sentiments will be reflected in employees' comments and actions, such as carelessness and unconcern. Management must redress it with understanding and empathy. Management should show that it listens, acts, and appreciates employee input. Furthermore, through its decisions and actions, management should put employees' priorities above those of the organization's—not only in matters relating to their work but also those relating to their personal lives. This may mean an organization doing more than just holding an annual employee picnic or running a feature on employees in a company's newsletter to get their families involved in the well-being of the organization. One CEO achieved this in a unique way. Instead of a Christmas card, Per-Olof Loof, chief executive of Sensormatic Electronics Corporation of Boca Raton, Florida, sent his 5,500 employees a CD of his inspirational song "Do It Again," praising and inspiring employees for all that they had done for the company during last year (*Wall Street Journal*, 2000).

An organization will very effectively lift its employees' morale if it sacrifices an order, delays a shipment, or even takes a loss on an account to accommodate the personal needs of its employees. Employees never forget their employer's actions leading to its sacrifices for their personal needs. It conveys that the act of sacrificing is a two-way street—that their organization does for them as they do for it. This sentiment will commit them to pay back significantly more than what would be needed to offset the loss incurred by the company in making such a sacrifice.

Organizations can also gain their employees' commitment and concern for it by involving their families in organizational life—socially and economically. During the last decade, many organizations formulated family-friendly policies to achieve this. These policies recognize the fact that, since families are important to their employees, they should be important to the company as well. Those organizations can touch employees' feelings by bringing their families into the organizational fold. Involving families and significant others in organizational life will increase their understanding of what takes place at work. Families will not only become more tolerant of the sacrifices that employees make at work for the organization but may even encourage engaging further in behavior that leads to productive outcomes for the organization. This practice will reduce the stress on employees by the convergence of the employees' and families' interests in the organization. The employees will enjoy more freedom from their families to engage in work-related activities or put in extra effort in getting the work done at or away from home.

The State of Helplessness

A sense of apathy commonly rules employees' behavior when they know what is wrong with their organization and what is needed to fix it, but, somehow, are convinced that they are not being permitted by the system to do that. A diagnosis of helplessness can be confirmed on hearing statements like "Our problems are too complex," "We can never deliver on time," and "Nothing changes here." In fact, the feeling of helplessness renders even the most loyal and willing employees ineffective. A prolonged apathy turns into helplessness. It is a psychological state whereby one accepts inefficacy not from a lack of ability, or even empowerment, but from a lack of cooperation from the one who is to benefit from the action. A continued sense of helplessness can take away initiative, confidence, and, in the end, ironically, even the ability to do a good job. This can bring an organization to a tragic state—a serious sickness that will end in its demise. In this case, financial incentives, such as another pay raise or an increase in bonus, may not work. To cure a state of helplessness of this magnitude, it is advisable that the organization encourage its employees to undertake any initiatives and assignments, even the ones at which the manager knows that they are likely to fail. Only a couple of failures, or the "breaking" of things, like these will replace helplessness with empowerment and apathy with creativity. This will act as a therapy to cure helplessness.

An organization can also do a number of other things to reduce the sense of helplessness among its employees. One important action requires abolishing "in" and "out" groups. Every employee should feel that his opinion counts and that he is as able to help the organization in whatever way he can as anyone else working for it.

ORGANIZATION FACTORS

How a knowledge workgroup is organized can have a positive or negative impact on its employees' morale. Its structure and how it conducts its business can contribute to the problem or diffuse it. This is why a common practice among organizations operating in knowledge environments is to model their organizations after successful firms in their sector. Before employees develop a low morale problem, they set as a reference for comparison organizations that are operating in the knowledge sector of their economy. More often than not, such firms are those that are in head-on competition with their organization. Therefore, the assessment in pursuit of curing low morale requires a thorough understanding of the organization's structure, procedures, and operating policies with a view to their impact on the employee morale. If an organization can ensure that its operations and structure do not have any built-in factors such as these, then its managers can work to easily dam the eroding morale among its employees. The built-in factors could be very specific to organizations requiring individual assessment. Nevertheless, the ones most prevalently causing this problem are discussed in the following sections.

Self-Select Coworkers and Teammates

As we have already seen, contemporary knowledge assignments are so large and complex that their solutions are possible only if organizations deploy cohesive teams that can exert their concerted effort. It is important for them to make sure that these teams are formed and are allowed to operate only if *all* of their members feel excited about working on them. The selection of who will work with whom is very important for the success of these teams. The importance of a preferred coworker in curing low morale cannot be overemphasized in these organizations. According to a recent study (Smith, 2000), one preference factor in selecting and staying on a job for 86 percent of workers age 50 and above was enjoyable coworker relationships. Earning a high salary ranked sixth on this list. Preferred coworkers and team members can make working together fun and solving tough problems a breeze. One sign that a team will produce is if its members work together and ignore boundaries established by rank, age, gender, and other demographic and organizational factors.

Utilize Talent to the Fullest

The other organizational factor that can contribute to low morale among employees has to do with the poor utilization of the talent they have to offer. In addition to increasing organizational productivity, feeling excited about what they do and using their talent to the fullest increases their creativity—an important input to high employee morale.

In general, all employees have to *feel* that they get *interesting* assignments. Since most employees in knowledge organizations possess education at higher levels and specialized skills, they expect to get assignments that make use of these skills and help them build further on them. Therefore, their managers have to see that they are challenged and their skills are fully utilized. If their intellect is not used to the fullest or if they see their colleagues not being fully utilized, they feel low and experience a morale problem. The utilization of employees' talent to their full satisfaction in roles that are clearly defined in terms of the contribution they make to achieve accepted goals will keep their morale high.

Structure and Organize Tasks

It is well known that most tasks in knowledge environments are unstructured, which could entail a lot of complexity and uncertainty. Even though people working in these organizations are aware of this fact, when they come across tasks that are left unknown and unorganized, they tend to have lower morale. As much as possible, managers of these tasks should define the work—if not fully, then within some established bounds—set milestones at which progress should be taken, and audit resource consumption and requirements.

Due to task uncertainty, it is likely that some assignments will actually have a longer duration than expected, whereas some others may not be finished at all. Even though it is very likely that this may not be due to a lack of effort and talent of the individual working on this assignment, nevertheless, when an employee faces such a situation, he is likely to blame himself and have a sense of rejection. This becomes one of the main causes of low morale in employees. A manager can carefully avoid such burnouts by providing assistance in successfully finishing these assignments without waiting for the employees to ask for it. It would be better still if the help is provided in a private and subliminal manner. All this cooperation and help made available to those who need them should be friendly, voluntary, and a sort of sharing without any consequences or strings. This will avoid burnouts, low morale, and declines in innovation and productivity.

Install Quick-Response Systems

To make sure that employee morale does not sag, organizations operating in a knowledge environment should design into their structure a standing quick-response system. Although any organization can benefit from a system that quickly and appropriately responds to needs from its environment, it becomes mandatory for knowledge organizations because of the pressure from the environment in which they operate.

We find that there are five functions that must be made part of a quick-response system specifically recommended for knowledge organizations:

1. *Put Out "Internal Fires."* This system should sense and put out "internal fires." It should rapidly respond to an organization's work-related needs, such as those from work centers, inputs, and feeder lines. If an employee is not performing well on his job, he is not going to have high morale.

2. *Respond to Employees' Personal Needs.* Since we believe that it is important for the organization to consider its employees holistically—in all their roles—rather than only in their roles as employees of the organization, a good quick-response system for them should also respond promptly and courteously to their personal needs in addition to the function covered in the previous section. If this is not done, most of the effort put into responding to the first set of needs will be futile.

3. *Respond to Customers and Markets.* This system should quickly and effectively respond to sudden demands due to market and customer needs. Fulfilling market needs in a timely manner and bringing satisfaction to customers gives employees a sense of achievement, job satisfaction, and the security that comes with a job well done—all the important ingredients needed to keep employee morale high. An organization should not expect to have satisfied employees for too long if its customers and market needs are not rapidly and effectively fulfilled. Employee morale will not be too low if customer and market problems are allowed to hang on.

4. *Provide Performance Feedback.* The fourth important function of such a system is to provide quick feedback to employees on their performance. It should regularly provide employees with results of their undertaking, preferably in an objective—not just phony words of praise or a pat on back—and perpetual manner, for example, what they did right, where they went wrong, what they should have done to avoid such wrongs, and any general changes to bring about further improvements in their performance. This is the minimum required to keep their morale up. Employee morale will be further lifted if the system tells them what reward, if any, they will get for their finished performance and what their cumulative reward would be with the new one added in there.

5. *Provide Means for Success.* The system should tell employees what new skills they can learn to better their ability to earn higher rewards and draw better satisfaction from their jobs. It should also tell how employees can acquire these recommended skills.

Direction as Needed

When working with people who are specialists in their areas and who probably know as much, or maybe more, on a topic as do their supervisors, then the latter must be very careful when it comes to understanding how to direct them. In many cases where these employees do not have answers to tricky problems, it is very likely that their supervisors may not have them either. In such circumstances, it is difficult to know if an employee needs direction; if a supervisor knows that he does, then the question arises on how to provide it. The reality in this situation is that not providing direction when and where it is genuinely needed will not only negatively affect the employee's output but will also have a negative impact on his morale. On the other hand, giving direction where it is not needed will amount to wasted time and unnecessary interference, which would do the opposite— hamper progress, reduce productivity, and lower employee morale.

In all contemporary organizations, but more importantly in knowledge organizations, to maintain employee morale it is important that the employees have a symbiotic-type relationship—one that is between equals—with their supervisors. It is not a coaching-type relationship, because that has some hierarchy and assumes that the supervisor can in fact coach the employee. Instead, this relationship should be a player-player relationship, in contrast to the coach-player type. From player-player relationships come direction in the form of friendly assistance that one is neither hesitant to ask for nor resistant to give. It becomes a truly give-and-take relationship—one takes sometimes and gives sometimes. There is give-and-take out of concern and affection, not organizational obligation. This type of direction wins and earns respect and keeps morale high for both, those who direct and those who receive direction.

SYNERGISTIC FACTORS

There are certain factors that may or may not contribute to employee morale by themselves in isolation; however, they provide a synergistic effect that with other organizational decisions and actions have been shown to enhance morale. Ethical management is probably the most important factor in this category. Engaging in philanthropic and humanitarian activities is another one. Individual organizations, through employee surveys or other formal studies, should find out factors in this category that are specifically applicable to them. Once these factors are recognized, organizations should then enhance their activities and visibility in these areas. Not only is this an act of conscience, it is a job of public relations that should be specifically targeted at employees to attain the goal of improving employee morale. Some of these important factors are discussed below in more detail.

Enhance Ethical Management

Employee exit interviews show that a recurring reason for leaving an organization is, "I was treated unfairly." It is obvious that when employees use the word "unfair," they implicate their company's lack of ethical practices. A survey reported by the Washington, D.C.–based Ethics Resource Center (ERC) states that 92 percent of the respondents who felt that their supervisors modeled ethical behavior felt that they were valued as employees (Leonard, 2000). The feeling of being valued has a high association with high morale, retention, and productivity. Knowledge environment firms can help improve their employees' morale by publishing and practicing an ethics code and implementing it in its full spirit. It is important to practice a published ethics code because there is nothing more detrimental to employee morale than an employer who violates his own published ethics code.

It is also important for organizations to have a meaningful ethics program. Such a program should be taken seriously by their top management, who should make sure that they live by it and enforce it on all who report to them. There should be ample communication and employee training on the program; otherwise, an ethics program could actually backfire. In fact, organizations should provide an ethics resource center and an advice line that employees may use to resolve their ethical dilemmas. ERC also reports that if employees perceive their employer's ethics statement as nothing more than a paper tiger, then morale will actually be lowered. Any ethics program will work as a good morale booster if firms have an ethics enforcement process in place that employees can avail without fear of retribution when they experience or notice gaps in practice and the firm's published ethics code.

Either because of the pressure from their industry or the government, it has become almost impossible for organizations to avoid setting ethical standards dealing with honesty, fairness, responsibility, and trust. By doing the right job in establishing and practicing ethical standards, they can turn ethical behavior into a big morale booster for their employees. Moreover, it will make it easier on management to make tough decisions and will help gain quick acceptance of them from their employees—both whom they affect and whom they don't.

Philanthropy and Humanitarianism

Organizations can improve their employees' morale by incorporating their employees' personalities in corporate acts of philanthropy and humanitarianism. Not only in America but also all over the world, people like to share and show a softer side of their behavior. When their employers do that, it awakens that part in them and makes them take their employers in a good stead. They feel more loyal and committed, work harder, succeed, and have their morale boosted. However, to be effective morale boosters, philanthropy and humanitarian programs have to be tailored, designed, and implemented in line with the specific reading that an organization gets from its employees in this regard. A caution is in order here. Many times such programs end up being a reflection of the priorities and preferences of top management, in which case they may serve the purpose of being philanthropic and humanitarian but may not win the hearts of their employees and therefore may not help boost their morale.

To make sure that such programs help boost employee morale, organizations should conduct a survey of their employees to study and develop a profile of their social pulse. It should be a public process that involves as many employees as show interest. There may be open meetings where they can reflect their choices. They may even be allowed to take a small part of the corporate philanthropy budget as a matching amount for donation to a charity or any other mission of their choosing—putting their name on it along with the organization's. Finally, what comes out of these studies should be used to set and administer the philanthropic and humanitarian goals of the organization. It is also important that each act is conspicuously displayed as an act from the employees of the organization.

Increase the Comfort Factor

The amount of time that knowledge environment employees spend at their desks and in their offices is larger than the time they spend anywhere else, including their homes. In these circumstances, it is important, for their morale and productivity, that employees feel comfortable at work—both physically and psychologically. Organizations may do whatever they can to bring an "at home" feeling to their employees. This may involve letting them choose where they want to work when they are at the firm's premises. Further, as much as possible, they should be permitted to work away from their offices. Let them redo their work areas as they please, and let the common areas be done jointly by those who use them. This may involve laying them out, decorating, coloring, selecting equipment, purchasing, and choosing the technology applications to be employed.

Organizations can also increase their employees' comfort factor and in turn morale by not enforcing work hours rigidly—making them stay at work until quitting time whether there is work to do or not. One of the biggest turnoffs of knowledge employees is the set work hours—in particular, staying at work when there is no work to do. Knowledge environment employees work long hours when there is a lot of work to do, but when there is no work or less than normal work, organizations should let them leave early or come in late without harboring any sense of guilt. In addition to increasing employee morale, it would be time well inventoried for those days when there will be more work than adequate time to finish it.

Organizations should work in ingenious ways to create alternate work places—breather places, escapes, and spaces with changed surroundings. These will help boost employee morale and regain creativity and productivity.

Trade and Professional Activities

Employees of organizations operating in a knowledge environment are specialists in their fields. They often contact their professional colleagues many times in the context of their work. Trade and professional activities let their colleagues, and managers, see the importance of what they are doing and contributing through the eyes of those whom they believe have the best ability to appreciate what they are doing.

In addition to the usual participation in society and trade activities, organizations can engage their knowledge employees in these by organizing professional meetings and seminars on their premises. They may also sponsor professional conferences and symposia with their involvement conspicuously displayed. Such activities and presence will refresh their energies, recharge them, encourage them to apply new techniques, and empower them to better handle their job. However, the most significant benefit of these actions would be an uplifting of morale. It will be one of the most effective investments these organizations can make in the development of their employees.

ASSESSMENT TOOLS

There are a number of techniques that an organization can employ to regularly monitor and assess its employees' morale. From our experience, we have observed that managers and supervisors almost always discern when their employees have low morale. However, because they mostly feel they are a part of the problem, they may refuse to accept its presence in their area. It could be because many times when their workers have low morale, the managers have it too. However, because of either this or the fear that the occurrence of low morale amounts to their failure, they provide justifications in an attempt to continue to engage in the denial of any low morale in their part of the organization. Behavior of this sort is very rational, as we have stated earlier in this chapter, and in most cases of low morale, managers feel helpless—although this is not fully true—in resolving the problem.

In addition to getting cues on low morale from usual employee behavior statistics, such as the rates of absenteeism, tardiness, going home early due to feeling sick, voluntary and involuntary termination of employment, work-related accidents, late deliveries, and low productivity, managers may ask external observers for expert opinions. A convenient though involved method for assessing employee morale is by administering instruments specifically designed for the purpose. One such instrument, useful when work is done in teams, was designed by Charney (1995). In it, he assesses morale in teams employing seven measures: involvement, cooperation, communication, organization, improvement, atmosphere, and leadership. It is available on the Internet (for which a reference is provided at the end of this text). A more complete tool to assess employee morale in knowledge environments is given in Instrument 11-1.

We can never overemphasize the importance of a healthy work environment in knowledge organizations, and the level of an individual employee's morale is an indication of how he is reacting to that environment. As we saw in this chapter, it is very important for managers of knowledge organizations to monitor morale among their employees and take individual initiatives to remedy low morale problems. Managers of individual departments and area

INSTRUMENT 11-1
Knowledge Employee Morale Meter

Job Title: _____ Department: _____ Organization: _____
Brief Job Description: _____
Analyst: _____ Date: _____ Comments: _____

Consider your organization, department, work, and work environment, and gather your feelings and observations about them and answer the following questions:

1. In your understanding, how well is your organization doing?

   ☐ A It is being well managed and is doing well.
   ☐ B It has some problems which, I believe, will be resolved before they pose a serious threat to the organization.
   ☐ C It has serious troubles and, at this stage, no one really knows how to fix them.

2. In your understanding, how well are other organizations in your industry doing?

   ☐ A They are being well managed and are doing well.
   ☐ B Some of them have problems, which I believe, will be resolved before they pose a serious threat to organization.
   ☐ C They all have serious troubles, and, at this stage, no one really knows when will they come out of them.

3. How stable is the workforce in your organization?

   ☐ A I feel well trained, equipped, and supported in doing my job.
   ☐ B There is a stable core of mostly old-time employees, but new ones come and go.
   ☐ C People are leaving left and right, I feel like I am the only one stuck here.

4. What do you think of your supervisor?

   ☐ A My supervisor is well trained, friendly with me, and supportive of my work.
   ☐ B He/she mostly leaves me alone.
   ☐ C He/she is merely an administrative head without any understanding of my field. Many times, he/she becomes a hindrance to my work performance.

(*continued*)

INSTRUMENT 11-1 (*continued*)

5. Is it common in your organization for employees to keep information of concern, such as poor performance, layoff, firing, etc., from the person whom it most affects?

    □ A No, I tell whatever I know to whomever it concerns. Everyone in our organization feels so close to each other, and freely tells whatever one knows.

    □ B Yes, but only in case of those people with whom I don't feel very close.

    □ C Yes, in my organization, we accept formal channels to give out information, such as meetings, or through other formal channels.

6. Are there many rumors floating around in your organization?

    □ A No, rumors are rare in our organization. We have efficient information sources.

    □ B Yes, but they mostly fly before big news comes out.

    □ C Yes, it is the only source of our information.

7. Are rumors in your organization just rumors?

    □ A Yes, almost all of them are rumors and we know that they are just rumors.

    □ B Most of them are rumors.

    □ C No, many turn into news later.

8. Are most of your communications with your supervisor through memos, or other written or formal means?

    □ A No. We communicate using all means. I feel free to walk into my boss's office and ask any question or say whatever without any fear of reprisal.

    □ B No, most of our meetings are spontaneous, in the halls, or at my work center.

    □ C Yes, almost always.

9. Are most communications from supervisors to employees in other organizations in your industry through memos, or other written or formal means?

    □ A No. They communicate using all means. The employees feel free to walk into their bosses' offices and ask them any questions or say whatever without any fear of reprisal.

    □ B No, most of their meetings are spontaneous, in the halls, or at their work centers.

    □ C Yes, almost always.

10. How are meetings conducted in your organization?

    □ A They are open, constructive, and everyone contributes.

    □ B They are short, and supervisor give out news and instructions.

    □ C Meetings are very rare in our organizations.

(*continued*)

INSTRUMENT 11-1 (*continued*)

11. Do people stop talking when a superior approaches?

☐ A   No, but we change to a neutral topic.
☐ B   Yes, but only when people are criticizing the approaching superior.
☐ C   Yes, everyone shuts up. There is too much doubting and blaming going around.

12. How do you generally feel at work?

☐ A   I feel very good and enjoy my work and colleagues.
☐ B   I feel all right.
☐ C   I mostly feel tired and exhausted in the mornings/early afternoons.

13. How do you feel about your job?

☐ A   I feel well trained, equipped, and supported in doing my job.
☐ B   There isn't much support, but somehow we get by.
☐ C   I know that there are problems, but there is little that I can do to help.

14. How are others performing in their jobs in your department?

☐ A   I am surrounded by people who are the best employees one could have.
☐ B   Some of them are doing well, whereas there are others who are doing poorly.
☐ C   They are doing a poor job because they are not trained to do the work assigned to them.

15. How do you know about new employees joining your organization?

☐ A   Our supervisor makes us meet new employees and asks us our opinion about them before they are hired in the company.
☐ B   We read about them and sometimes meet them before they join us.
☐ C   We meet and know about them when we see them working.

16. If you were promoted in the position of your supervisor, how will you do that job?

☐ A   I will do exactly what he/she is doing.
☐ B   I will make substantial changes in a number of areas.
☐ C   I will do things very different, and I know that I will do a better job.

17. Do you know that many mistakes are being made by employees in your organization and that these mistakes are being left unattended and unresolved?

☐ A   No. However, sometimes things do go wrong but we fix them in an orderly and timely fashion.
☐ B   Yes, but there are a few problems that are causing most of the lingering on errors.
☐ C   Yes, there are problems all over the organization, which seem to be being compounded with time.

(*continued*)

INSTRUMENT 11-1 (*continued*)

18. How upbeat is your supervisor on the future of the company?

    □ A He/she is convinced that our organization is doing fine and he keeps us informed about it.

    □ B Ours is such a large and disconnected organization that our supervisor cannot say anything credibly.

    □ C He/she is very dissatisfied about what is going on at levels above theirs.

19. Is griping and complaining in your department just usual "bitching" that you expect to go on in any organization like yours?

    □ A Yes, we have people who are constant complainers, mostly without any reason.

    □ B Yes, but only most of it. Some people have genuine concerns.

    □ C No, complaints people make in our organization reflect serious problems that need to be attended.

20. How is the general condition of the industry in which your organization belongs?

    □ A Most companies are doing fine and are hiring and growing.

    □ B Some are doing well, whereas some are not.

    □ C There is a general decline in the whole industry.

SCORING ON THE MORALE METER
Give a 1 for each "A" box scored, a 0 for each "B" box scored, and a −1 for each "C" box scored in all questions except 2, 9, and 20. For questions 2, 9, or 20, give a −1 for each "A" box scored, a 0 for each "B" box scored, and a 1 for each "C" box scored. Add up all the points. That is the morale score of the employee completing the questionnaire.

Score	What Type	Employee Morale
≥16	High Morale	Well set for creativity and high productivity
13–15	Good Morale	Improve to achieve best results.
10–12	Satisfactory	Improve for gains
7–9	Struggling	Expedite assessment and mending
<7	Low Morale	Rush for help

supervisors can play an important role, irrespective of the steps that an organization may take to redress the overall problems.

As a rule, managers should avoid linking all low morale problems to low compensation. Although this may be a factor, in knowledge organizations where remunerations are high, severe problems of low morale still prevail. In most cases, the first assumption of low morale should have to do with work and the work environment rather than anything else.

Once the low morale is diagnosed and its causes identified, there are many ways in which a manager can remedy this problem. Whereas a number of these specific steps are given in this chapter, topics covered in other chapters of this book broadly address the problem of low morale in knowledge organizations and suggest how managers can play an important role in addressing low morale problem by directly managing them.

REFERENCES

Business Bulletin: An ode to employees. *Wall Street Journal*, pp. A1, C5.

Charney, C. (1995). *The manager's tool kit: Practical tips for tracking 100 on-the-job problems* <http://www.knowledgecenters.versaware.com/notoc/getpage.asp?book=ManagerToolProb&page=062000205.asp>.

Ellison, S., & Delaney, K. (2000, October 30). Cap Gemini will use ads to boost profile, morale. *Wall Street Journal*, p. B12.

Leonard, S. (2000, October 10). Walking the talk. *HRMagazine, 45*, 256.

Smith, A.K. (2000, November 6). Charting your own course. *U.S. News & World Report*, pp. 56–65.

Thorton, E., & Timmons, H. (2000, November 20). The Street's punishing pay stubs. *Business Week*, pp. 154–155.

Turpin, J.R. (2000, July 24). Tech says they "don't get no respect." *Air Conditioning, Heating & Refrigeration News*, 1–29.

Zemke, R. (2000, August). What morale problem? *Training, 37*, 14–16.

SECTION V _____

FUTURE OF KNOWLEDGE
ORGANIZATIONS

Chapter 12

Knowledge Organizations in the Twenty-First Century

The need to develop an understanding about the future of knowledge work, workers, and the organizations whose functioning depends on knowledge—either as an important input in its system or its output—is obvious. This understanding will give organizations a direction about how to allocate their resources and how far ahead in the future to plan. In this chapter, we take a systematic look at the growth of knowledge in organizations and attempt to examine them from the past couple of centuries to the next decade or so.

ORGANIZATIONAL SUCCESS REQUISITES

To understand the importance of knowledge work and workers in organizations in the future, we need to do two things. First, we need to assess the evolution of the use of knowledge and the employment of knowledge workers in economic entities leading up to the present time. Second, since business and society have been so tightly intertwined due to their dependence on each other, we also need to study how their interaction has turned small craft shops into large corporations during this assessment period.

For this study to provide meaningful information, the period covered in this assessment should be long enough to serve as a valid basis for projecting the use of knowledge work over a time horizon in the future. We believe that if we examine the past couple of centuries, we will be able to know how organizations got to their present mode of operation and, therefore, we may be able to answer the question of where they are going from here. It is important to know when and how organizations started to use knowledge as a major input in the transformation of their products and services. This assessment and understanding about the appreciation and use of knowledge by organizations will shed light on the future of knowledge in organizations. For example, we will know how these organizations grow and, therefore, how the need for knowledge work, knowledge workers, and managers with specialized skills to manage them will also grow in society.

To further our understanding of the growth and development of organizations, we should study how human input to transformation systems of economic entities has changed over this study period. Because these economic entities have been identified using different names and have existed in different shapes and sizes from time to time, we should include all transformation organizations small and large, in whatever form they have existed, in understanding the type of human input that they need for their success. For this assessment, we divide the study period into three major eras as given by the following sections.

The Skills Era

Until the nineteenth century, human society all over the world was primarily agrarian. Most of the economic entities of this period, directly or indirectly, were related to agricultural products. The primary human input in these systems were skills relating to growing, marketing, distributing, and storing agricultural products. The art of performing these tasks was passed on from one generation to the next—mostly from father to son. More than anything else, it was experience that mattered the most in developing the ability to have excellent performance of these tasks. All nonagricultural products were created by independent artisans and small craft shops. The skills essential in the creation of goods in this category, mostly achieved on a unit-by-unit basis, were acquired by artisans and tradesmen by apprenticeship under the guidance of master craftsmen who had many years of experience in their trades.

The performance of artisans, tradesmen, and craftsmen in the conversion of products and services depended very much on the individual skills that they acquired during their apprenticeship. Since skills were what mattered the most, both for success at being an independent contractor and for working at one of the craft shops (these being the marketable skills of the time), people worked to acquire these skills. Success in life depended on how well one acquired the skills. The two most important ingredients of prosperity in the skills era were possession of these skills and hard work. Anyone who had the skills and was willing to work hard succeeded. Accordingly, a societal value system was built around this theme.

Another important characteristic of this era was the emphasis of individual work and skills in the conversion processes of the time. Most of the economic entities during this time were operated individually or in small groups. Almost no goods and services required group or organized effort in their conversion. Group initiatives, skills, and team efforts were of no major importance.

The nineteenth century was truly a period where skills made all the difference to people individually and to society as a whole. It was an era where the skilled craftsmen ruled. Mankind by then had not developed technology to engage in mass production of goods to have any significant impact on human lifestyle or livelihood.

For the economic entities of the era, the main tool of business competition was skills that their artisans and craftsmen had. The business was won using unique and superior skills that they reflected in their products.

The Machine-Tool Technology Era

In the early twentieth century, mechanization of the agricultural farm relieved a large number of people from agricultural jobs to explore other employment options. However, these options could become available only by the acquisition of skills that were marketable in the conversion of the goods and service sectors of the economy. Formal trade schools and vocational institutions sprang up to meet the needs of the population. In a matter of a couple of decades, there were a large number of skilled people ready to make goods and provide services that were in demand during that time.

Then there was a second factor that, when combined with the above phenomenon, provided all that was sufficient to transform the economic entities of the last century and to pull the socioeconomic system out of the skills era. This factor was the increased disposable income in the hands of farmers and landowners because of the higher efficiency of farms due to mechanization. The increase was sufficient to fuel demand for goods and services and therefore expand opportunities for those who could convert and distribute products and services that were in demand. There were many who could afford to acquire "products" and many who could supply them. The stage was set for the "producers" to fight for "customers" and for customers to "shop around."

This was the beginning of a long period of fierce competition among producers to win over and hold on to customers. Producers would do anything to achieve this goal. They needed to make their operations more efficient and customer- and market-responsive to be successful. They wanted to do to their shops what they had done to their farms—mechanization. To cut costs so that they could undersell their competitors, they redesigned tools to become machine tools—cutting and shaping tools with electric motors and automation mechanisms that replaced human muscle and skills. Craft shops of the nineteenth century became mass production centers called factories. It was the start of the machine-tool technology era. Machines did everything. Machines were grouped with machines. They were interlocked to further increase their efficiency. The proud skilled artisans and craftsmen were useful only if they could learn how to adapt their skills to the machines and fit in mass-producing interlocked man-machine systems, better known as assembly lines. In most cases, the value of their abilities to the organization was as good as that of workers hired fresh off the street.

The concept of mass production had been developed. Every transformation system from here on in had to handle large identical items to be able to produce them at a low cost and therefore successfully compete in the market-place. Compared to the advancement that had occurred in product conversion systems during the twentieth century, the economic entities of the nineteenth century were quite primitive. Society had transformed itself from agrarian to industrial, where the skills that mattered were the ones relating to the harness-ing of power and the operating of machines in concert with many others. An individual could not do much without working in coordination with others. The individual skills of the previous century had lost all importance.

To be successful in the machine era, one had to acquire an understanding of science and technology, in particular, conversion technology, such as that relating to the engineering and allied professions. To prosper in this era, one had to go to a four-year college—preferably an engineering school—and work for an organization that was a market leader in its industry. It was an era of engineers. To attain success in the position, one had to learn how to work on a team, how to get along with coworkers, and, more than anything else, how to work smart and not just hard.

The organizations of the machine technology era competed based on the superior machine technology that they deployed in their conversion processes. Machine-tool technology provided them with cost reduction, which they passed along to their customers at lower-selling prices, thereby gaining cus-tomers from their competitors. Since the machine-tool technology was very expensive, efficient organizations of this era were highly capital-intensive.

The Knowledge Era

The invention of the electronic computer has made it possible to put to productive application for the benefit of mankind virtually all knowledge in all fields of human learning. It began with applications of knowledge that was acquired in understanding humans and the human environment, in the form of science and technology. Although the invention of the electronic computer occurred in the early parts of the second half of the twentieth century, its use to improve the quality of human life had started primarily only during the last decade of the twentieth century. With every year during this decade, the use of the electronic computer has been expanding and stretching too far into human life at a rate higher than that at any time in the past.

The last decade of the twentieth century has seen the start of a new era of organizations for which knowledge and, more precisely, wisdom—the ability to acquire knowledge and transform it into applications to fulfill societal needs or solve human problems—mattered more than the conversion skills of the nineteenth century or the mass-production machine technology of the twen-tieth. That is why we recognize this period as the start of the knowledge era.

The organizations of this era, with the use of the computer and knowledge, in many ways created new products and services either to fulfill a need that was not even recognized until now or to fulfill an old need with precision or at low cost. They also reshaped their transformation systems that, while maintaining the cost-efficiency benefits of the mass production technology of the twentieth century, have allowed enough flexibility to permit development and application of individual human skills, knowledge, enterprise, and initiatives that were possible only in the pre–machine-tool technology era of the twentieth century.

During this era, organizations succeeded based on their ability to create a structure and environment that encouraged individual efforts in transforming their knowledge into marketable applications that have enhanced the quality of human life or have improved the efficiency of their processes.

Those individuals who had more up-to-date knowledge were more able to perform and succeed in their jobs in organizations of the knowledge era. For individual success in a job in this era, one needed more than the knowledge that comes from a four-year college education. In fact, to be able to make a real contribution in one's position in a knowledge organization, one needed graduate school education in specialized fields of study—not professional studies. The knowledge era organizations would get the most contribution from employees with the maximum years of graduate education, perhaps to a terminal level. A few such individuals could support the whole organization.

The tool of marketplace competition in the knowledge era is knowledge—more appropriately, wisdom. An organization's main competitive advantage in this era is based on the pool of knowledge employees that it built and the ability that they collectively have to come up with applications of knowledge as and when needed. Whereas the mass production organizations of the twentieth century were highly capital-intensive, knowledge organizations are labor-intensive. A big part of their budget goes to maintaining a knowledgeable labor force.

KNOWLEDGE AND THE TWENTY-FIRST CENTURY

Even though the onset of the knowledge era was in the last decade of the twentieth century, the full-fledged start of this era is still in the future. Its full bloom will actually occur during the first quarter of the twenty-first century. Evolving through the early stages of the last century, almost all organizations of the twenty-first century will eventually become fully driven by knowledge and wisdom. In fact, in its full bloom, the knowledge era will truly be the wisdom era. The possession of knowledge is not what will give organizations an advantage in the marketplace, but instead how much wisdom the organization has—that is, how much ability it has to connect knowledge with life in so many of its facets.

Organizations that survive beyond the first two decades of the twenty-first century will be knowledge organizations to a great extent. Some of these will be very heavily knowledge work-based, while some others will be less so. However, all of them will utilize knowledge work as a significant part of managing their operations. The greater the knowledge component in an organization is, the greater its market stability and financial health will be.

To prepare themselves for the changes due to the increase in knowledge work in organizations of all types, managers will have to train themselves and set up their organizations to be responsive to them. They should regularly monitor certain knowledge-relevant aspects of their operations to assess if their organization is transforming itself into a knowledge organization and if it is turning knowledge into applications.

There are certain generic measures that all managers of knowledge organizations should take to assess how their organization is progressing in transforming itself, or maintaining itself, as a knowledge organization. Following this paragraph, we provide some of these generic measures. Of course, managers may add other items to this list or exclude some if they find them to be not relevant to their operations. They should also see that the readings on these measures progressively increase for their organization as it advances in the twenty-first century. A steady improvement in these measures will be essential for success in the twenty-first century. To be more objective, they may decide to take readings on the same measures for their competitors or main rivals in an attempt to maintain their lead. The process may be repeated on a periodic basis, maybe once every year. Four of these measures are explained below.

Precise Products and Services

The integration of knowledge in organizational operations can be reflected in many ways—in a firm's product and service lines, processes employed for their conversion or production, employee satisfaction, and lower costs. The first test that an organization should perform to assess the extent to which it is transforming itself into a knowledge organization is a check on its product line. It should look at its products and services and assess if they have become more precise and more powerful in serving the functions that they are supposed to perform. This would be a good test of the incorporation of knowledge work since precision and power in applications developed require incorporation of state-of-the-art knowledge in the field. An example of a precise product may be in the form of a painkiller that eliminates pain only in a particular joint of the body rather than throughout the whole body. Another example may be an antibiotic that will kill a particular organism only in a particular organ of the body rather than attack all organisms in all parts of the body.

Knowledge should move product and service lines from the general to the specialized, from the specialized to the subspecialized, and from the subspecialized to the sub-subspecialized, and so forth. The extent to which an organization's products and services are pointed, precise, and powerful indicates the amount of knowledge that it is using in its managing of the firm. The process of making products and services more powerful, pointed, and precise should continue incessantly in a knowledge organization.

Efficient Transformation System

Ambitious organizations also utilize knowledge in running their operations more effectively and efficiently just as they use it to redo their product and service line. The deployment of current knowledge in the transformation of products and services is not indicative of the fact that an organization is keeping up with the advancements in knowledge relating to its processes through acquisition of state-of-the-art conversion technology; typically, it also shows how up-to-date it is with knowledge relevant to its firm. Many knowledge organizations design or customize their own transformation technology for the use in their processes. Many times, they may acquire what is available on the market for all members of their industry and adapt, modify, and upgrade it by marrying it to their knowledge of the process technology. In some cases, knowledge organizations may have their own proprietary conversion technology that will give them an edge over their competitors in the marketplace. These organizations realize a higher efficiency in the transformation of their goods and services, which will be very evident in the reduction in their costs of doing business that they pass on to their customers to gain market share.

Specialist Workforce

To continue its pace with knowledge relating to product and service lines, and transformation processes in its field, a knowledge organization will have to maintain a workforce that possesses up-to-date knowledge. Since employees are the most important resource of a knowledge organization, it should continue to search for talent in colleges and in the labor force throughout the world. It knows that if it brings in employees who possess the requisite knowledge, they will be able to find in a synergistic way marketable applications of the knowledge that they possess. Further, to enhance the knowledge level of their current employees, a knowledge organization must provide formal training. This way, the organization does not only raise the bar on those entering its employment, it also keeps all of its labor force at an up-to-date knowledge level. It will make communication and cooperation among employees more conducive. Overall, the workforce will become more educated. There will be a growing number of highly educated specialists, holding higher academic credentials, such as master's and doctoral degrees.

Hefty Compensation Packages

Because knowledge organizations recruit employees who possess up-to-date knowledge, typically they pay their employees at the highest rates in the economy. This is how they attract and retain a knowledge workforce. These organizations also have a greater disparity in the compensation packages of their employees: Some receive extremely high compensations, whereas others receive much lower ones, but mostly the compensation is based on the contribution that they make to the organization. There will be a greater disparity in worker compensation based on the level of their education: Those with higher credentials will make more money than those lacking them.

Secondly, knowledge organizations have very few employees who belong in the nonknowledge classification. Many of them may not have any in the nonknowledge classification.

FUTURE CHALLENGES IN MANAGING KNOWLEDGE ORGANIZATIONS

We have learned in previous chapters that the management of knowledge organizations is quite different from the management of traditional organizations. Moreover, we know that the main differences in these management styles are due to the differences in the work that organizations perform and the workers they have. We have also learned how knowledge work is different from traditional work and how knowledge workers are not like other workers.

Even though we have covered a number of important aspects of managing knowledge organizations and have provided guidance to their managers on how to manage employees more effectively, there are a number of areas that we have not covered. More work is needed to help strengthen the lack of applicable techniques that are usable in these areas. The following section contains some of the aspects of managing knowledge organizations in which research to develop theories or more specific adaptations of existing management theories applicable to knowledge environments is needed.

Performance Evaluation

We have known previously that every knowledge work assignment is unique and therefore hard to assess. This nature of knowledge work makes it impossible to establish any objective standards to measure the output or its quality. Making serious attempts to do performance evaluations can create more problems and headaches for management than provide answers on how to improve it or to the employees on how best they can do their job. Since about half-a-century ago, when service work was becoming an important part of organizations, managers have been grappling with the question of the assessment and performance evaluation of service employees, which is still continuing. Many organizations engage in pseudoevaluations of service work and somehow satisfy their routine. However, they are aware that a true assessment of this work is not taking place.

Knowledge work is much tougher to assess than service work and a lot tougher to assess than any other work. Until now, no research has been done that would help a manager establish objective standards to measure knowledge work. Moreover, there seems to be no chance in the near future of any research coming down the line. Whatever efforts are put in this direction during the knowledge era will be a contribution to the profession of knowledge management.

Feedback Systems

Seeking feedback to whatever humans do is natural, and proper feedback can become a very meaningful incentive. It can also become a source of achieving further improvement in work. All knowledge organizational managers are aware of this, but due to the difficulty in the very nature of knowledge work, they also know that there is not much that they can do in this regard. As we have already seen, knowledge work is very difficult to assess and hence almost impossible for the manager to objectively review and give feedback. There is always a risk of making a wrong assessment and giving feedback that may disserve the basic aim of the feedback.

In spite of the difficulty, there should be some way to have knowledge workers receive feedback on their performance so that they can go on with what they are doing with or without any changes.

The best way to provide feedback to a knowledge worker is through the work itself. Knowledge organizations must develop technology for building a system into the work itself so that the worker does get an objective feedback on the progress he has made on the assignment and how good a job he is doing. This type of feedback will require a unique system for each assignment. There is a need for research in this area also. Any effort on how to have the work provide feedback to its doer will make an important contribution to the field of managing knowledge workers.

One way to let knowledge workers receive feedback on the progress of the work itself can be achieved by breaking large, endless, uncertain jobs into small, manageable, time-bound assignments whose sizes can be easily tracked and monitored either by feedback modules built into the work systems or manually by their operators. This way, the completion of a part of a large, complex job can provide an automatic feedback to the operator, which will be instantaneous, credible, and from the work itself.

CONCLUSION

The area of managing people performing knowledge work, or of managing knowledge organizations, is so new and wide open that any research on this topic is likely to make a contribution to the field. The pressure on managers of these organizations is great because the environmental turbulence makes it practically impossible for them to put any meaningful effort in this direction. Research in this area will have to be conducted in an organized fashion, by creating a professional society of academics and practitioners. It may also be conducted under the auspices of university-based research centers. Corporate research and development departments can also make meaningful contributions to the knowledge in this area; however, due to the desire of corporations to use their findings to benefit only their bottom line, it will not be of much benefit to advancing the profession of knowledge organization management. Corporate effort in this direction may be best carried out by creating a consortium of corporations that fund a joint entity that conducts research in this area and gives its findings and results to its members before releasing them to the public at large.

No matter how the effort to build this field is put together, there are two certainties. First, it will take many years and a lot of effort to develop a workable theory on managing knowledge organizations. This book is among the early efforts along this direction. It may be the start of a management-disciplined research that will go on for a long time. Second, the future work will be almost all knowledge work, and it belongs to knowledge workers.

Glossary

Baby Boomers All persons born after World War II ended. Most of them are now in their late forties and fifties.

Brick-and-Click This is a name for the mixed-model businesses that maintain brick-and-mortar operations while making use of the Internet for further enhancing their business.

Brick-and-Mortar This is a nomenclature describing a traditional business organization. The term is used more in the context of e-business to describe an organization that does not engage in earning its revenue primarily from on-line means. These days, a number of brick-and-mortar operations, in particular retail organizations, do combine their largely traditional retail operations with some on-line shopping.

Data Mining Information drawn from every click by Web browsers through powerful computers and software is then stored in data warehouses and mined for a few nuggets to lure Web browsers to shop.

Decision Complexity The complexity of a decision is directly measured by the number of people or tasks that it affects. A decision is complex if its effect is going to be widely affecting the work or personal lives of many people.

Decision Size The size of a decision is directly determined by the number of people involved in making it. When taken in the context of consensus decision making, it equals the number of people who either provide direct input or actually make it.

E The letter, which stands for "electronic," denotes a prefix that connotes direct or indirect association with knowledge, electronics, and automation in organization, in particular the Internet or Web. E-mail first popularized this letter. Today its meaning is more related to the Internet and Web rather than electronics.

E-Business This represents a compendium of electronic computer activities for developing, promoting, and transacting goods and services through the medium of the Internet. (The word is synonymous with e-commerce, which is more popular in Europe.)

Followship This is the leadership that emerges from the follower side—followers entrusting someone to lead them. It allows leader-led power to flow in the opposite direction. Rather than a leader exercising power to influence the behavior of his followers, followship occurs when followers of a leader give power to him to influence them.

Gen Xers   Also known as Generation X, these are children of the Baby Boomer generation born before 1977. Novelist Douglas Coupland in his novel, by that title, coined the term Generation X.

Generation Y   They constitute people born between 1977 and later until the 1990s—late offspring of the Baby Boomer generation.

Independent Contractor   Any entity accorded the responsibility for the accomplishment of a work sector in full is an independent contractor. It is used in the generic sense. An individual, group of individuals, or an organization can be called an independent contractor.

Knowledge Employees   Employees of any organization whose primary job responsibilities involve knowledge work.

Knowledge Organization   An organization whose primary input is knowledge and/ or whose primary output is knowledge. This organization derives its revenue primarily through the activities described by knowledge work. (See definition of *Knowledge Work*.)

Knowledge Organization Leadership   The art of helping employees of knowledge organizations establish and realize their personal goals and in the process realize their organizational goals, since they have to have significant congruence in knowledge organizations.

Knowledge Organization Management   Managers of a knowledge organization whose primary job functions include planning and organizing of knowledge work and controlling and leading of knowledge employees.

Knowledge Project   A knowledge project is any activity or group of activities that is not performed in a knowledge organization on a regular basis, or it is the work or a segment of work that is organized as the manager deems fit. The term project may or may not be taken in the same sense as it is taken in project management.

Knowledge Scheduling   A positive scheduling system primarily recommended for knowledge organizations that gives a lot of latitude to employees and objectively lets them set times when they start or stop working.

Knowledge Widget   Products or services, such as electronic, computer, or conventional, that come from a knowledge organization are termed knowledge widgets.

Knowledge Work   Working to tame, apply, use, and develop applications with or without electronic computers and technology to bring out applications—products and services—is knowledge work. It includes the science, technology, arts, information technology, and Internet-related activities, such as research and development, engineering, sciences, technology, the arts, and all other creative pursuits in organizations. Knowledge work has very little or no structure and mostly cannot be standardized, or predesigned, especially by the ones who are not going to be the actual doers of the work. Each individual knowledge work should be unique and require the ingenuity of the doer in its accomplishment.

Knowledge Work Module   A knowledge work module is a connected piece of a complex whole that in some known way is complete, simple, and independent but embodies all the requisite detail for its completeness.

Nexters   People born between 1964 and 1977. This is another way to identify Generation X.

Operating Work   Any work that is structured, standardized, and carried out according to a preconceived design and method is operating work. It is usually routine work that is repetitive in nature or is a replication of another work.

Vision   An imaginative insight into a subject or situation in time that others find attractive as well as credibly achievable is labeled vision.

Work Environment   All factors and forces that control worker and work accomplishment, over which the worker has no or little control, especially in the short-term, are grouped as work environment. Some examples of work environment may be work schedule, specified method, timing, procedures, and supervisor.

Index

About the Author

A.D. AMAR is Professor of Management at the Stillman School of Business, Seton Hall University. Also director and editor of *The Mid-Atlantic Journal of Business*, he has published more than 50 articles in other periodicals as well. He holds a degree in engineering and management engineering, an MBA from Baruch College and a doctorate in business from City University of New York. Among his clients as a consultant at various times are General Motors, VW/Audi USA, the Social Security Administration, and The Human Resource Administration of the City of New York.